OUR FAMILY LINKS
TO THE
SHOWMEN'S GUILD

www.irishancestors4u.com

By

Kathleen Merryweather
nee Green

Published by Irish Ancestors 4U Ltd
Irish Ancestors 4U Ltd Copyright © 2013
www.irishancestors4u.com
Printed by Joshua Horgan Print & Design
Date 10th November 2013
First print of this volume
ISBN Number 978-0-9562976-3-1

DISCLAIMER

The material and information contained in this Publication are for general information purposes only. You should not rely upon the material or information in the Publication as a basis for making any business, legal or any other decisions.

Whilst we endeavour to keep the information up to date and correct, IRISH ANCESTORS 4U LTD makes no representations or warranties of any kind, express or implied about the completeness, accuracy, reliability, suitability or availability with respect to the Publication or the information, products, services or related graphics contained on the Publication for any purpose. Any reliance you place on such material is therefore strictly at your own risk.

IRISH ANCESTORS 4U LTD will not be liable for any false, inaccurate, inappropriate or incomplete information presented in the Publication. Certain links in this Publication will lead to other Publications which are not under the control of IRISH ANCESTORS 4U LTD. When you access these you will leave this Publication. IRISH ANCESTORS 4U LTD has no control over and accepts no liability in respect of materials, products or services available on any Publication which is not under the control of IRISH ANCESTORS 4U LTD.

To the extent not prohibited by law, in no circumstances shall IRISH ANCESTORS 4U LTD be liable to you or any other third parties for any loss or damage (including, without limitation, damage for loss of business or loss of profits) arising directly or indirectly from your use of or inability to use, this Publication or any of the material contained in it.

For the sake of clarity, IRISH ANCESTORS 4U LTD accept absolutely no responsibility for the information, products, services or related graphics contained in the Publication and any reliance you place on such material is therefore strictly at your own risk. These disclaimers and exclusions shall be governed by and construed in accordance with English law.

INTRODUCTION TO THE BOOK

The purpose of this book is to record and widely publicize historical and factual information on my family links to the Showmen's Guild.

Records such as the Census Returns, courtesy of The National Archives (United Kingdom), provide a valuable insight into their culture, social standing, education, occupations, relationships with others, as well as painting a picture of their lives and confirming who they were and how they were related.

In respect to baptismal marriages and deaths records, most of the information has come directly from the original record. However, on occasions Ancestry.co.uk, Findmypast.uk and The latter Day Saints family search have been consulted.

The focus has been on the facts and not the original source of the information. In many cases this source has been difficult to identify as information has been recreated, repeated, published in a secondary form, not referenced and/or moved several times from a place of keeping. Not knowingly misquoting the original source would be inappropriate and misleading. For this reason, where the sources of information are unclear they have been excluded.

The sheer amount of information and family lines have been difficult to present in an 'easy to read' format, particularly in the restricted pages of a book. However, a family outline and a family tree line drawing have been produced before the main body of the detail to assist with identification of particular lines within the family units. The preceding numbers for each individual relate to the generation number line. Siblings have not been recorded chronologically but recorded for ease of presentation for reading purposes.

Finally, for those who like to proof read there may well be some typos but the factual information is as it is!

ACKNOWLEDGEMENTS

- The Showmen's Guild of Great Britain
- The Showmen's Guild of Great Britain – Lancashire, Cheshire and North Wales Section.
- Dr. Vanessa Toulmin, National Fairground Archive, University of Sheffield
- Cheshire Archives and Local Studies
- St. Helen's Church, Witton, Northwich, Cheshire – Parish Records
- St. Wilfred's Church, Davenham, Northwich, Cheshire – Parish Records
- St. Mary's Parish Church, Chester, Cheshire – Parish Records
- St. Mary's and All Saints' Church, Great Budworth, Cheshire – Parish Records
- St Oswald's Church (Cathedral), Chester – Parish Records
- St John The Baptist Church, Chester - Parish Records
- St. Werburgh's, Chester – Parish Records
- Holy Trinity, Hulme, Lancashire – Parish Records
- St. Stephen's,Salford, Lancashire – Parish Records
- St. Bartholomew, Salford, Lancashire – Parish Records
- St. Peter, Addingham, Yorkshire. – Parish Records
- All Saints, Wakefield, Yorkshire. – Parish Records
- St. Lawrence, Adwick le Street, Doncaster, Yorkshire – Parish Records
- Findmypast .co.uk
- Ancestry .co.uk
- The National Archives of United Kingdom – Census Returns
- Cheshire Quarter Sessions and Assizes Records
- Cheshire and Flint Assizes Records
- Diocese of Chester Parish Register
- The Chester Courant Newspaper
- The Chester Chronicle Newspaper
- The National Library of Australia
- The State Library of Western Australia
- The Inquirer & Commercial News
- The State Library of South Australia
- The Perth Gazette
- The Independent Journal of Politics and News (Australia)
- The State Library of New South Wales
- The Sydney Morning Herald
- The City of Perth Library (Australia)
- The State Library of Tasmania
- The South Australian Parliament Legislation Council
- Quarter Sessions, Perth, Australia.
- The South Australian Advertiser
- The Salford City Reporter
- Salford Archives and Library
- The World's Fair Newspaper
- The Era Newspaper
- The Northwich Independent Newspaper
- Northwich Library, Cheshire
- Manchester Collegiate Church / Cathedral – Parish Records
- Manchester Library, Archives and Local Studies
- Richard Griffiths' Primary Valuation of Ireland 1848-1864
- The National Archives of Ireland – Tithe Applotment Books
- The British Newspaper Archive

ACKNOWLEDGEMENTS

- Ellesmere Port Library, Cheshire
- Ellesmere Port Pioneer Newspaper
- Doncaster Archives
- Durham Mining Museum
- Genealogical Society of Utah, Church of Jesus Christ of the Latter Day Saints
- John Fearns, Genealogist
- Kenneth Salt, Genealogist
- Gilbert and Julie Dixon,Genealogists
- Joan Tapner, Genealogist

Five Generations of Our Family

Table of Contents

Chapter One

THE DEAN FAMILY

Dean Family Outline

Joseph DEAN (circa 1700-) [2232].

---

1. James DEAN (circa 1720-) [323].
Sp. Mary BUCKLEY (circa 1720 -) [355].
   2. Mary DEAN (1760 -) [919].
   2. Ann DEAN (1755-) [921].
   Sp. John WINSTANLEY (-) [1713].
   2. Susannah DEAN (1753-1815) [1711].
   Sp. Peter LEIGH (-) [1712].
   2. James DEAN (1758-) [2104].
   2. Sarah DEAN (1752-1801) [577].
   Sp. Thomas FALLOWS (-) [483], son of Thomas FALLOWS (-) [484] and Ann (-) [485].
      3. Nancy FALLOWS (1779-) [486].
      3. John FALLOWS (1780-) [487].
   Sp. George BOWYER (1750-1833) [488], son of George BOWYER (circa 1715-) [356] and Mary
      HOLLAND (-) [357].
      3. James BOWYER (1785-) [489].
      3. George BOWYER (1787-1843) [490]..
      3. Elizabeth BOWYER (1789-) [491].
      3. Sarah BOWYER (1791-) [492].
   2. Joseph DEAN (1750-) [272].
   Sp. Mary BOWYER (circa 1750-) [273], dau. of George BOWYER (1715-) [356] and Mary HOLLAND (
      -) [357].
SEE BOWYER FAMILY
      3. Nancy DEAN (1802-) [340].
      3. Female/Margaret/Sarah DEAN (1795-) [478].
      3. Thomas DEAN (circa 1796-1881) [501].
      3. Joseph DEAN (1786-) [997].
      3. James (Senr) DEAN (1789-1871) [45].
      Sp. Martha JACKSON (1794-1875) [46], dau. of Thomas JACKSON (1760-) [281] and Martha
         BRATHERTON (1764-) [282].
SEE BRATHERTON FAMILY
         4. James (Toffee) DEAN (1834-1899) [44].
         Sp. Jane BOSTOCK (1833-1870) [85], dau. of Josiah BOSTOCK (1791-1838) [210] and Mary
            YARWOOD (1794-) [211].
SEE BOSTOCK AND YARWOOD FAMILY
            5. Betsy DEAN (1852-1911) [33].
            Sp. Robert DIXON (1849-1916) [34], son of Philip DIXON (1819-) [42] and Elizabeth DUTTON
               (1822-) [209].
SEE DIXON AND DUTTON FAMILY
            5. James DEAN (1861-) [52].
            5. Thomas DEAN (1855-) [54].
            Sp. Lucy Emily BERROW (1855-1915) [682].
               6. William Thomas DEAN (1874-1943) [686].
               Sp. Susannah TURNER (1874-1909) [696].
                  7. Emily DEAN (1896-1925) [697].
                  Sp. David CARTER (-) [923].
                     8. Joseph CARTER (1919-1980) [924].
                     8. Susannah CARTER (1921-1921) [925].
                     8. Mary F CARTER (1922-1922) [926].
                  7. Thomas DEAN (1901-1902) [698].
                  7. Doris DEAN (1903-1905) [699].
               Sp. Catherine (Kate) TYRELL (-) [700].

7. Doris DEAN (1916-) [701].
7. Albert Edward DEAN (1930-1932) [702].
6. James DEAN (1875-1934) [687].
Sp. Ellen OLLERTON (-) [703].
7. Thomas DEAN (1897-1915) [704].
7. Mary Ann DEAN (1900-) [705].
7. Margaret DEAN (1902-1982) [706].
7. Hannah DEAN (1905-1915) [707].
7. Susannah DEAN (1909-1997) [708].
7. James DEAN (1911-) [709].
7. Robert DEAN (1915-) [710].
7. Thomas DEAN (1917-) [711].
7. Emily DEAN (1920-) [712].
6. Jane DEAN (1879-) [688].
Sp. Peter BARNES (-) [713].
7. Julia BARNES (1900-) [714].
7. Sarah BARNES (1904-) [715].
7. Lily BARNES (1906-) [716].
7. Peter BARNES (1909-) [717].
7. Jane BARNES (1913-) [718].
7. James BARNES (1919-) [719].
7. John BARNES (1912-1913) [720].
7. Edward BARNES (1922-) [721].
6. Julie DEAN (1881-1958) [689].
Sp. James CHADWICK (1881-1940) [722].
7. Thomas CHADWICK (1906-) [723].
7. James CHADWICK (1909-) [724].
7. Clara CHADWICK (1913-1914) [725].
7. Elizabeth CHADWICK (1914-) [726].
7. Jane CHADWICK (1916-) [727].
7. Julia CHADWICK (1916-) [728].
7. Richard CHADWICK (1911-1917) [729].
6. William DEAN (1885-1972) [690].
Sp. Ethel WARNER (1886-1963) [730].
7. Edna DEAN (1908-1974) [731].
Sp. Herbert Roy Gareth HANSON (1904-1993) [739].
7. Harold DEAN (1911-1982) [732].
7. Amy DEAN (1913-1956) [733].
7. Estella DEAN (1915-1985) [734].
6. Henry DEAN (1886-1890) [691].
Sp. Margaret ASPEY (1890-1971) [735].
7. Harry DEAN (1910-) [736].
7. Emily DEAN (1913-) [737].
6. Richard DEAN (1890-1908) [692].
6. Robert DEAN (1888-1915) [693].
Sp. Alice SELDON (-) [738].
6. Clara DEAN (1892-1892) [694].
6. David DEAN (1895-1900) [695].
5. Female (1851-) [56].
5. Mary DEAN (1858-) [202].
Sp. Robert HANCOCK (1857-) [203], son of Robert HANCOCK (circa 1828-) [270] and Sarah
    Ann (circa 1829-) [271].
6. Robert M HANCOCK (1880-) [204].
6. Sarah HANCOCK (1878-) [594].
Sp. Male NOBLE (-) [595].
7. Colin NOBLE (-) [596].
5. Martha DEAN (1867-1936) [253].
Sp. John William COOPER (1865-1940) [254], son of Solomon COOPER (-) [2368] and Fanny
    HULL.(-) [2369].
6. Nora COOPER (-) [2366].

Sp. John FITZSIMMONS (-) [2367].
6. Gilbert COOPER (-) [2370].
5. Margaret DEAN (1860-1862) [363].
5. James DEAN (1865-) [681].
Sp. Mary Elizabeth MILLNER (1876-) [749].
6. Charles DEAN (1896-) [750].
6. Thomas E DEAN (1901-) [751].
6. James DEAN (1897-) [1685].
Sp. Alice Margaret PARTINGTON (circa 1842-) [359].
4. Thomas DEAN (1824-) [58].
Sp. Elizabeth BRACKILOW (-) [265].
5. Margaret DEAN (1847-) [266].
Sp. Thomas COULTHURST (1846-) [959], son of Thomas COULTHURST (-) [960].
6. Elizabeth COULTHURST (1865-) [961].
4. Martha DEAN (1831-) [59].
Sp. Thomas PLANT (1829-) [214].
5. Martha PLANT (1857-) [60].
Sp. (unknown).
6. Margaret PLANT (-) [600].
5. Joseph PLANT (1853-) [679].
5. Cornelius PLANT (1855-) [680].
4. Mary DEAN (1837-) [62].
4. Margaret DEAN (1829-) [216].
4. Susannah DEAN (1827-) [267].
4. Elizabeth DEAN (1816-) [480].
4. Joseph DEAN (1832-) [503].
4. Joseph DEAN (1819-) [922].
3. John DEAN (1783-) [274].
Sp. Mary EVANS (-) [275].
4. Joseph DEAN (1815-) [317].
4. Mary DEAN (1817-) [318].
4. Betsy DEAN (1820-) [319].
4. Sarah DEAN (1824-) [320].
4. Helen DEAN (1827-) [321].
4. Robert DEAN (1830-) [322].
Sp. Elizabeth (1839-) [362].
4. James DEAN (1835-) [367].
4. John DEAN (1822-) [368].
Sp. Ann (1829-) [369].
5. Sarah Ann DEAN (1845-) [370].
5. Thomas DEAN (1846-) [371].
5. William DEAN (1849-) [372].
5. James DEAN (1853-) [1769].
4. Hannah DEAN (-) [473].
4. Charlotte DEAN (-) [475].
4. William DEAN (-) [476].
3. George DEAN (1793-) [276].
Sp. Hannah ORMSON (-) [277].
4. Mary DEAN (1829-) [324].
4. Sarah DEAN (1831-1833) [325].
4. William DEAN (1833-) [326].
4. James DEAN (1835-1836) [327].
4. Joseph DEAN (1824-) [328].
3. William DEAN (1798-) [278].
Sp. Charlotte WRENCH (-) [279].
4. Mary Ann DEAN (1823-1824) [329].
4. John DEAN (1825-) [330].
4. Ann DEAN (1826-) [331].
4. Samuel DEAN (1831) [332].
4. Martha DEAN (1822-1834) [333].

4. Sarah DEAN (1839-1840) [907].
3. Mary DEAN (1795-) [290].
Sp. Thomas BALDWIN (-) [291].
        4. Thomas BALDWIN (1819-) [292].
        4. Betty BALDWIN (1816-) [334].
        4. John BALDWIN (1819-) [335].
        4. Joseph BALDWIN (1821-) [336].
        4. Mary BALDWIN (1824) [337].
        4. James BALDWIN (1834-) [338].
        4. Fanny BALDWIN (1835) [339].

Dean Lineage

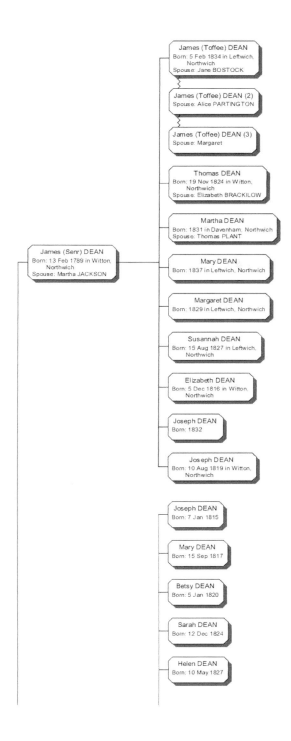

James (Senr) DEAN
Born: 13 Feb 1789 in Witton, Northwich
Spouse: Martha JACKSON

James (Toffee) DEAN
Born: 5 Feb 1834 in Leftwich, Northwich
Spouse: Jane BOSTOCK

James (Toffee) DEAN (2)
Spouse: Alice PARTINGTON

James (Toffee) DEAN (3)
Spouse: Margaret

Thomas DEAN
Born: 19 Nov 1824 in Witton, Northwich
Spouse: Elizabeth BRACKILOW

Martha DEAN
Born: 1831 in Davenham, Northwich
Spouse: Thomas PLANT

Mary DEAN
Born: 1837 in Leftwich, Northwich

Margaret DEAN
Born: 1829 in Leftwich, Northwich

Susannah DEAN
Born: 15 Aug 1827 in Leftwich, Northwich

Elizabeth DEAN
Born: 5 Dec 1816 in Witton, Northwich

Joseph DEAN
Born: 1832

Joseph DEAN
Born: 10 Aug 1819 in Witton, Northwich

Joseph DEAN
Born: 7 Jan 1815

Mary DEAN
Born: 15 Sep 1817

Betsy DEAN
Born: 5 Jan 1820

Sarah DEAN
Born: 12 Dec 1824

Helen DEAN
Born: 10 May 1827

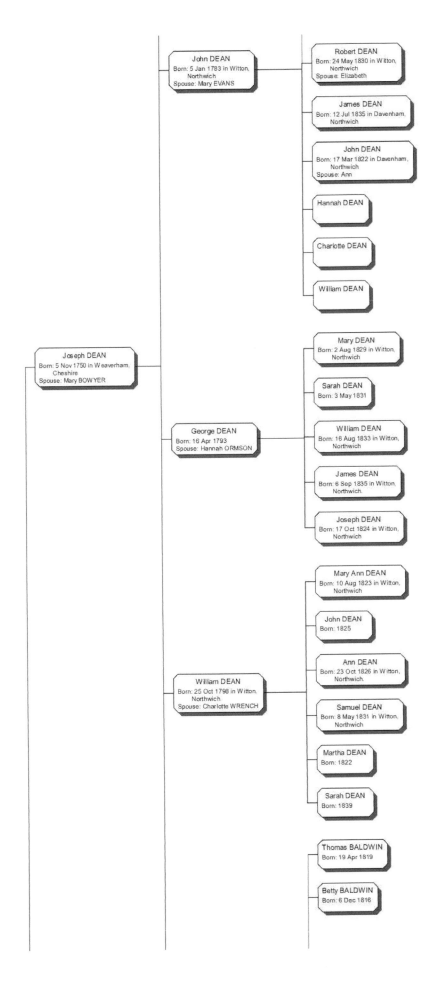

Joseph DEAN
Born: 5 Nov 1750 in Weaverham, Cheshire
Spouse: Mary BOWYER

John DEAN
Born: 5 Jan 1783 in Witton, Northwich
Spouse: Mary EVANS

Robert DEAN
Born: 24 May 1830 in Witton, Northwich
Spouse: Elizabeth

James DEAN
Born: 12 Jul 1835 in Davenham, Northwich

John DEAN
Born: 17 Mar 1822 in Davenham, Northwich
Spouse: Ann

Hannah DEAN

Charlotte DEAN

William DEAN

George DEAN
Born: 16 Apr 1793
Spouse: Hannah ORMSON

Mary DEAN
Born: 2 Aug 1829 in Witton, Northwich

Sarah DEAN
Born: 3 May 1831

William DEAN
Born: 16 Aug 1833 in Witton, Northwich

James DEAN
Born: 6 Sep 1835 in Witton, Northwich.

Joseph DEAN
Born: 17 Oct 1824 in Witton, Northwich

William DEAN
Born: 25 Oct 1798 in Witton, Northwich
Spouse: Charlotte WRENCH

Mary Ann DEAN
Born: 10 Aug 1823 in Witton, Northwich

John DEAN
Born: 1825

Ann DEAN
Born: 23 Oct 1826 in Witton, Northwich.

Samuel DEAN
Born: 8 May 1831 in Witton, Northwich

Martha DEAN
Born: 1822

Sarah DEAN
Born: 1839

Thomas BALDWIN
Born: 19 Apr 1819

Betty BALDWIN
Born: 6 Dec 1816

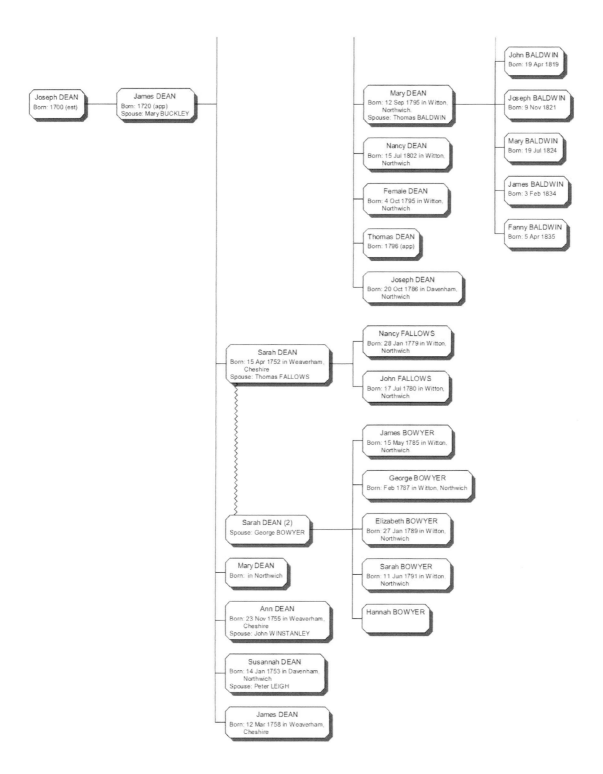

Joseph DEAN
Born: 1700 (est)

James DEAN
Born: 1720 (app)
Spouse: Mary BUCKLEY

Mary DEAN
Born: 12 Sep 1795 in Witton, Northwich.
Spouse: Thomas BALDWIN

John BALDWIN
Born: 19 Apr 1819

Joseph BALDWIN
Born: 9 Nov 1821

Mary BALDWIN
Born: 19 Jul 1824

James BALDWIN
Born: 3 Feb 1834

Fanny BALDWIN
Born: 5 Apr 1835

Nancy DEAN
Born: 15 Jul 1802 in Witton, Northwich

Female DEAN
Born: 4 Oct 1795 in Witton, Northwich

Thomas DEAN
Born: 1796 (app)

Joseph DEAN
Born: 20 Oct 1786 in Davenham, Northwich

Sarah DEAN
Born: 15 Apr 1752 in Weaverham, Cheshire
Spouse: Thomas FALLOWS

Nancy FALLOWS
Born: 28 Jan 1779 in Witton, Northwich

John FALLOWS
Born: 17 Jul 1780 in Witton, Northwich

James BOWYER
Born: 15 May 1785 in Witton, Northwich

George BOWYER
Born: Feb 1787 in Witton, Northwich

Elizabeth BOWYER
Born: 27 Jan 1789 in Witton, Northwich

Sarah DEAN (2)
Spouse: George BOWYER

Sarah BOWYER
Born: 11 Jun 1791 in Witton, Northwich

Mary DEAN
Born: in Northwich

Ann DEAN
Born: 23 Nov 1755 in Weaverham, Cheshire
Spouse: John WINSTANLEY

Hannah BOWYER

Susannah DEAN
Born: 14 Jan 1753 in Davenham, Northwich
Spouse: Peter LEIGH

James DEAN
Born: 12 Mar 1758 in Weaverham, Cheshire

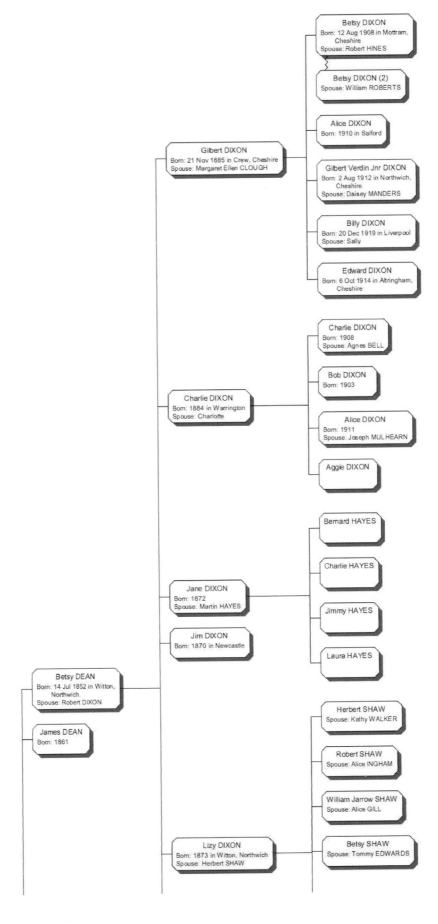

Betsy DIXON
Born: 12 Aug 1908 in Mottram, Cheshire
Spouse: Robert HINES

Betsy DIXON (2)
Spouse: William ROBERTS

Alice DIXON
Born: 1910 in Salford

Gilbert Verdin Jnr DIXON
Born: 2 Aug 1912 in Northwich, Cheshire
Spouse: Daisey MANDERS

Billy DIXON
Born: 20 Dec 1919 in Liverpool
Spouse: Sally

Edward DIXON
Born: 6 Oct 1914 in Altringham, Cheshire

Gilbert DIXON
Born: 21 Nov 1885 in Crew, Cheshire
Spouse: Margaret Ellen CLOUGH

Charlie DIXON
Born: 1908
Spouse: Agnes BELL

Bob DIXON
Born: 1903

Alice DIXON
Born: 1911
Spouse: Joseph MULHEARN

Aggie DIXON

Charlie DIXON
Born: 1884 in Warrington
Spouse: Charlotte

Bernard HAYES

Charlie HAYES

Jimmy HAYES

Laura HAYES

Jane DIXON
Born: 1872
Spouse: Martin HAYES

Jim DIXON
Born: 1870 in Newcastle

Herbert SHAW
Spouse: Kathy WALKER

Robert SHAW
Spouse: Alice INGHAM

William Jarrow SHAW
Spouse: Alice GILL

Betsy SHAW
Spouse: Tommy EDWARDS

Betsy DEAN
Born: 14 Jul 1852 in Witton, Northwich.
Spouse: Robert DIXON

James DEAN
Born: 1861

Lizy DIXON
Born: 1873 in Witton, Northwich
Spouse: Herbert SHAW

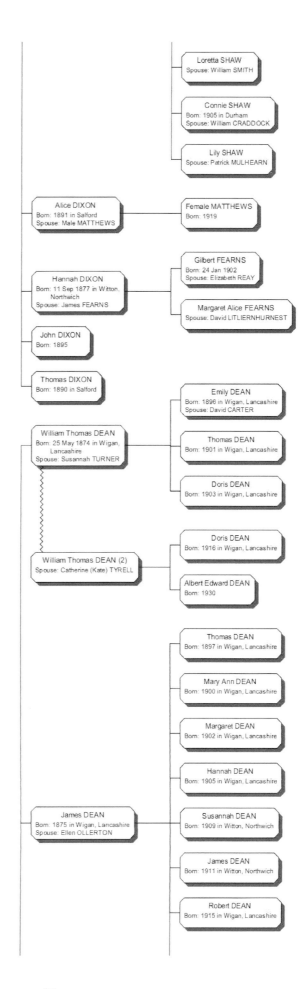

Loretta SHAW
Spouse: William SMITH

Connie SHAW
Born: 1905 in Durham
Spouse: William CRADDOCK

Lily SHAW
Spouse: Patrick MULHEARN

Alice DIXON
Born: 1891 in Salford
Spouse: Male MATTHEWS

Female MATTHEWS
Born: 1919

Hannah DIXON
Born: 11 Sep 1877 in Witton, Northwich
Spouse: James FEARNS

Gilbert FEARNS
Born: 24 Jan 1902
Spouse: Elizabeth REAY

Margaret Alice FEARNS
Spouse: David LITLIERNHURNEST

John DIXON
Born: 1895

Thomas DIXON
Born: 1890 in Salford

William Thomas DEAN
Born: 25 May 1874 in Wigan, Lancashire
Spouse: Susannah TURNER

Emily DEAN
Born: 1896 in Wigan, Lancashire
Spouse: David CARTER

Thomas DEAN
Born: 1901 in Wigan, Lancashire

Doris DEAN
Born: 1903 in Wigan, Lancashire

William Thomas DEAN (2)
Spouse: Catherine (Kate) TYRELL

Doris DEAN
Born: 1916 in Wigan, Lancashire

Albert Edward DEAN
Born: 1930

Thomas DEAN
Born: 1897 in Wigan, Lancashire

Mary Ann DEAN
Born: 1900 in Wigan, Lancashire

Margaret DEAN
Born: 1902 in Wigan, Lancashire

Hannah DEAN
Born: 1905 in Wigan, Lancashire

James DEAN
Born: 1875 in Wigan, Lancashire
Spouse: Ellen OLLERTON

Susannah DEAN
Born: 1909 in Witton, Northwich

James DEAN
Born: 1911 in Witton, Northwich

Robert DEAN
Born: 1915 in Wigan, Lancashire

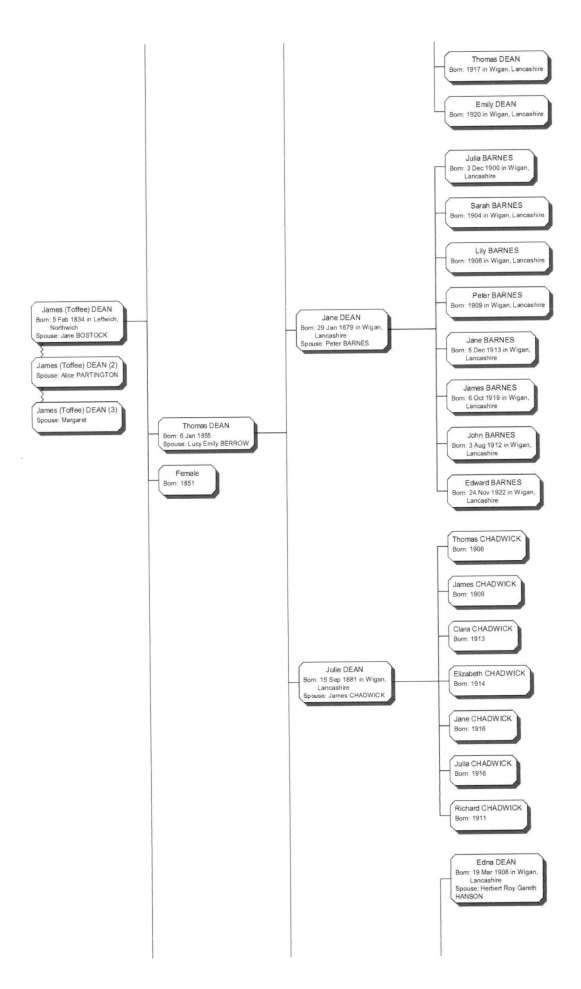

James (Toffee) DEAN
Born: 5 Feb 1834 in Leftwich, Northwich
Spouse: Jane BOSTOCK

James (Toffee) DEAN (2)
Spouse: Alice PARTINGTON

James (Toffee) DEAN (3)
Spouse: Margaret

Thomas DEAN
Born: 6 Jan 1855
Spouse: Lucy Emily BERROW

Female
Born: 1851

Jane DEAN
Born: 29 Jan 1879 in Wigan, Lancashire
Spouse: Peter BARNES

Julie DEAN
Born: 15 Sep 1881 in Wigan, Lancashire
Spouse: James CHADWICK

Thomas DEAN
Born: 1917 in Wigan, Lancashire

Emily DEAN
Born: 1920 in Wigan, Lancashire

Julia BARNES
Born: 3 Dec 1900 in Wigan, Lancashire

Sarah BARNES
Born: 1904 in Wigan, Lancashire

Lily BARNES
Born: 1906 in Wigan, Lancashire

Peter BARNES
Born: 1909 in Wigan, Lancashire

Jane BARNES
Born: 5 Dec 1913 in Wigan, Lancashire

James BARNES
Born: 6 Oct 1919 in Wigan, Lancashire

John BARNES
Born: 3 Aug 1912 in Wigan, Lancashire

Edward BARNES
Born: 24 Nov 1922 in Wigan, Lancashire

Thomas CHADWICK
Born: 1906

James CHADWICK
Born: 1909

Clara CHADWICK
Born: 1913

Elizabeth CHADWICK
Born: 1914

Jane CHADWICK
Born: 1916

Julia CHADWICK
Born: 1916

Richard CHADWICK
Born: 1911

Edna DEAN
Born: 19 Mar 1908 in Wigan, Lancashire
Spouse: Herbert Roy Gareth HANSON

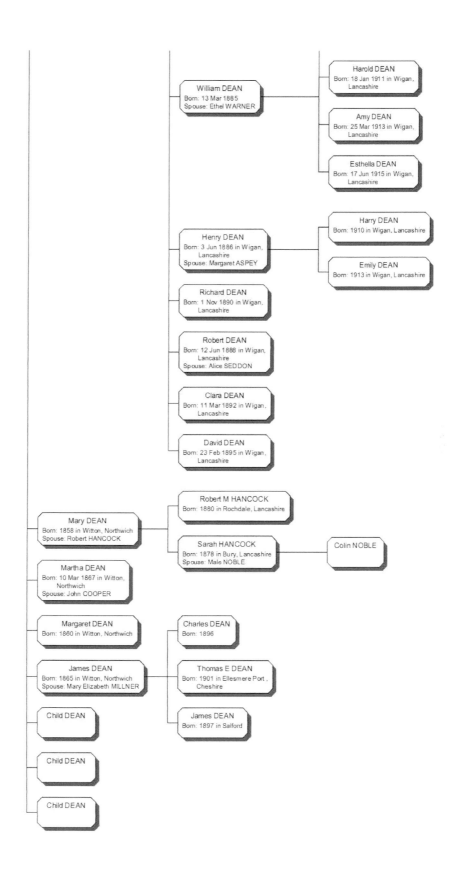

William DEAN
Born: 13 Mar 1885
Spouse: Ethel WARNER

Harold DEAN
Born: 18 Jan 1911 in Wigan, Lancashire

Amy DEAN
Born: 25 Mar 1913 in Wigan, Lancashire

Esthella DEAN
Born: 17 Jun 1915 in Wigan, Lancashire

Henry DEAN
Born: 3 Jun 1886 in Wigan, Lancashire
Spouse: Margaret ASPEY

Harry DEAN
Born: 1910 in Wigan, Lancashire

Emily DEAN
Born: 1913 in Wigan, Lancashire

Richard DEAN
Born: 1 Nov 1890 in Wigan, Lancashire

Robert DEAN
Born: 12 Jun 1888 in Wigan, Lancashire
Spouse: Alice SEDDON

Clara DEAN
Born: 11 Mar 1892 in Wigan, Lancashire

David DEAN
Born: 23 Feb 1895 in Wigan, Lancashire

Mary DEAN
Born: 1858 in Witton, Northwich
Spouse: Robert HANCOCK

Robert M HANCOCK
Born: 1880 in Rochdale, Lancashire

Sarah HANCOCK
Born: 1878 in Bury, Lancashire
Spouse: Male NOBLE

Colin NOBLE

Martha DEAN
Born: 10 Mar 1867 in Witton, Northwich
Spouse: John COOPER

Margaret DEAN
Born: 1860 in Witton, Northwich

Charles DEAN
Born: 1896

James DEAN
Born: 1865 in Witton, Northwich
Spouse: Mary Elizabeth MILLNER

Thomas E DEAN
Born: 1901 in Ellesmere Port, Cheshire

James DEAN
Born: 1897 in Salford

Child DEAN

Child DEAN

Child DEAN

Joseph DEAN (circa 1700-) [2232]. Hartford, Cheshire. Unfortunately, no confirmed birth or marriage details have been found for Joseph. However, the following have been added for interest as one reference may apply.

- Joseph DEAN of Lostock, Cheshire, Farmer in 1750.
- Joseph DEAN Marr Mary HIGNETT, 6 Dec 1728, St. Wilfred's, Davenham, Northwich, Cheshire. Joseph was noted as a Grocer of Northwich and Mary Hignett was of Davenham.
- Joseph DEAN Marr Martha Plumbley 20 Feb 1734, St. Helen's, Witton, Northwich, Cheshire.

1. **James DEAN (circa 1720-) [323].** Hartford, Cheshire. Born circa 1720, Hartford, son of Joseph Dean of Hartford. Although no actual birth or marriage details have been found for James, there are two particular references confirming the Dean family are of Hartford, Cheshire.

- Ann Dean baptised in 1755, recorded as the daughter of James Dean of Hartford. Additionally, Ann married John WINSTANLEY. The Winstanley family are confirmed as being connected to this particular Dean family
- Joseph Dean, baptised 5 Nov 1750, Weaverham, father James Dean of Hartford. Joseph Married Mary Bowyer.

James Dean married a Mary. Although not evidenced it is thought this was Mary Buckley, 27 Dec 1739, Weaverham, both were noted as living in Weaverham. There was also a James DEAN of Witton, Northwich, a labourer in 1742, who also had a daughter called Ann, baptised 1750 and a James DEAN of Sandiway in 1758. Sandiway was transferred from Weaverham Civil Parish in 1936. It is possible all the references refer to the same James.

Sp. Mary BUCKLEY (circa 1720 -) [355]. Born circa 1720.

2. **Mary DEAN (1760 -) [919].** Baptised 17 Aug 1760, St Helen's, Witton, Northwich.
2. **Ann DEAN (1755-) [921].** Baptised 1761, St. Helen's, Witton, Northwich. Ann Marr John WINSTANLEY. Anne's parents were James Dean of Hartford. There was also an Ann Dean baptised St. Helen's, Witton, Northwich 23 Dec 1750, born to James Dean of Witton, Labourer.
Sp. John WINSTANLEY (-) [1713].

2. **Susannah DEAN (1753-1815) [1711].** Baptised 14 Jan 1753, St. Wilfred's. Davenham, Northwich. Susannah Marr Peter LEIGH, 29 Apr 1788, St. Wilfred's, Davenham, Northwich. Susannah died Mar 1815, buried 1 Apr 1815, St Helen's, Witton, Northwich.
Sp. Peter LEIGH (-) [1712].

2. **James DEAN (1758-) [2104].** Baptised 12 Mar 1758, Weaverham. James' father is noted as James Dean of Sanidway. It is not clear if this James is part of this particular family but has been included as Sandiway did transfer from Weaverham Civil Parish. In addition, James may well have been living in Sandiway at this time.
2. **Sarah DEAN (1752-1801) [577].** Baptised 15 Apr 1752, Weaverham. Dau of James and Mary Dean of Leftwich, Northwich.

Sarah Marr Thomas FALLOWS, shoemaker, Northwich, son of Thomas and Ann Fallows of Leftwich. 8 Feb 1778, St. Wilfred's, Davenham, Northwich. Witnesses John Dean and Samuel Cliffe. Sarah later went on to marry George Bowyer.

References for the children born to Thomas Fallows and Sarah Dean and the children born to Sarah Dean and George Bowyer confirm that Sarah did marry Thomas Fallows and George Bowyer.

Sarah died Jan 1801, age 49, buried 10 Jan 1801, St Helen's, Northwich.

Sp. Thomas FALLOWS (-) [483], son of Thomas FALLOWS (-) [484] and Ann (-) [485].

3. **Nancy FALLOWS (1779-) [486].** Baptised 28 Jan 1779, St. Helen's, Witton, Northwich.

3. **John FALLOWS (1780-) [487].** Baptised 17 Jul 1780, St. Helen's, Witton, Northwich. Parents Thomas Fallows and Sarah. Thomas's parents noted as Thomas Fallows and Ann's parents noted as James and Mary Dean of Leftwich.

After the death of Thomas FALLOWS, Sarah DEAN (1752-1801) [577] Marr George BOWYER, 21 June 1784, St. Wilfred's, Davenham, Leftwich, Northwich.

Sp. George BOWYER (1750-1833) [488], son of George BOWYER (circa 1715-) [356] and Mary HOLLAND (-) [357]. Baptised 6 May 1750, Weaverham.

3. **James BOWYER (1785-) [489].** Born 15 May 1785, baptised 5th June 1785, St. Helen's, Witton, Northwich.
3. **George BOWYER (1787-1843) [490].** Born Feb 1787, baptised Mar 1787, St. Helen's, Witton, Northwich. George died 21 Dec 1843, buried St. Helen's, Witton, Northwich.
3. **Elizabeth BOWYER (1789-) [491].** Born 27 Jan 1789, baptised 7th March 1789, St. Helen's, Witton, Northwich.
3. **Sarah BOWYER (1791-) [492].** Born 11 Jun 1791, baptised 26th June 1791, St. Helen's, Witton, Northwich.

2. **Joseph DEAN (1750-) [272].** Baptised 5 Nov 1750, Weaverham. Joseph's father is recorded as James Dean of Hartford. Joseph moved within the local area and had a number of careers during his life. For example he is noted as living in Witton, Northwich, Davenham, Shurlock, Weaverham and Leftwich. In 1780 he was recorded as a Flatman and a Salt Miner and in 1789, when his son was born he was recorded as a Rock Getter in Lordship. Joseph Marr Mary BOWYER. There are two references from three different sources. The July dates are likely to be the Bann reading dates.

Joseph Marr Mary BOWYER 11 Jul 1780, Weaverham. Joseph was recorded as a Flatman of the Parish of Davenham Joseph signed his name and Mary made an x as her mark.

Joseph Marr Mary BOWYER 11 Jul 1780, Weaverham. Joseph was recorded as a Salt Miner of the Parish of Davenham. Joseph signed his name and Mary made an x as her mark. Witnesses John Massey and John Dutton.

Joseph Marr Mary BOWYER, 24 Aug 1780, Weaverham. Joseph was recorded as a Flatman of the Parish of Davenham. Joseph signed his name and Mary made an X as her mark.

Sp. Mary BOWYER (circa 1750-) [273], dau. of George BOWYER (1715-) [356] and Mary HOLLAND (-) [357]. George Bowyer, baptised 6 Jan 1715, Weaverham, Cheshire, parent noted as Daniel Bowyer.

SEE BOWYER FAMILY

3. **Nancy DEAN (1802-) [340].** Born 15 Jul 1802, baptised 7 Aug 1802, St. Helen's, Witton, Northwich. Dau of Joseph Dean and Mary Bowyer.
3. **Female Margaret/Sarah DEAN (1795-) [478].** Baptised 4 Oct 1795, St. Helen's, Witton, Northwich. The name of this female was unreadable. However, the following details appeared ".......... dau of Joseph Dean of Shulock, a Waller, son of James and Mary Dean, of Northwich, Mary dau of George Bowyer and Mary of Weaverham". Other references might suggest the name was Margaret and or Sarah.
3. **Thomas DEAN (circa 1796-1881) [501].** Born circa 1796. Son of Joseph Dean and Mary Bowyer. Thomas died 27 Sep 1881, age 85, buried St Wilfred's, Davenham. Thomas' baptismal records do not seem to be available however, his death details confirm his parents.
3. **Joseph DEAN (1786-) [997].** Born 20 Oct 1786, baptised 12 Nov 1786, St. Wilfred's, Davenham, Leftwich, Northwich. Son of Joseph Dean and Mary Bowyer.
3. **James (Senr) DEAN (1789-1871) [45].** Born 13 Feb 1789, baptised 7 March 1790, St. Helen's, Witton, Northwich. Son of Joseph Dean and Mary Bowyer. James was a Confectioner in Leftwich. James Marr Martha JACKSON, 24 Aug 1818, St Mary's and All Saints, Great Budworth. Witnesses Joseph Cooper and Robert ....

1841 English Census, Longrow, Leftwich, Northwich
James DEAN, head, Confectioner of Leftwich, married, age 50, born 1791, Martha DEAN, wife, married, age 49, Thomas DEAN, son, age 15, Susan DEAN, dau, age 13, Margaret DEAN, dau, age 11, Martha DEAN, dau, age 9, James DEAN, son, age 7, Mary DEAN, dau, age 4.

1851 English Census, London Road, Leftwich, Northwich
James DEAN. age 62, head, Confectioner, Martha DEAN, wife, age 60, James DEAN, son, age 16, Labourer, Martha DEAN, age 19, Dressmaker, Mary DEAN, age 14, Confectioner's daughter, Margaret DEAN, granddaughter, age 3.

1861 English Census, London Road, Davenham, Leftwich, Northwich
James DEAN, head, age 72, born 1789, Witton, Sugar Boiler, Martha DEAN, wife, age 67, born 1794, Hartford, Margaret DEAN, granddaughter, age 14, born 1847, Leftwich, Northwich.

1871 English Census, London Road, Davenham, Leftwich, Northwich
James DEAN, head, age 82, born 1779, Witton, Confectioner, Martha DEAN, wife, age 78, born 1793.

James died 11 Dec 1871, age 82, Leftwich, buried 14 Dec 1871, St. Wilfred's Davenham, Cheshire. In the grave yard at St. Wilfred's, Davenham is a very old grave with a broken stone. The stone was full of writing but most of this has worn away. However, at the bottom of the stone says: Martha Dean beloved wife of the above James Dean who died in 1871.

Death certificate
Registration District Northwich, death in the sub-district of Northwich in the County of Chester, 11 Dec 1871, Leftwich Lane, Leftwich, James Dean, male, age 81, Confectioner, Old age certified as reason for death, the mark of Martha Dean present at the death Leftwich Lane, Leftwich, registered 16 Dec1871.

> **Sp. Martha JACKSON (1794-1875) [46],** dau. of Thomas JACKSON (1760-) [281] and Martha BRATHERTON (1764-) [282]. Baptised 18 Apr 1794, St. Helen's, Witton, Northwich. Thomas Jackson, Waller of Castle. Thomas Jackson, born 1760, was the son of Thomas born circa 1745 and Elizabeth Jackson. Thomas Jackson, born circa 1745, was son of Richard Jackson, born circa 1715 and Elizabeth.

SEE BRATHERTON FAMILY

Before Martha married James Dean, Martha had a daughter called Elizabeth born 5 Dec 1816. Mother, Martha Jackson, residing at Witton cum Twambrooks. No father noted. Mother's parents Thomas and Martha Jackson. Elizabeth was baptised 30 Aug 1823.

Martha died 13 Jan 1875, in the Workhouse, Leftwich, Northwich, age 84, Confectioner's wife. Buried St. Wilfred's Parish Church, Davenham, Northwich.

Death certificate
Registration District of Northwich, death in the sub- district of Northwich in the County of Chester, 13 January 1875, in the Workhouse of Leftwich, Martha Dean, female, age 84 years, widow of James Dean, Confectioner. Cause of death old age, 2 years certified. Signature, description and residence of informant, Martha Plant, daughter, Leftwich Lane, Leftwich, registered 9 February 1875.

> **4. James (Toffee) DEAN (1834-1899) [44].** Born 5 Feb 1834, Leftwich, Northwich. Baptised 23 Feb 1834, St. Helen's, Witton, Northwich. Parents James Dean of Leftwich a Flatman and Martha his wife. James was affectionately known as Toffee Dean.

JIMMY DEAN

James (Toffee) Dean. A Founder Member of The Showmen's Guild and its President 1894 – 95 - 99. Born 1834, James died 27 Sep 1899. Courtesy of National Fairground Archive, University of Sheffield Library.

The History of Fairs

The following are extracts from an article written by Dr Vanessa Toulmin and have been included courtesy of Dr. Vanessa Toulmin, National Fairground Archive, University of Sheffield.

"Fairs or hiring fairs as they were known were originally established as a place where people would gather to look for employment and where employers would go to secure labour. The fairs were a huge social gathering within the community and local people would sell their wares and produce. There would also be an element of entertainment. The origins of fairs are in pagan customs especially seasonal gatherings for festivals and trade. Many fairs and festivals were later incorporated into the Christian calendar and were usually held on a set date often associated with a Saint's feast day. Close to 5,000 fairs were granted royal charters during the middle ages.

The start of hiring fairs or mops (as they are known in the Midlands) can be traced to the fourteenth century with the passing of the Statute of Labourers in 1351 by Edward III. Their original purpose was the hiring of labourers. Even at the hiring fairs, however, a trade and amusement element was usually present. These Statute fairs or Mops still continued in their original purpose until the end of the nineteenth century. However, over the last few centuries the amusement element took over and the fairs, as we know them today, became totally for amusement".

"Those working and living with the fairs became a 'nomadic people' travelling from place to place, particularly during the summer months. During the winter months these 'nomadic people' became static in various places in moveable dwellings".

The following extract is courtesy of The Showmen's Guild and The Showmen's Guild – Lancashire, Cheshire and North Wales Section - 'History of The Showmen's Guild'

The Moveable Dwellings Bill

"Public reactions to nomadic communities have seldom been sympathetic and have more often been marked by fear, suspicion, hostility and social rejection. Between 1884 and 1891 an evangelist George Smith referred to members of this nomadic community as the 'dregs of society' and proposed legislation to restrict the movement and lifestyle of these people. He was successful in bringing about restrictions on the movement of barge dwellers in 1884.

In 1888, George Smith introduced the Moveable Dwellers Bill into Parliament. This Bill would force the registration of all moveable dwellings and compulsory school attendance of all Gypsy's and van dwellers and the introduction of a series of regulations concerning the number of people permitted in a given living space. It also sought to empower local councils to enter and inspect dwellings and regulate so called 'moral irregularities'. These proposals aroused so much anger and hostility that Smith was chased out of Birmingham, and had to be given police protection in Leicester and Northampton!

The Van Dwellers Protection Association

In 1889 the leading Showmen of the day gathered at a meeting held in the Black Lion Hotel in Salford. From this and other gatherings, The Van Dwellers' Protection Association was born, to safeguard and protect the interests of fairground people. The fairground community arranged public meetings across the country, distributed information pamphlets and collected petitions to Parliament. In the first year, a membership fund received donations from over 500 Showmen to fight George Smith's Bill. The Moveable Dwellings Bill was finally defeated in 1894.

The Showmen's Guild

The Van Dwellers Protection Association came to be re-named over the following years as The Showmen's Guild and formally registered in 1917. The Showmen's Guild continues to act as a professional body and Employers' Trade Union for the Showmen of Great Britain protecting the way of life of the fairground families. From the early efforts of the Van Dwellers Protection Association to the 20th and 21st Century activity of the Showmen's Guild, Showmen have developed a strong and very effective organisational network. This network is further sustained by the Showmen's newspaper, The World's Fair, first issued in 1904".

Founder Members

Amongst those who gathered at the Black Lion Hotel in Salford in 1889, were two of the founder members, James Dean, affectionately known as Toffee Dean and J W Bostock. It was in the upstairs rooms of the Black Lion Hotel in Salford where the inauguration of what is now known as The Showmen's Guild took place.

James Dean was born in Leftwich, Northwich, Cheshire in 1834. He was the youngest son of James Dean, born in 1789, a confectioner of Leftwich, Cheshire. James carried on in a similar business to his father making toffee, sweets, rock, nougat and brandy snaps which he sold on stalls at the fairgrounds. James married Jane Bostock a family member of another of the founder members, who was also from the Northwich area. Folklore recalls James moved from Northwich to Salford in the mid 1800s and joined the van dwellers. James died in 1899 and is buried at St Helen's Church, Witton, Northwich, Cheshire. The Grave stone of James (Toffee) Dean reads -

"This Memorial is the Living Tribute of the Showmen of the United Kingdom to James Dean, One of the Founders of their Trade Defence Society. The Showmen's Guild, of which he was Honorary Secretary 1891-1893 and President 1894-1895 and 1899. He won the respect and admiration of his fellow Fairground Traders and Amusement Caters and left behind him a signal example of unselfish devotion to the good of others".

J W Bostock, also a founder member and a close relation to Jane Bostock, wife of James Dean. In 1890, J W Bostock was appointed as the first official President. J W Bostock, BT Burnett, J Dean, J Clayton and J Walker were recorded as presidents between 1890 and 1899. Honorary Secretaries recorded at this time were J. Dean, R. Dixon (son in law of James Dean), G.T. Salva and T. Hurst.

In the 1841 English Census, Longrow, Leftwich, Northwich and the 1851 English Census, London Road, Leftwich, Northwich, James was living with his parents.

James Marr Jane BOSTOCK 14 Jun 1852, St Mary's and All Saints, Parish Church of Great Budworth in the County of Chester.

Marriage certificate
14 June 1852, James Dean, age 20, bachelor, Confectioner, residence Castle, father, James Dean, Confectioner. married Jane Bostock, age 19, residence Castle, father, Josiah Bostock, Waterman. Marriage solemnised at the Parish Church in the Parish of Great Budworth in the County of Chester. Mary Bostock and Mark Rayner were the witnesses. Mary Bostock made an X as her mark.

1861 English Census, Leftwich, Witton Street, Witton, Northwich
James DEAN, head, age 27, Sugar Boiler, Jane DEAN, wife, age 27, Betsy DEAN, dau, age 8, Thomas DEAN, son, age 6, Mary DEAN, dau, age 3, Margaret, DEAN, dau, age 7 months.

James made sweets and toffees in a factory located in Pipemaker's Yard, Witton, Northwich. The factory was two cottages knocked into one. The exact location of Pipemaker's Yard is not known, although, one source thought it may now be known as Yate's Yard.

After Jane's death in 1870, the 1871 English Census would suggest James (Toffee) Dean remarried to a Margaret. However, no trace of this marriage has been found.

1871 English Census, Bebbington's Yard, Witton, Northwich
James DEAN, head, married, age 37, male, Fruiter Hawker, born Witton, Northwich, Margaret DEAN, wife, married, age 29, Fruiter Hawker, born Manchester, Lancashire, James DEAN, age 6 years, scholar, born Witton, Northwich, Martha DEAN age 3, born Witton, Northwich.

James left Witton, Northwich about 10 years before his death and joined the van dwellers in Salford. James was the President of and one of the founder members of the Van Dwellers Association, later to be known as the Showmen's Guild.

James Dean had what is known in the fairground world as a 'panam'. A panam is a 'joint' (a stall that sells sweets, rock, nougat, brandy snaps, toffee etc.,) so called because a white smock/coat pinny and a white panama hat would always be worn.

It appears that by 1873, James had remarried to Alice PARTINGTON, 4 Sept 1873, Manchester Cathedral.

Marriage certificate
4 September 1873, Manchester Cathedral, James Dean aged 38, Widower, labourer, living Dulcie Bridge. Father James Dean, Labourer, married Alice Partington, age 22, spinster, living Dulcie Bridge, father William Partington, Porter. Witnesses John and Alice Radford.

1881 English Census, 1 Dixon Street, Greengate, Salford, Lancashire
James DEAN, head, married, age 47, born 1834, Northwich, Printer, Alice DEAN, wife, age 35, born 1846, Manchester, James DEAN, son, age 16, born 1865, Northwich, Martha DEAN, dau, age 14, born 1867, Northwich.

1891 English Census, 102 Macclesfield Road, Nether Alderley, Knutsford
James DANE, head, married, age 57, born 1834, Northwich, Fruiterer, Alice DANE, wife, age 41, born 1850, Manchester.

The following English Census details for Alice Partington have been added

1861 English Census, 2 Rowe Street, Manchester
William PARTINGTON, head, age 49, Railway Porter, born Manchester, Jane PARTINGTON, wife, age 35, Charwoman, born Preston, Lancashire, Alice PARTINGTON, dau, age 9, born Manchester, Edward PARTINGTON, son, age 8, born Manchester, William PARTINGTON, son, age 2, born Manchester.

1871 English Census, 39 Longworth Street, Manchester
Francis BROOKS, Head, age 30, unmarried, Groom, born Wakefield, Alice PARTINGTON, lodger, age 21, unmarried, Mill Hand, born Manchester.

James died 27 Sep 1899, age of 67, 5 Church Brow, Mottram in Longsdale, Cheshire. (His age should have said 65). He is buried at St Helen's, Witton, Northwich.

Northwich Independent Newspaper dated Wednesday 4th October 1899 "One of the founder members of the Showmen's Guild".
"Funeral of a former Northwich Tradesman Prominent among showmen, On Monday afternoon the remains of Mr James Dean age 67 years, who died on the previous Wednesday at Mottram, were interned in Witton Churchyard, Northwich. The deceased was a native of the town, being the youngest son of the late Mr James Dean confectioner, Leftwich, which business deceased followed about 10 years. After that he removed to Manchester, his postal address being Flat Iron Market, Manchester. He joined those who visit fairs and became a leader of the dwellers in vans. When Mr Smith introduced his movable dwelling bill, which was feared would have a disastrous effect upon showmen and others, the Van Dwellers Protection Association was established and Mr Dean was appointed President which position he continued to occupy up to his death. By his earnest and conscientious efforts he gained the respect and esteem of the nomadic fraternity. The news of his demise created general regret and the funeral was attended by about 100 people among whom he had laboured for so many years. They came from all quarters. The attendance would have been larger but for the fact that Monday was the opening of the greatest fair of the year. Numerous telegrams and letters were received expressing regret at being unable to attend the obsequies. The mourners travelled by train from Manchester to Northwich. The service was conducted by the Rev T Horne. Hon. Chaplain to the Showmen's Guild, whilst in church he delivered an address in which he dwelt upon the useful work performed by their departed brother on behalf of all associated with their particular department in life. He always did what he could to benefit the community by who he was surrounded, and had won for himself their love. The speaker trusted that many present would try and follow in his footsteps. Amongst those present were: Mrs Dean (widow), Mr and Mrs Robert Dixon, Mr Thomas Dean, Mrs Hancock Jnr., Mrs Cooper, Mrs Hayes, Mrs Shaw, Mr Charles and Gilbert Dixon, Mr R Hancock, Mr John Cooper, Mr W Shaw, Mr Dean Jnr., Mrs Walker, Mr and Mrs Wright, Mr John Cordwell, Mr and Mrs Mitchell, Mrs Jewell, Mrs Williams, Mr P Collins, Mr Bennion, Mr and Mrs Clarke, Mrs Gallaghan, Mr and Mrs Holmes, Mr Goodwin, Mr Green, Mrs Milner, Mr Thomas Hurst, Mr Holmes, Mr and Mrs Black, Mr and Mrs Dillon, Mrs Darlington, Mr McGuiness, Mr and Mrs White, Mrs Massey, Mr Bucannon, Mrs Hartlington, Mr and Mrs Leo, Mr Robert Whitehead, Mr Turner, Mr West and Mr Charles Howard, Solicitor to the Van Dwellers and Showmen's Association. The bearers were Messrs Clayton, Walker, Darlington and Dillon. The wreaths were numerous and beautiful, the donors including the following: Mrs Dean (widow), Mr Fred Bikley, Mr and Mrs P Collins, Mrs Hartlingon, Mr and Mrs Dean, Mrs Collins (Jnr.,) Mrs and Miss S Holmes, Mr and Mrs Shaw, Mr and Mrs Clarke, Mr John Collins (Jnr), Mrs Holmes, Mr and Mrs James Goodwin, Mrs Mitchell, Mr and Mrs Robert Williams, Mr and Mrs Greatrex, Mrs Birk, Mr and Mrs Hancock, Mr and Mrs Symonds, Mr and Mrs George Walker, Mr and Mrs Cordwell (sen), Mrs Jennings, Mr and Mrs George White, Mr and Mrs Cooper, Mr and Mrs Whiting, Mr and Mrs James Dean, Mr Sheldon, Mr Charles Howard, Mr H Hammesley, Mr James Dean, Mrs Jewell, Mr and Mrs Robert Hancock, Mr B Newall and Mr and Mrs Black".

Will of James Dean
This is my last will and testament made this eighth day of September 1899 I bequeath to my son James Dean (1) my brown mare and harness with wagon and all accompaniments (2) the twenty four foot stall and all accessories also to my son in law John Cooper number two wagon with horse harness and accessories also the dray with all its belongings to my son in law Robert Hancock the rest of my property to be divided equally between my children I humbly submit my soul to God trusting in His Mercy thereby appoint Robert Dickson to be sole EXECUTOR to this my last will and testament and I bequeath the sum of twenty five pounds to him from my estate before it is divided (signed) James Dean 8/9/99 witnesses Isaac Shaw - John Roodhouse. Affidavit of due execution filed on the 14th day of October 1899 Probate of this will was granted to Robert Dixon the sole Executor. DEATH ON OR AFTER 1ST JANUARY 1898 Be it known that James Dean of No 5 Church Brow Mottram in the County of Chester died on the 27th day of September 1899 at No 5 Church Brow aforesaid AND BE IT FURTHER KNOWN that at the date here under written the last will and testament of the said deceased was proved and registered in the Principal Probate Registry of Her Majesty's High Court of Justice, and that administration of all the estate which by law devolves to and vests in the personal representative of the said deceased was granted by the aforesaid Court to Robert Dixon (in the will written Dickson) of the Flat Iron Market Blackfriars Street Salford in the County of Lancaster Showman the

sole Executor named in the said will dated the 14 day October 1899 Value of estate £164. Value of Personal Estate £113.10.6.

The grave stone of James (Toffee) Dean reads -
This Memorial is the Living Tribute of the Showmen of the United Kingdom to James Dean, One of the Founders of their Trade Defence Society. The Showmen's Guild of which he was Hon. Sec. 1891-1893. President 1894-1895 and 1899. He won the respect and admiration of his fellow Fairground Traders and Amusement Caters and left behind him a signal example of unselfish devotion to the good of others.

> **Sp. Jane BOSTOCK (1833-1870) [85]**, dau. of Josiah BOSTOCK (1791-1838) [210] and Mary YARWOOD (1794-) [211]. Jane's baptismal details have not been found. However, Mary Yarwood remarried after the death of Josiah Bostock to George Fairhurst and Jane appears in the following 1841 English Census.

SEE BOSTOCK AND YARWOOD FAMILY

1841 English Census, Crown Inn Farm House, Witton Street, Witton Cum Twanbrook, Great Budworth George FAIRHURST, age 45, Publican. born Cheshire, Mary FAIRHURST, wife, age 40, born Cheshire, Fanny BOSTOCK, dau, age 12, born Cheshire, James BOSTOCK, son, age 10, born Cheshire, Jane BOSTOCK, dau, age 8, born Cheshire, Mary BOSTOCK, dau, age 6, born Cheshire.

Jane died 22 June 1870, 15 Owens Court, Bridgewater Street, Deansgate, Manchester. Owens Court was one of the worse slums in Manchester. There was no running water, any water had to be carried from a communal well. There were two toilets for between 150/160 people. It is not clear why Jane was there as her abode was Witton. Jane may have been on a local fair ground or visiting when she was taken ill.

Death Certificate
Registration District Manchester, death in the sub-district of Deansgate, Manchester in the County of Lancaster, Jane Dean died 22 June 1870, 15 Owens Court, Bridgewater Street, Manchester, age 36, wife of James Dean a Hawker. Cause of death cancer uteri certified, signature, description and residence of informant X is the mark of Elizabeth Jones present at the death 15 Owens Court, Bridgewater Street, Manchester. Registered 23 June 1870, signature of registrar William Thomason.

Jane is buried at St Helen's, Witton, Northwich, not in the same grave as James Dean but in another grave close to the church and near the edge of the cemetery. The records from the burials at St Helens, Witton state: Jane dead, abode Witton, buried 26 June 1870 age 36 years.

> **5. Betsy DEAN (1852-1911) [33].** Baptised 14 Jul 1852, St. Helen's, Witton, Northwich. Dau of James Dean and Jane Bostock.

Betsy DEAN 1852 – 1911. Courtesy of National Fairground Archive, University of Sheffield Library.

Birth Certificate

Betsy, born 14 Jul 1852, Northwich, father, James Dean, Confectioner, mother, Jane Dean formerly Bostock. Signature, description and residence of informant was Jane Dean, mother, Witton, registered 16 Aug 1852 William Newall was the registrar.

Betsy Marr Robert DIXON, 9 Feb 1869, St John's Church, Parish of Burslem, Stoke on Trent, Staffordshire.

Marriage Certificate

9 Feb 1869, the Parish Church in the Parish of Burslem in the County of Stafford. Robert Dixon, age 19, bachelor, Labourer, residence Burslem, father Philip Dixon, Labourer, married Elizabeth Dean, age 17, spinster, residence Burslem, father James Dean, cabinet maker. Witnesses Alexander Taylor and Emily Howland. Both Robert and Elizabeth made an X each as their mark.

Betsy died 10 Jan 1911, age 54, Trinity Market Place, Salford. Buried 16 Jan 1911, in the family plot at Weaste Cemetery, Salford. Her death was reported in the Salford City Reporter January 14th 1911, "Dixon Elizabeth dearly beloved wife of Robert Dixon of the Flat Iron Market, Salford".

> **Sp. Robert DIXON (1849-1916) [34]**, son of Philip DIXON (1819-) [42] and Elizabeth DUTTON (1822-) [209].

SEE DIXON AND DUTTON FAMILY

5. **James DEAN (1861-) [52].** Born 1861. Son of James Dean and Jane Bostock.
5. **Thomas DEAN (1855-) [54].** Baptised 6 Jan 1855, St. Helen's, Witton, Northwich. Son of James Dean and James Bostock. There appear to be references which record a Thomas born 1852 and 1855. It is likely they are the same Thomas and the birth years were recorded incorrectly. Thomas Marr Lucy Emily BERROW, 5 Feb 1874, Warrington.
Sp. Lucy Emily BERROW (1855-1915) [682].

> 6. **William Thomas DEAN (1874-1943) [686].** Baptised 25 May 1874, Wigan, Lancashire. Son of Thomas Dean and Lucy Emily Berrow. William Marr firstly Susannah TURNER, 31 Jul 1895, Wigan, Lancashire and secondly Marr Catherine (Kate) TYRELL, 19 Apr 1915, Wigan, Lancashire. William Thomas died 22 Dec 1943.
> **Sp. Susannah TURNER (1874-1909) [696].**

> > 7. **Emily DEAN (1896-1925) [697].** Baptised 1896, Wigan, Lancashire. Emily Marr David CARTER, 13 Jun 1919, Wigan, Lancashire. Emily drowned at Bursough, Lancashire, 8 Aug 1925.
> > **Sp. David CARTER (-) [923].**

> > > 8. **Joseph CARTER (1919-1980) [924].** Born 1919. Died 18 Nov 1980, Wigan, Lancashire.
> > > 8. **Susannah CARTER (1921-1921) [925].** Born 1921, Wigan, Lancashire. Died 1921, 11 days old.
> > > 8. **Mary F CARTER (1922-1922) [926].** Born 1922, Wigan, Lancashire. Died 30 Jun 1922.

> > 7. **Thomas DEAN (1901-1902) [698].** Born 1901, Wigan, Lancashire. Died 13 Jan 1902.
> > 7. **Doris DEAN (1903-1905) [699].** Born 1903, Wigan, Lancashire. Died 28 Jun 1905, Wigan, Lancashire.

William Thomas DEAN (1874-1943) [686], married secondly Catherine TYRELL

> **Sp. Catherine (Kate) TYRELL (-) [700].**

> > 7. **Doris DEAN (1916-) [701].** Born 1916, Wigan, Lancashire.
> > 7. **Albert Edward DEAN (1930-1932) [702].** Born 1930. Died 7 Jul 1932, Wigan, Lancashire.

6. **James DEAN (1875-1934) [687].** Born 1875, Wigan, Lancashire. Son of Thomas Dean and Lucy Emily Berrow. James Marr Ellen OLLERTON, 23 Sep 1896, Wigan, Lancashire. Died 17 Mar 1934.
Sp. **Ellen OLLERTON (-) [703].**

  7. **Thomas DEAN (1897-1915) [704].** Born 1897, Wigan, Lancashire. Died 1915.
  7. **Mary Ann DEAN (1900-) [705].** Born 1900, Wigan, Lancashire.
  7. **Margaret DEAN (1902-1982) [706].** Born 1902, Wigan, Lancashire. Died 1982.
  7. **Hannah DEAN (1905-1915) [707].** Born 1905, Wigan, Lancashire. Died 1915,of burns.
  7. **Susannah DEAN (1909-1997) [708].** Born 1909, St. Helen's, Witton, Northwich. Died 1997.
  7. **James DEAN (1911-) [709].** Born 1911, St. Helen's, Witton, Northwich.
  7. **Robert DEAN (1915-) [710].** Born 1915, Wigan, Lancashire.
  7. **Thomas DEAN (1917-) [711].** Born 1917, Wigan, Lancashire.
  7. **Emily DEAN (1920-) [712].** Born 1920, Wigan, Lancashire.

6. **Jane DEAN (1879-) [688].** Baptised 29 Jan 1879, Wigan, Lancashire. Dau of Thomas Dean and Lucy Emily Berrow. Jane Marr Peter BARNES, 26 Nov 1898, Wigan, Lancashire.
Sp. **Peter BARNES (-) [713].**

  7. **Julia BARNES (1900-) [714].** Baptised 3 Dec 1900, Wigan, Lancashire.
  7. **Sarah BARNES (1904-) [715].** Born 1904, Wigan, Lancashire.
  7. **Lily BARNES (1906-) [716].** Born 1906, Wigan, Lancashire.
  7. **Peter BARNES (1909-) [717].** Born 1909, Wigan, Lancashire.
  7. **Jane BARNES (1913-) [718].** Baptised 5 Dec 1913, Wigan, Lancashire.
  7. **James BARNES (1919-) [719].** Baptised 6 Oct 1919, Wigan, Lancashire.
  7. **John BARNES (1912-1913) [720].** Baptised 3 Aug 1912, Wigan, Lancashire. Died 29 Jan 1913.
  7. **Edward BARNES (1922-) [721].** Baptised 24 Nov 1922, Wigan, Lancashire.

6. **Julie DEAN (1881-1958) [689].** Baptised 15 Sep 1881, Wigan, Lancashire. Dau of Thomas Dean and Lucy Emily Berrow. Julie Marr James CHADWICK, 26 May 1906, Wigan, Lancashire. Julie died 25 Jun 1958.
Sp. **James CHADWICK (1881-1940) [722].**

  7. **Thomas CHADWICK (1906-) [723].** Born 1906.
  7. **James CHADWICK (1909-) [724].** Born 1909.
  7. **Clara CHADWICK (1913-1914) [725].** Born 1913. Clara died 1 Jan 1914, age 5 months.
  7. **Elizabeth CHADWICK (1914-) [726].** Born 1914.
  7. **Jane CHADWICK (1916-) [727].** Born 1916, Twin.
  7. **Julia CHADWICK (1916-) [728].** Born 1916, Twin.
  7. **Richard CHADWICK (1911-1917) [729].** Born 1911. Died 2 Mar 1917, age 5 months.

6. **William DEAN (1885-1972) [690].** Baptised 13 Mar 1885. Son of Thomas Dean and Lucy Emily Berrow. William Marr Ethel WARNER, 12 Jun 1907, Wigan, Lancashire. Died 29 Jan 1972.
Sp. **Ethel WARNER (1886-1963) [730].**

William Dean born 1885 and Ethel
Warner born 1886.
Married 12th June 1907, Wigan,
Lancashire. Courtesy of Joan Tapner
nee Hanson

William Dean born 1885.
Courtesy of Joan Tapner nee Hanson

Ethel Dean nee Warner wife of William
Dean, with daughter Edna born 1908,
son Harold born 1911. Courtesy of Joan
Tapner nee Hanson

7. **Edna DEAN (1908-1974) [731].** Baptised 19 Mar 1908, Wigan, Lancashire. Edna Marr Herbert Roy Gareth HANSON, 22 Sep 1931, Carlisle, Cumberland. Edna died 18 Nov 1974, Wallasey, Wirral, Cheshire.
Sp. Herbert Roy Gareth HANSON (1904-1993) [739].

7. **Harold DEAN (1911-1982) [732].** Baptised 18 Jan 1911, Wigan, Lancashire. Harold died 29 Mar 1982, Carlisle, Cumberland.

Harold Dean 1911-1982, son of William Dean and Ethel Warner. Courtesy of Joan Tapner nee Hanson

7. **Amy DEAN (1913-1956) [733].** Baptised 25 Mar 1913, Wigan, Lancashire. Died 3 Mar 1956, Carlisle, Cumberland.

Amy Dean 1913-1950, daughter of William Dean and Ethel Warner. Courtesy of Joan Tapner nee Hanson

7. Estella DEAN (1915-1985) [734]. Baptised 17 Jun 1915, Wigan, Lancashire. Died 15 Oct 1985, Carlisle, Cumberland.

Estella Dean 1915-1935, daughter of William Dean and Ethel Warner. Courtesy of Joan Tapner nee Hanson

6. Henry DEAN (1886-1890) [691]. Baptised 3 Jun 1886, Wigan, Lancashire. Son of Thomas Dean and Lucy Emily Berrow. Henry died 1890. Henry Marr Margaret ASPEY, 18 Dec 1909, Wigan, Lancashire.
Sp. Margaret ASPEY (1890-1971) [735].

    7. Harry DEAN (1910-) [736]. Born 1910, Wigan, Lancashire.
    7. Emily DEAN (1913-) [737]. Born 1913, Wigan, Lancashire.

6. Richard DEAN (1890-1908) [692]. Baptised 1 Nov 1890, Wigan, Lancashire. Son of Thomas Dean and Lucy Emily Berrow. Richard died 29 Aug 1908.
6. Robert DEAN (1888-1915) [693]. Baptised 12 Jun 1888, Wigan, Lancashire. Son of Thomas Dean and Lucy Emily Berrow. Robert Marr Alice SELDON, 1911, Wigan, Lancashire. Robert died 1915.
Sp. Alice SEDDON (-) [738].

6. Clara DEAN (1892-1892) [694]. Baptised 11 Mar 1892, Wigan, Lancashire. Dau of Thomas Dean and Lucy Emily Berrow. Clara died 8 Dec 1892.
6. David DEAN (1895-1900) [695]. Baptised 23 Feb 1895, Wigan, Lancashire. Son of Thomas Dean and Lucy Emily Berrow. David died 21 Jul 1900.

    5. Female (1851-) [56]. Born 1851. Dau of James Dean and Jane Bostock.
    5. Mary DEAN (1858-) [202]. Born 1858, Northwich. Dau of James Dean and Jane Bostock. Mary Marr Robert HANCOCK 1879, Salford, Lancashire.

1871 English Census, Navigation Road, Castle, Northwich
Mary J MILLS, dau, age 11, scholar, Thomas MILLS, son, age 9, scholar, Margaret MILLS, dau, age 4, Mary DEAN (boarder), age 13, born Leftwich .(in temporary charge of family, in absence of parents in Liverpool), Samuel L MILLS, son, age 2.

    Sp. Robert HANCOCK (1857-) [203], son of Robert HANCOCK (circa 1828-) [270] and Sarah Ann (circa 1829-) [271].

1881 English Census,15 Dawson Street ,Heap, Bury, Lancashire.
Robert HANCOCK, head, married, age 53, Travelling Co, born, Bury, Lancashire, Sarah Ann HANCOCK, wife, married, age 52, housewife, born Rochdale, Lancashire, Robert HANCOCK, son, married, age 24, Travelling Co, born Haywood, Lancashire, Mary HANCOCK, wife, married, age 23, Traveller's wife, born Northwich, Sarah Jane HANCOCK, dau, age 3, scholar, born Bury, Lancashire, Robert M HANCOCK, son, age 1, born Rochdale, Lancashire.

> 6. **Robert M HANCOCK (1880-) [204].** Born 1880, Rochdale, Lancashire.
> 6. **Sarah HANCOCK (1878-) [594].** Born 1878, Bury, Lancashire.
> **Sp. Male NOBLE (-) [595].**
> > 7. **Colin NOBLE (-) [596].**

> 5. **Martha DEAN (1867-1936) [253].** Baptised 10 Mar 1867, St. Helen's, Witton, Northwich. Dau of James Dean and Jane Bostock. In the 1871 English Census of Bebbington's Yard, Witton, Northwich. Martha Marr John COOPER, 1884, Salford. Martha died 16 Feb 1936, Warrington.
> **Sp. John William COOPER (1865-1940) [254].** Born 1865. Son of Solomon Cooper (-) [2368] and Fanny Hull (-) [2369], who married 29 Sept 1884, Salford. John died 6 Aug 1940, Warrington.

Nora Fitzsimmons nee Cooper and family. Courtesy of Jean Berry nee Fitzsimmons

> 6. **Nora COOPER (-) [2366].** Nora married John FITZSIMMONS
> **Sp. John FITZSIMMONS (-) [2367].**
> 6. **Gilbert COOPER (-) [2370].**

> 5. **Margaret DEAN (1860-1862) [363].** Born 1860, Witton, Northwich. Dau of James Dean and Jane Bostock. Margaret died 1862, age 17 months.
> 5. **James DEAN (1865-) [681].** Born 1865, Witton, Northwich. Son of James Dean and Jane Bostock. James was living with his parents in 1871 English Census, Bebbington's Yard,

Witton, Northwich and in the 1881 English Census, 1 Dixon Street, Greengate, Salford. James Marr Mary Elizabeth MILLNER, 1877, Blackley, Lancashire

1901 English Census for Manchester (Harpurey Ward) (Living in Travelling Caravans) Queens Road Fairground, Salford
James DEAN, age 36, travelling confectioner, retired, born 1864/5 Northwich, Mary E DEAN, wife, age 24, born 1876 Blackley, Charles DEAN, son, age 4, born Salford, Thomas E DEAN, son, age 4 months, born Ellesmere Port.

> Sp. Mary Elizabeth MILLNER (1876-) [749]. Born Blackley, Lancashire. Mary Elizabeth Dean, nee Millner, remarried in 1910, Prestwich, Lancashire, to William Ryan. In the 1911 English Census James Dean, born 1897, Salford, son, was living with them.

>> 6. Charles DEAN (1896-) [750]. Born 1896, Salford, son of James Dean and Mary Elizabeth Millner.
>> 6. Thomas E DEAN (1901-) [751]. Born 1901, Ellesmere Port , son of James Dean and Mary Elizabeth Millner.
>> 6. James DEAN (1897-) [1685]. Born 1897, Salford, son of James Dean and Mary Elizabeth Millner.

> 4. Thomas DEAN (1824-) [58]. Born 19 Nov 1824, Witton, Northwich. Baptised 3 Dec 1824, St. Helen's, Witton, Northwich. Son of James, Flatman of Northwich and Martha Dean. Thomas became a cabinet maker. Thomas was living with his parents in 1841 English Census, Longrow, Leftwich, Northwich. Thomas Marr Elizabeth BRACKLOW.
> Sp. Elizabeth BRACKILOW (-) [265].

>> 5. Margaret DEAN (1847-) [266]. Baptised 12 Sept 1847, St. Wilfred's, Davenham, Leftwich, Northwich. In the 1851 English Census, London Road, Leftwich, Margaret living with her grandparents. Margaret Marr Thomas COULTHURST, 19 Feb 1865, Leftwich, Northwich.
>> Sp. Thomas COULTHURST (1846-) [959], son of Thomas COULTHURST (-) [960].

Marriage certificate
Margaret Dean, age 17, single, residence Leftwich, married 19th Feb 1865. Thomas Coulthurst, age 19, single, his father Thomas Coulthurst, her father Thomas Dean.

1871 English Census. Hut (temporary structure) on Portland Street, Manchester
Thomas COULTHURST, head, age 24, b1846, Tin Plate Worker, born Fleetwood, Lancashire, Margaret COULHURST, wife, age 23, born 1847, Northwich, Elizabeth COULTHURST, dau, age 5, born 1865 Northwich.

>> 6. Elizabeth COULTHURST (1865-) [961]. Born 1865, Northwich.

> 4. Martha DEAN (1831-) [59]. Born 1831, Davenham, Northwich. Baptised 1 Jan 1831, Parish of Astbury, Cheshire. Parents Joseph Dean and Martha of Astbury, Cheshire. Martha Marr Thomas PLANT, 1852. Martha was living with her parents in 1841 English Census, Longrow, Leftwich, Northwich and the 1851 English Census, London Road, Leftwich, Northwich. Martha Marr Thomas PLANT.
> Sp. Thomas PLANT (1829-) [214].

The following Census records Thomas Plant before his marriage to Martha.

1851 English Census, London Road, Davenham, Leftwich, Northwich
James PLANT, head, age 26, Sarah PLANT, wife, age 22, John PLANT, son, age 8, Mary PLANT, dau, Thomas PLANT, brother, age 22, Carpenter.

1861 English Census, London Road, Davenham, Leftwich, Northwich
Thomas PLANT, head, married, age 31, born 1830, Leftwich, Shipwright, Martha PLANT, wife, age 29, born 1832, Leftwich, Joseph PLANT, son, age 8, born 1853, Leftwich, Cornelius PLANT, son, age 6, born 1855, Leftwich, Martha PLANT, dau, age 4, born 1857, Leftwich, Northwich.

1871 English Census, London Road, Davenham, Leftwich, Northwich
Thomas PLANT, head, married, age 41, born 1830, Leftwich, Shipwright, Martha PLANT, wife, age 39, born 1832, Leftwich, Joseph PLANT, son, age 18, born 1853, Leftwich, Cornelius PLANT, son, age 16, born 1855, Leftwich, Martha PLANT, dau, age 14, born 1857, Leftwich, Northwich.

At the time of Martha's mother's death in 1871, Martha's residence was Leftwich Lane, Leftwich

1881 English Census, 157 London Road, Davenham, Leftwich, Northwich
Thomas PLANT, head, married, age 50, Ship Carpenter, born Davenham, Martha PLANT, wife, married, age 49, born Davenham, Martha PLANT, dau, unmarried, age 24, tobacconist, born Davenham.

      5. Martha PLANT (1857-) [60]. Born 1857, Davenham, Northwich. Tobacconist.
      Sp. (unknown).

          6. Margaret PLANT (-) [600].

      5. Joseph PLANT (1853-) [679]. Born 1853, Leftwich, Northwich. Joseph was living with his parents in 1861 English Census, London Road, Davenham, Leftwich, Northwich and the 1871 English Census, London Road, Davenham, Leftwich, Northwich
      5. Cornelius PLANT (1855-) [680]. Born 1855, Leftwich, Northwich. Cornelius was living with his parents in 1861 English Census, London Road, Davenham, Leftwich, Northwich and the 1871 English Census, London Road, Davenham, Leftwich, Northwich

   4. Mary DEAN (1837-) [62]. Born 1837, Davenham, Leftwich. Confectioner's daughter. Dau of James Dean and Martha Jackson. Mary was living with her parents in 1841 English Census, Longrow, Leftwich, Northwich and the 1851 English Census, London Road, Leftwich, Northwich
   4. Margaret DEAN (1829-) [216]. Born 1829, Leftwich, Northwich. Baptised 20 Sept 1829, St. Helen's, Witton, Northwich. Dau of James, Flatman of Leftwich and Martha Dean. Residence noted as Northwich. Margret was living with her parents in 1841 English Census, Longrow, Leftwich, Northwich.
   4. Susannah DEAN (1827-) [267]. Born 15 Aug 1827, Leftwich, Northwich. Baptised 2 Sept 1827, St. Helen's, Witton, Northwich. Residence noted as Northwich. Dau of James Dean and Martha Jackson. Susannah was living with her parents in 1841 English Census, Longrow, Leftwich, Northwich.
   4. Elizabeth DEAN (1816-) [480]. Born 5 Dec 1816, Witton, Northwich. Baptised 30 Aug 1823, St. Helen's, Witton. Elizabeth was born before James Dean and Martha Jackson married. There is no father's name on her certificate. Mother's name Martha Jackson, dau of Thomas and Martha Jackson, residing at Witton cum Twanbrooks, Northwich.
   4. Joseph DEAN (1832-) [503]. Born 1832. Baptised 31 Aug 1832, St. Helen's, Witton, Northwich, son of James Dean, Flatman of Northwich and Martha Dean. In a large old book for St Helens, Witton, was noted the birth of a Josue/Joseph Dean, born in 1832 and he was listed as working in Pipemaker's Yard in Witton,. Josue/Joseph was a brother of James (Toffee) Dean.
   4. Joseph DEAN (1819-) [922]. Born 10 Aug 1819, Leftwich, Northwich. Baptised 18 Aug 1819, St. Helen's, Witton, Northwich. Son of James Dean and Martha Jackson.

  3. John DEAN (1783-) [274]. Born December 1782. Baptised 5 Jan 1783, St. Helen's, Witton, Northwich. Parents Joseph Dean and Mary Bowyer from Witton cum Twambrooks, Northwich. John Marr Mary EVANS, 21 Aug 1809, St Mary's and All Saints, Great Budworth, Cheshire.
  Sp. Mary EVANS (-) [275].

1851 English Census, London Road, Leftwich, Northwich
John DEAN, head (widower) age 70, Fireman, born Leftwich, James DEAN, son, age 15.

      4. Joseph DEAN (1815-) [317]. Born 7 Jan 1815. Baptised 12 Jan 1815.
      4. Mary DEAN (1817-) [318]. Born 15 Sep 1817. Baptised 5 Oct 1817.
      4. Betsy DEAN (1820-) [319]. Born 5 Jan 1820. Baptised 27 Jan 1820.
      4. Sarah DEAN (1824-) [320]. Born 12 Dec 1824. Baptised 2 Feb 1825.
      4. Helen DEAN (1827-) [321]. Born 10 May 1827. Baptised 3 Jun 1827.

4. **Robert DEAN (1830-) [322].** Born 24 May 1830, Witton, Northwich. Baptised 27 Jun 1830, St. Helen's, Witton, Northwich. Robert Marr Elizabeth
Sp. Elizabeth (1839-) [362].

1861 English Census York Buildings, Leftwich, Northwich.
Robert DEAN, head, age 32, Salt Labourer, born Leftwich, Elizabeth DEAN, wife, age 22, born Warrington.

4. **James DEAN (1835-) [367].** Born Davenham, Leftwich. Baptised 12 Jul 1835, St. Wilfred's, Witton, Northwich. Son of John Dean and Mary Evans. James was living with his father in 1851 English Census, London Road, Leftwich, Northwich.
4. **John DEAN (1822-) [368].** Baptised 17 Mar 1822, St. Wilfred's, Davenham, Northwich. Son of John Dean and Mary Evans. John Marr Ann.
Sp. Ann (1829-) [369].

1851 English Census, London Road, Leftwich
John DEAN, head, age 29, salt labourer, born Leftwich, Ann DEAN, wife, age 31, Sarah Ann DEAN, dau, age 6, Thomas DEAN, son, age 4, William DEAN, son, age 2.

5. **Sarah Ann DEAN (1845-) [370].** Baptised 12 Jan 1845, St. Wilfred's, Davenham, Northwich. Sarah Ann living with parents in the 1851 English Census, London Road, Leftwich, Northwich.
5. **Thomas DEAN (1846-) [371].** Baptised 6 Dec 1846, St. Wilfred's, Davenham, Northwich. Thomas was living with his parents in the 1851 English Census, London Road, Leftwich, Northwich.
5. **William DEAN (1849-) [372].** Born 1849. William was living with his parents in 1851 English Census, London Road, Leftwich, Northwich.
5. **James DEAN (1853-) [1769].** Born 7 Aug 1853, Baptised St. Wilfred's, Witton, Northwich.

4. **Hannah DEAN (-) [473].** Dau of John Dean and Mary Evans.
4. **Charlotte DEAN (-) [475].** Dau of John Dean and Mary Evans.
4. **William DEAN (-) [476].** Son of John Dean and Mary Evans.

3. **George DEAN (1793-) [276].** Born 16 Apr 1793. Baptised 15 May 1793, St. Helen's, Witton, Northwich. Son of Joseph Dean and Mary Bowyer, Lordship, Rockgetter. George grandson of James and Mary Dean of Leftwich, Mary dau of George and Mary Bowyer of Weaverham. George Marr Hannah ORMSON, 7 Aug 1822, St Wilfred's, Davenham, Northwich.
Sp. Hannah ORMSON (-) [277].

4. **Mary DEAN (1829-) [324].** Born 16 Jul 1829, baptised 2 Aug 1829, St. Helen's, Witton, Northwich.
4. **Sarah DEAN (1831-1833) [325].** Born 3 May 1831, baptised 19 Jun 1831, St. Helen's, Witton, Northwich. Died 8 Apr 1833, of small pox 1 year 9 months old. Buried St Helen's Witton, Northwich.
4. **William DEAN (1833-) [326].** Born 16 Aug 1833, baptised 1 Sep 1833, St. Helen's, Witton, Northwich.
4. **James DEAN (1835-1836) [327].** Baptised 6 Sep 1835, St. Helen's, Witton, Northwich. James died 12 Feb 1836, of a weakness 5 months old. Buried St Helen's Witton, south side.
4. **Joseph DEAN (1824-) [328].** Baptised 17 Oct 1824, St. Helen's, Witton, Northwich .

3. **William DEAN (1798-) [278].** Born 25 Oct 1798, Leftwich, baptised 18 Nov 1798, St. Helen's, Witton, Northwich. Son of Jospeh Dean and Mary Bowyer. William Marr Charlotte WRENCH, 20 Mar 1819, Knutsford.
Sp. Charlotte WRENCH (-) [279].

4. **Mary Ann DEAN (1823-1824) [329].** Born 10 Aug 1823, baptised 24 Aug 1823, St. Helen's, Witton, Northwich. Mary Ann died 17 Jan 1824, of Convulsions first year of life. Buried St Helen's Witton, Northwich.
4. **John DEAN (circa 1825-) [330].** Born circa 1825.
4. **Ann DEAN (1826-) [331].** Born 23 Oct 1826, baptised 5 Nov 1826, St. Helen's, Witton, Northwich.

4. **Samuel DEAN (1831) [332].** Baptised 8 May 1831, St. Helen's, Witton, Northwich.
4. **Martha DEAN (1822-1834) [333].** Born 1822, death age and birth do not match. Could have been 2 Martha's. Martha died 21 Sep 1834, of a chink cough. age 1. Buried St Helen's, Witton, Northwich.
4. **Sarah DEAN (1839-1840) [907].** Born 1839. Died 29 Apr 1840, water on the brain 9 months old. Buried St Helen's Witton, Northwich.

3. **Mary DEAN (1795-) [290].** Born 12 Sep 1795, baptised 4th October 1795, St. Helen's, Witton, Northwich. Dau of Joseph Dean and Mary Bowyer. Mary Marr Thomas BALDWIN.
Sp. Thomas BALDWIN (-) [291].

4. **Thomas BALDWIN (1819-) [292].** Born 19 Apr 1819, baptised 16 May 1819.
4. **Betty BALDWIN (1816-) [334].** Born 6 Dec 1816, baptised 22 Dec 1816.
4. **John BALDWIN (1819-) [335].** Born 19 Apr 1819, baptised 16 May 1819. Twin.
4. **Joseph BALDWIN (1821-) [336].** Born 9 Nov 1821, baptised 25 Nov 1821.
4. **Mary BALDWIN (1824) [337].** Baptised 19 Jul 1824.
4. **James BALDWIN (1834-) [338].** Born 3 Feb 1834, baptised 2 Mar 1834.
4. **Fanny BALDWIN (1835) [339].** Baptised 5 Apr 1835.

Gilbert Fearns Set of Chair Planes - Grandson of Betsy Dean and Robert Dixon.
Courtesy of John Fearns

Mitchell's Ark (a speedway). Courtesy of John Fearns

Chapter Two

THE BRATHERTON FAMILY

Bratherton Family Outline

James BRATHERTON (circa 1690-)

---

1. James BRATHERTON (circa 1690-) [2115].
Sp. Martha WOODCOCK (-) [2126].
   2. Thomas BRATHERTON (1726-) [2127].
   2. James BRATHERTON (1721-) [2128].
   2. Richard BRATHERTON (1731-) [2034].
   Sp. Elizabeth LOWE (-) [2039].
      3. Martha BRATHERTON (1764-) [282].
      Sp. Thomas JACKSON (circa 1760 -) [281]. Son of Thomas Jackson (circa 1740 -) [2229] and
          Elizabeth (-) [2376].
        4. Martha JACKSON (1794 -1875) [46].
       Sp. James (Senr) DEAN (1789-1871) [45]. Son of Joseph DEAN (1750-) [272] and Mary
          BOWYER (circa 1750-) [273].
SEE DEAN AND BOWYER FAMILY
        4. Sarah/Sally JACKSON (1801-1856) [283].
       Sp. James WHITEHEAD (-) [284].
        4. Thomas JACKSON (1796 -) [493].
        4. Margaret JACKSON (1799-) [494].
       Sp. John WEBB (-) [495].
        4. Marie JACKSON (1791-) [2377].
        4. George JACKSON (-) [496].
       Sp. Mary WILKINSON (-) [497].
        4. Martha JACKSON (1789-) [2114].
      3. Richard BRATHERTON (1771-) [2035].
      3. Hannah BRATHERTON (1775-) [2036].
      3. William BRATHERTON (1779-) [2038].
      3. Peggy BRATHERTON (1765-1767) [2113].
      3. Thomas BRATHERTON (1780-) [2123].
      3. James BRATHERTON (1768-) [2116].
      Sp. Margaret GERRARD (1769-1824) [2117].
        4. Richard BRATHERTON (1791-) [2118].
        4. Betty BRATHERTON (1796-) [2119].
        4. Thomas BRATHERTON (1799-1801) [2120].
        4. James BRATHERTON (1805-) [2121].
        4. Marin BRATHERTON (-1798) [2122].
        4. William BRATHERTON (-1803) [2124].
        4. George BRATHERTON (1793-) [2125].

Bratherton Lineage

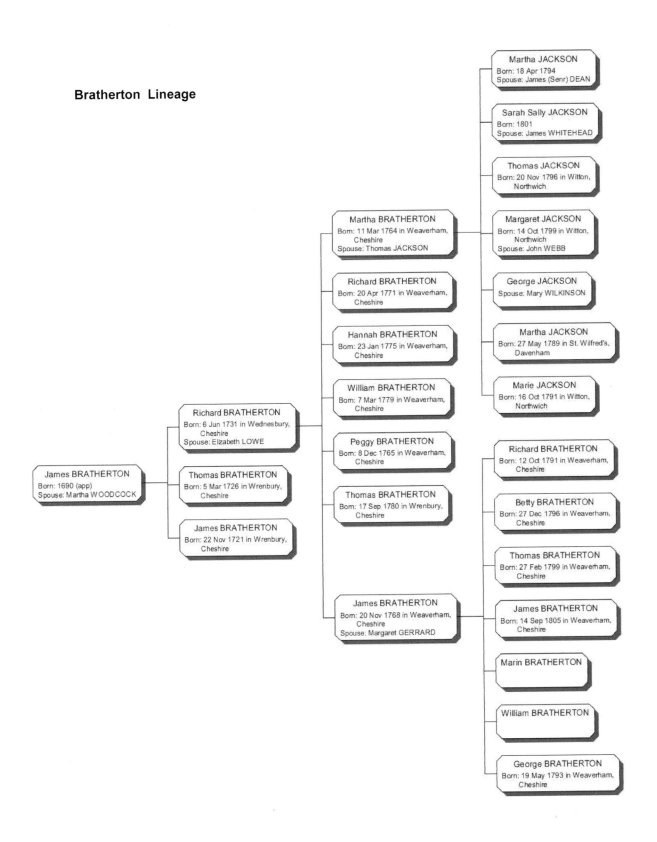

Martha JACKSON
Born: 18 Apr 1794
Spouse: James (Senr) DEAN

Sarah Sally JACKSON
Born: 1801
Spouse: James WHITEHEAD

Thomas JACKSON
Born: 20 Nov 1796 in Witton, Northwich

Margaret JACKSON
Born: 14 Oct 1799 in Witton, Northwich
Spouse: John WEBB

George JACKSON
Spouse: Mary WILKINSON

Martha JACKSON
Born: 27 May 1789 in St. Wilfred's, Davenham

Marie JACKSON
Born: 16 Oct 1791 in Witton, Northwich

Martha BRATHERTON
Born: 11 Mar 1764 in Weaverham, Cheshire
Spouse: Thomas JACKSON

Richard BRATHERTON
Born: 20 Apr 1771 in Weaverham, Cheshire

Hannah BRATHERTON
Born: 23 Jan 1775 in Weaverham, Cheshire

William BRATHERTON
Born: 7 Mar 1779 in Weaverham, Cheshire

Peggy BRATHERTON
Born: 8 Dec 1765 in Weaverham, Cheshire

Thomas BRATHERTON
Born: 17 Sep 1780 in Wrenbury, Cheshire

Richard BRATHERTON
Born: 6 Jun 1731 in Wednesbury, Cheshire
Spouse: Elizabeth LOWE

Thomas BRATHERTON
Born: 5 Mar 1726 in Wrenbury, Cheshire

James BRATHERTON
Born: 1690 (app)
Spouse: Martha WOODCOCK

James BRATHERTON
Born: 22 Nov 1721 in Wrenbury, Cheshire

Richard BRATHERTON
Born: 12 Oct 1791 in Weaverham, Cheshire

Betty BRATHERTON
Born: 27 Dec 1796 in Weaverham, Cheshire

Thomas BRATHERTON
Born: 27 Feb 1799 in Weaverham, Cheshire

James BRATHERTON
Born: 20 Nov 1768 in Weaverham, Cheshire
Spouse: Margaret GERRARD

James BRATHERTON
Born: 14 Sep 1805 in Weaverham, Cheshire

Marin BRATHERTON

William BRATHERTON

George BRATHERTON
Born: 19 May 1793 in Weaverham, Cheshire

James BRATHERTON (circa 1690-)

1. **James BRATHERTON (circa 1690-) [2115].** Born circa 1690. No baptismal details have been found for James. The surname has a number of spellings, in particular Brotherton. James Marr Martha WOODCOCK, 7 Feb 1720, Wrenbury, Cheshire. Both were noted as residing in Wrenbury. James was noted as a shoemaker of Sound in 1727, when his son Thomas was born.

The following have been noted as possible branches of this family
Sarah Brotherton baptised 21 Aug 1720, Wrenbury, parents William and Elizabeth of Sound
Martha Bratherton baptised 8 Oct 1727, Wrenbury, parents William and Elizabeth of Sound
George Bratherton baptised 13 May 1723, Wrenbury, son of Elizabeth Broatherton of Bramhall
Martha Bratherton baptised 17 Aug 1755, Wrenbury, parents George and Dorothy of Sound
Thomas Bratherton baptised 23 Aug 1730, Coddington, parents John and Priscilla, labourer of Barton
Mary Bratherton baptised 1741, parent John of Coddington
Richard Bratherton baptised 25 May 1760, Wrenbury, parents Thomas and Dorothy of Sound
Thomas Bratherton buried 13 Aug 1730, Wrenbury, Cheshire
Thomas Bratherton Marr 23 Sept 1700, Wrenbury to Anne Ellis
William Bratherton married 14 Jul 1657, Wrenbury to Prudence Palin
John Bratherton married Katharine Capper, 3 Jan 1677, Wrenbury

Sp. Martha WOODCOCK (-) [2126].

2. **Thomas BRATHERTON (1726-) [2127].** Baptised 5 Mar 1726, Wrenbury, born to James and Martha Bratherton, shoemaker of Barton, Cheshire.
2. **James BRATHERTON (1721-) [2128].** Baptised 22 Nov 1721, Wrenbury, born to James and Martha Bratherton, residence Sound, Cheshire.
2. **Richard BRATHERTON (1731-) [2034].** Baptised 6 Jun 1731, Wrenbury, born to James and Marther Bretherton, residence Sound, Cheshire. Richard Marr Elizabeth LOWE, 29 Jul 1763, Weaverham, Cheshire. Both noted as being from Weaverham. Witnesses James Shallcross and G Rathbone. Richard and Elizabeth moved from Sound and took up residence in Cuddington, Cheshire by the time their first daughter Martha was born in 1764.

Sp. Elizabeth LOWE (-) [2039].

The actual baptismal record for Elizabeth has not been confirmed. The following registrations have been included as one of these is likely to be the correct registration for Elizabeth

- Female Lowe baptised 29 May 1727, Weaverham, born to Thomas Lowe and Elizabeth. Much of this record is unreadable.
- Elizabeth Lowe baptised 27 Feb 1733, Weaverham, born to John Lowe, Farmer of Bay Lane, Weaverham and his wife Hannah
- Elizabeth Lowe baptised 27 Mar 1734, Weaverham, born to Samuel Lowe, Farmer of Sandiway and his wife Elizabeth

3. **Martha BRATHERTON (1764-) [282].** Baptised 11 Mar 1764, Weaverham, parents residence noted as Cuddington, Cheshire. Dau of Richard Bratherton and Elizabeth Lowe. Martha (Brotherton) Marr Thomas JACKSON, 28 June 1784, Weaverham. Witnesses Samuel Heppard, Richard Bratherton and John Cartwright. Both recorded as being of Weaverham.

   There is a record for Martha Bratherton Marr Thomas JACKSON, 20 Nov 1796, St Helens, Witton Northwich. In 1794, Thomas was recorded as residing in Witton cum Twambrooks, Northwich. Considering the Bratherton family are, at this stage, from the Weaverham area it is likely the marriage in 1784 is correct. In addition some of their children were born before 1794.

Sp. Thomas JACKSON (circa 1760 -) [281]. Son of Thomas Jackson , born circa 1740 and Elizabeth. Thomas Jackson born circa 1740, son of Richard Jackson born circa 1715 and Elizabeth.

4. **Martha JACKSON (1794 -1875) [46].** Baptised 18 Apr 1794, St. Helen's, Witton, Northwich. Dau of Thomas Jackson, Waller of Castle and Martha. Thomas' parents Thomas Jackson and Elizabeth. Martha Bratherton's parents Robert Bratherton and Elizabeth Lowe. Martha Marr James (Senr) DEAN.

Sp. James (Senr) DEAN (1789-1871) [45], son of Joseph DEAN (1750-) [272] and Mary

BOWYER (circa 1750-) [273].

SEE DEAN AND BOWYER FAMILY

4. **Sarah JACKSON (1801-1856) [283].** Born 1801, Witton. Sarah, age 25, Sarah Marr James WHITEHEAD, 7 Aug 1826, St. Helen's, Witton, Northwich. James was 26 years old. Witnesses Thomas Sayer and William Swindall. Sarah died 5 Aug 1856, Witton Cum Twambrooks, age 63, father Thomas Jackson, mother, Martha, Spouse James Whitehead

Sp. James WHITEHEAD (-) [284].

4. **Thomas JACKSON (1796-) [493].** Baptised 20 Nov 1796, born to Thomas Jackson, Waller of Hartford and Martha. Thomas' parents were Thomas Jackson and Elizabeth.

4. **Margaret JACKSON (1799-) [494].** Baptised 14 Oct 1799, St. Helen's, Witton, Northwich. Parents residence noted as Witton cum Twanbrooks. Margaret Marr John WEBB.

Sp. John WEBB (-) [495].

4. **Marie JACKSON (1791-) [2377].** Baptised 16 Oct 1791, St. Helen's, Witton, Northwich. Parents residence noted as Witton cum Twanbrooks. Dau of Thomas Jackson of Hartford, Rockgetter and Martha Bratherton. Thomas's parents are Thomas Jackson and Elizabeth . Martha Bratherton's parents are Robert Bratherton and Elizabeth Lowe.

4. **George JACKSON (-) [496].** George Marr Mary WILKINSON.

Sp. Mary WILKINSON (-) [497].

4. **Martha JACKSON (1789-) [2114].** Born 27 May 1789, Baptised 26 Oct 1789, St. Wilfred's, Davenham, Northwich, born to Thomas and Martha Jackson of Wharton. Martha died circa 1790. There is no evidence link this record to this family but has been noted for interest.

3. **Richard BRATHERTON (1771-) [2035].** Born 20 Apr 1771, baptised 5 May 1771, Weaverham. Residence of parents was Cuddington, Cheshire.

3. **Hannah BRATHERTON (1775-) [2036].** Baptised 23 Jan 1775, Weaverham. A further reference states baptised 23 Jan 1774, Weaverham. Residence of parents was Cuddington.

3. **William BRATHERTON (1779-) [2038].** Born 4 Feb 1779, baptised 7 Mar 1779, Weaverham. Residence of parents was Cuddington.

3. **Peggy BRATHERTON (1765-1767) [2113].** Baptised 8 Dec 1765, Weaverham. Residence of parents was Cuddington, Margaret died May 1767, Buried 22 May 1767, Weaverham. Father was noted as Richard Bratherton.

3. **Thomas BRATHERTON (1780-) [2123].** Baptised 17 Sep 1780, Wrenbury, Cheshire. Parents Richard and Eliza Bratherton.

3. **James BRATHERTON (1768-) [2116].** Baptised 20 Nov 1768, Weaverham. Residence of parents was noted as Cuddington. James Marr Margaret GERRARD, 16 Feb 1790, Weaverham. James died June 1837, age 68, buried 26 Jun 1837, Weaverham.

Sp. Margaret GERRARD (1769-1824) [2117].

4. **Richard BRATHERTON (1791-) [2118].** Born 12 Oct 1791, baptised 30 Oct 1779, Weaverham, born to James and Margaret Bratherton of Sandiway, Cheshire.

4. **Betty BRATHERTON (1796-) [2119].** Born 27 Dec 1796, baptised 17 Jan 1796, Weaverham. Parent's residence was Cuddington. Dau of James and Margaret Bratherton.

4. **Thomas BRATHERTON (1799-1801) [2120].** Born 27 Feb 1799, baptised 17 Mar 1799, Weaverham, born to James and Margaret Bratherton of Cuddington. Thomas died Feb 1801, buried 23 Feb 1801, Weaverham.

4. **James BRATHERTON (1805-) [2121].** Born 14 Sep 1805, baptised 15 Sept 1805, Weaverham, born to James and Margaret Bratherton of Cuddington.

4. **Marin BRATHERTON (-1798) [2122].** Died Mar 1798, buried 11 Mar 1798, Weaverham, dau of James and Margaret Bratherton.

4. **William BRATHERTON (-1803) [2124].** Died Jan 1803, buried 15 Jan 1803, Weaverham, parents James and Margaret Bratherton.

4. **George BRATHERTON (1793-) [2125].** Born 19 May 1793, Sandiway, baptised 2 Jun 1793, Weaverham. Parents James and Margaret Bratherton of Sandway.

Chapter Three

THE BOWYER FAMILY

Bowyer Family Outline

George BOWYER (circa 1650-)

1. George BOWYER (circa 1650-) [2139].
Sp. (unknown).
   2. Daniel BOWYER (1676-) [2162].
   2. Daniel BOWYER (1678-) [573].
   Sp. Joanna ROBEY (1678-) [2129].
      3. George BOWYER (1715-) [356].
      Sp. Mary HOLLAND (1720-) [357].
         4. Mary BOWYER (circa 1750-) [273].
         Sp. Joseph DEAN (1750-) [272], son of James DEAN (circa 1720-) [323] and Mary BUCKLEY
           (circa 1720-) [355].
SEE DEAN FAMILY
         4. George BOWYER (1750-1833) [488].
         Sp. Sarah FALLOWS nee DEAN (1752-1801) [577], dau. of James DEAN (circa 1720-) [323] and
           Mary BUCKLEY (circa 1720-) [355].
           5. James BOWYER (1785-) [489].
           5. George BOWYER (1787-1843) [490].
           5. Elizabeth BOWYER (1789-) [491].
           5. Sarah BOWYER (1791-) [492].
           5. Hannah BOWYER (-1785) [2161].
         Sp. (unknown).
         4. Daniel BOWYER (1740-) [2132].
         Sp. Mary WILLIAMS (-) [2141].
         4. Catherine BOWYER (1743-) [2133].
         4. Hannah BOWYER (1747-) [2375].
      3. Elizabeth BOWYER (1719-) [2134].
      3. Sara BOWYER (1703-) [2135].
      3. Child BOWYER (1704-) [2136].
      3. George BOWYER (1713-) [2137].
      3. Hanna BOWYER (1710-) [2138].
      3. Marie BOWYER (1707-) [2148].
   2. Samuel BOWYER (-) [2149].
   Sp. Mary (-) [2150].
      3. Joseph BOWYER (1719-) [2151].
      3. Mary BOWYER (1716-) [2152].
      3. Martha BOWYER (1713-) [2153].
      3. Ester BOWYER (1725-) [2154].
   2. Joseph BOWYER (1680-) [2140].
   Sp. Sara (-) [2143].
      3. Sarah BOWYER (1719-) [2142].
      3. Robert BOWYER (1718-) [2144].
      3. Robert BOWYER (1721-) [2145].
      3. Joseph BOWYER (1707-) [2146].
      3. Sarah BOWYER (1712-) [2147].
      3. Joseph BOWYER (-1787) [2156].
      3. Mary BOWYER (1724-) [2157].
      3. Rebecca BOWYER (1731-) [2158].
      3. James BOWYER (1727-) [2159].

Bowyer Lineage

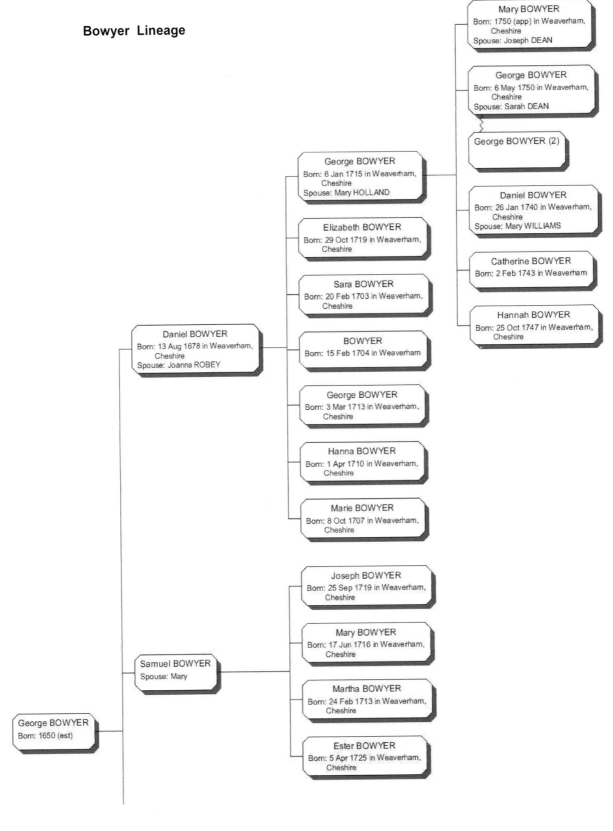

Mary BOWYER
Born: 1750 (app) in Weaverham, Cheshire
Spouse: Joseph DEAN

George BOWYER
Born: 6 May 1750 in Weaverham, Cheshire
Spouse: Sarah DEAN

George BOWYER (2)

Daniel BOWYER
Born: 26 Jan 1740 in Weaverham, Cheshire
Spouse: Mary WILLIAMS

Catherine BOWYER
Born: 2 Feb 1743 in Weaverham

Hannah BOWYER
Born: 25 Oct 1747 in Weaverham, Cheshire

George BOWYER
Born: 6 Jan 1715 in Weaverham, Cheshire
Spouse: Mary HOLLAND

Elizabeth BOWYER
Born: 29 Oct 1719 in Weaverham, Cheshire

Sara BOWYER
Born: 20 Feb 1703 in Weaverham, Cheshire

BOWYER
Born: 15 Feb 1704 in Weaverham

George BOWYER
Born: 3 Mar 1713 in Weaverham, Cheshire

Hanna BOWYER
Born: 1 Apr 1710 in Weaverham, Cheshire

Marie BOWYER
Born: 8 Oct 1707 in Weaverham, Cheshire

Daniel BOWYER
Born: 13 Aug 1678 in Weaverham, Cheshire
Spouse: Joanna ROBEY

Joseph BOWYER
Born: 25 Sep 1719 in Weaverham, Cheshire

Mary BOWYER
Born: 17 Jun 1716 in Weaverham, Cheshire

Martha BOWYER
Born: 24 Feb 1713 in Weaverham, Cheshire

Ester BOWYER
Born: 5 Apr 1725 in Weaverham, Cheshire

Samuel BOWYER
Spouse: Mary

George BOWYER
Born: 1650 (est)

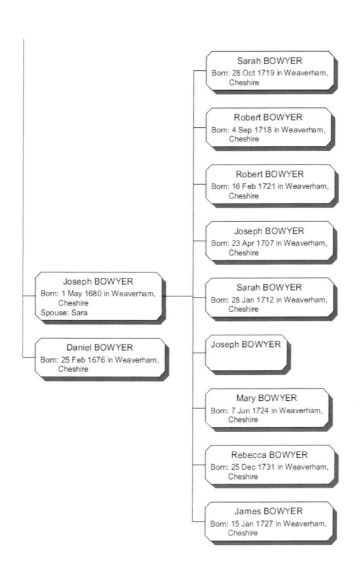

Sarah BOWYER
Born: 28 Oct 1719 in Weaverham, Cheshire

Robert BOWYER
Born: 4 Sep 1718 in Weaverham, Cheshire

Robert BOWYER
Born: 16 Feb 1721 in Weaverham, Cheshire

Joseph BOWYER
Born: 23 Apr 1707 in Weaverham, Cheshire

Sarah BOWYER
Born: 28 Jan 1712 in Weaverham, Cheshire

Joseph BOWYER

Mary BOWYER
Born: 7 Jun 1724 in Weaverham, Cheshire

Rebecca BOWYER
Born: 25 Dec 1731 in Weaverham, Cheshire

James BOWYER
Born: 15 Jan 1727 in Weaverham, Cheshire

Joseph BOWYER
Born: 1 May 1680 in Weaverham, Cheshire
Spouse: Sara

Daniel BOWYER
Born: 25 Feb 1676 in Weaverham, Cheshire

George BOWYER (circa 1650-)

1. George BOWYER (circa 1650-) [2139]. The surname Bowyer has a number of different spellings, such as Boyer and Bayer
Sp. (unknown).

2. Daniel BOWYER (1676-) [2162]. Baptised 25 Feb 1676, Weaverham, son of George Bowyer.
2. Daniel BOWYER (1678-) [573]. Baptised 13 Aug 1678, Weaverham, son of George Bowyer. Daniel Marr Joanna ROBEY, 12 May 1703, Weaverham.
Sp. Joanna ROBEY (1678-) [2129]. Baptised 17 Aug 1678, Weaverham, dau of Henry ROBY (-) [2130].

3. George BOWYER (1715-) [356]. Baptised 6 Jan 1715, Weaverham, son of Daniel, Bowyer and Joanna Robey. Parent's residence noted as Weaverham. George Marr Mary HOLLAND, 10 Apr 1740, Weaverham.
Sp. Mary HOLLAND (1720-) [357]. There are two possible birth references for Mary.

Mary Holland baptised 13 Mar 1720, Weaverham, father Joseph Holland of Weaverham
Mary Holland baptised 27 Jun 1712, Weaverham, father William Holland of Weaverham

If Mary was born in 1712, she would have been 28 years old when she married and 38 when her son George was born. The correct Mary is likely to have been the one born in 1720, to Joseph Holland of Weaverham, as she would have been 20 years old when she married and 30 years old when her son George was born.

Unfortunately, no mother's name or father's occupation was noted on Mary's baptismal details. However, it is possible that her father was Joseph Holland, baptised 21 Mar 1697, Great Budworth and his father was also recorded as Joseph Holland who was baptised 15 June 1651, Little Budworth, parents noted were John Holland and Grace.

The following are possibly Mary's siblings

Anne baptised 26 Jul 1724, Weaverham to Joseph, Shoemaker of Weaverham and Anne
Anne baptised 7 Aug 1726, Weaverham, born to Joseph, Shoemaker of Weaverham and Anne
Joseph baptised 20 May 1733, Weaverham born to Joseph, Shoemaker of Weaverham and Anne
Elizabeth, baptised 1 Oct 1738, Weaverham, father Joseph of Weaverham, no occupation give or name of the mother.

4. Mary BOWYER (circa 1750-) [273]. Born circa 1750, Weaverham. Mary Marr Joseph DEAN, Weaverham.
Sp. Joseph DEAN (1750-) [272], son of James DEAN (circa 1720-) [323] and Mary (possibly) BUCKLEY (circa 1720-) [355]. Baptised 5 Nov 1750, Weaverham, Parent's residents Hartford.

SEE DEAN FAMILY

4. George BOWYER (1750-1833) [488]. Baptised 6 May 1750, Weaverham. In 1780, George was recorded as being of Weaverham. George died 1 Apr 1833, age 80, buried St. Helen's, Witton, Northwich. George Marr Sarah DEAN, 21 Jun 1784, Davenham, Northwich. George was recorded as a Rockgetter.
Sp. Sarah DEAN (1752-1801) [577], dau. of James Dean and Mary Buckley of Leftwich. Sarah had previously been married to Thomas FALLOWS (-) [483].

5. James BOWYER (1785-) [489]. Born 15 May 1785, baptised 5 June 1785, St. Helen's, Witton, Northwich. Parents George Bowyer and Sarah. George son of George and Mary Bowyer. Sarah's parents were James and Mary Dean of Leftwich.
5. George BOWYER (1787-1843) [490]. Born Feb 1787, baptised Mar 1787, St. Helen's, Witton, Northwich. George died 21 Dec 1843, buried St. Helen's, Witton, Northwich.
5. Elizabeth BOWYER (1789-) [491]. Born 27 Jan 1789, baptised 7 Mar 1789, St. Helen's, Witton, Northwich. Parents George Bowyer and Sarah. George son of George and Mary Bowyer. Sarah's parents James and Mary Dean of Leftwich.

5. **Sarah BOWYER (1791-) [492].** Born 11 Jun 1791, baptised 26 June 1791, St. Helen's, Witton, Northwich. Parents George Bowyer and Sarah. George son of George and Mary Bowyer. Sarah's parents James and Mary Dean of Leftwich.

5. **Hannah BOWYER (-1785) [2161].** Died Mar 1785, infant. Buried 14 Mar 1785, Weaverham. Parents George Bowyer and Sarah.

4. **Daniel BOWYER (1740-) [2132].** Baptised 26 Jan 1740, Weaverham. Daniel Marr Mary WILLIAMS.
Sp. Mary WILLIAMS (-) [2141].

4. **Catherine BOWYER (1743-) [2133].** Baptised 2 Feb 1743, Weaverham.

4. **Hannah BOWYER (1747-) [2375].** Baptised 25 Oct 1747, Weaverham.

3. **Elizabeth BOWYER (1719-) [2134].** Baptised 29 Oct 1719, Weaverham. Dau of Daniel Bowyer and Joanna Robey.

3. **Sara BOWYER (1703-) [2135].** Baptised 20 Feb 1703, Weaverham. Dau of Daniel Bowyer and Joanna Robey

3. **Child BOWYER (1704-) [2136].** Baptised 15 Feb 1704, Weaverham. Child only noted, of Daniel Bowyer and Joanna Robey.

3. **George BOWYER (1713-) [2137].** Baptised 3 Mar 1713, Weaverham. Son of Daniel Bowyer and Joanna Robey.

3. **Hanna BOWYER (1710-) [2138].** Baptised 1 Apr 1710, Weaverham. Dau of Daniel Bowyer and Joanna Robey.

3. **Marie BOWYER (1707-) [2148].** Baptised 8 Oct 1707, Weaverham. Dau of Daniel Bowyer and Joanna Robey.

2. **Samuel BOWYER (-) [2149].**
Sp. Mary (-) [2150].

3. **Joseph BOWYER (1719-) [2151].** Baptised 25 Sep 1719, Weaverham.

3. **Mary BOWYER (1716-) [2152].** Baptised 17 Jun 1716, Weaverham.

3. **Martha BOWYER (1713-) [2153].** Baptised 24 Feb 1713, Weaverham.

3. **Ester BOWYER (1725-) [2154].** Baptised 5 Apr 1725, Weaverham.

2. **Joseph BOWYER (1680-) [2140].** Baptised 1 May 1680, Weaverham, son of George Bowyer, residence Cuddington.
Sp. Sara (-) [2143].

3. **Sarah BOWYER (1719-) [2142].** Baptised 28 Oct 1719, Weaverham, son of Josiah Bowyer, Shoemaker, residence Cuddington.

3. **Robert BOWYER (1718-) [2144].** Baptised 4 Sep 1718, Weaverham, son of Josiah Bowyer.

3. **Robert BOWYER (1721-) [2145].** Baptised 16 Feb 1721, Weaverham, son of Josiah and Sarah.

3. **Joseph BOWYER (1707-) [2146].** Baptised 23 Apr 1707, Weaverham, son of Joseph Bowyer.

3. **Sarah BOWYER (1712-) [2147].** Baptised 28 Jan 1712, Weaverham, dau of Joseph Bowyer of Weaverham.

3. **Joseph BOWYER (-1787) [2156].** Died Jun 1787, buried 16 Jun 1787, Weaverham, father Joseph Bowyer.

3. **Mary BOWYER (1724-) [2157].** Baptised 7 Jun 1724, Weaverham.

3. **Rebecca BOWYER (1731-) [2158].** Baptised 25 Dec 1731, Weaverham. Parent's residence Weaverham.

3. **James BOWYER (1727-) [2159].** Baptised 15 Jan 1727, Weaverham. Parent's residence Gorstich, Cheshire, Father Shoemaker.

Chapter Four

THE BOSTOCK FAMILY

Bostock Family Outline

Ottiwell BOSTOCK (circa 1665 -)

---

1. Ottiwell BOSTOCK (circa 1665 -) [2065].
Sp. (unknown).
   2. Maria BOSTOCK (1694-) [2066].
   2. Peter BOSTOCK (1708-) [2067].
   2. John BOSTOCK (1691-1771) [2040].
   Sp. Ann MALBONE (1702-1744) [2057], dau. of John MALBONE (-) [2102].
      3. Anna BOSTOCK (1729-1787) [2061].
      3. William (Gulielmus) BOSTOCK (1726-1808) [2062].
      Sp. Martha BOTTOMS (1737-1816) [2068], dau. of Robert BOTTOMS (1712-1777) [2058] and Martha
         HIND (-) [2059].
SEE BOTTOMS FAMILY
         4. Mary BOSTOCK (1758-) [2069].
         4. Ann BOSTOCK (1759-) [2070].
         4. Thomas BOSTOCK (1769-) [2071].
         4. William BOSTOCK (1767-) [2072].
         4. William BOSTOCK (1769-) [2073].
         4. Robert BOSTOCK (1771-1772) [2074].
         4. Ann BOSTOCK (1773-1773) [2075].
         4. Robert BOSTOCK (1774-1781) [2076].
         4. Charlotte BOSTOCK (1776-1776) [2077].
         4. James BOSTOCK (1777-) [2078].
         4. Mary BOSTOCK (1779-) [2079].
      3. Marie BOSTOCK (1722-) [2063].
      3. Sara BOSTOCK (1724-) [2064].
      3. Philip BOSTOCK (1732-1802) [412].
      Sp. Ellen BOTTOMS (1732-1786) [461], dau. of Robert BOTTOMS (1712-1777) [2058] and Martha
         HIND (-) [2059].
SEE BOTTOMS FAMILY
         4. James BOSTOCK (1756-1827) [255].
         Sp. Fanny CARTER (1757-1829) [262], dau. of Isaiah CARTER (circa 1710-) [413] and Hannah
            PENKIN (1718-) [414].
            5. Josiah BOSTOCK (1791-1838) [210].
            Sp. Mary YARWOOD (1794-) [211], dau. of James YARWOOD (1760-1838) [263] and Mary
               DUTTON (1759-1840) [264].
SEE YARWOOD AND DUTTON FAMILY
               6. Jane BOSTOCK (1838-1870) [85].
               Sp. James (Toffee) DEAN (1834-1899) [44], son of James (Senr) DEAN (1789-1871) [45]
                   and Martha JACKSON (1794-1875) [46].
SEE DEAN FAMILY
               6. Mary BOSTOCK (1835-) [212].
               Sp. Aaron APPLETON (-) [2080].
               6. Sarah BOSTOCK (1819-) [242].
               Sp. James RAYNOR (-) [2399].
               6. Ellen BOSTOCK (1823-1827) [243].
               6. Helen BOSTOCK (1823-1826) [244].
               6. James BOSTOCK (1831-1852) [245].
               6. Fanny BOSTOCK (1829-1883) [246].
               Sp. Mark RAYNOR (1826-) [379].
                   7. Mark RAYNOR (1869-) [380].
                   7. Eleanor RAYNOR (1862-) [381].
                   Sp. Albert SIDDIS (-) [383].

       7. John RAYNOR (1854-) [382].

       7. Joseph RAYNOR (1846-) [384].

       7. Mary RAYNOR (1852-) [391].

       7. James RAYNOR (1856-) [392].

       7. Samuel RAYNOR (1858-) [393].

       7. Elizabeth RAYNOR (1860-) [394].

     6. John BOSTOCK (-) [415].

  5. James BOSTOCK (1797-1872) [256].

Sp. Sarah THOMPSON (1799-1872) [257], dau. of John THOMPSON (-) [2081] and Hannah (-) [2082].

     6. Stephen BOSTOCK (1819-) [2084].

       7. William BOSTOCK (1838-1891) [354].

     Sp. Jane (1847-1922) [2105].

     6. Thomas BOSTOCK (1821-) [2085].

     6. James BOSTOCK (1823-) [2086].

     6. Fanny BOSTOCK (1840-) [2087].

     6. Hannah BOSTOCK (1825-) [2088].

     Sp. Henry WAINWEARING (-) [2089].

     6. Thomas BOSTOCK (1838-) [2090].

     6. James BOSTOCK (1827-) [2091].

     Sp. Ann ECCLESTON (1825-) [2092].

     6. John BOSTOCK (1829-) [2093].

     Sp. Elizabeth HOLLAND (1833-) [2094].

       7. James BOSTOCK (1852-) [2111].

       7. Joseph BOSTOCK (1855-) [2112].

     6. Sarah BOSTOCK (1831-) [2095].

     6. Mary BOSTOCK (1836-) [2096].

     6. Josiah BOSTOCK (1834-) [2097].

     6. Simon BOSTOCK (1835-) [2098].

     6. Jane BOSTOCK (1823-) [2109].

  5. Ellen BOSTOCK (1785-) [258].

     6. Frances BOSTOCK (1819-) [2083].

  5. Jane BOSTOCK (circa 1791-1856) [342].

Sp. Samuel VERNON (1796-) [343], son of John VERNON (-) [349] and Fanny (-) [350].

     6. Hannah VERNON (1827-) [344].

     6. Jane VERNON (1822-) [345].

     6. Francis Carter VERNON (1816-1850) [348].

     6. James VERNON (1819-) [470].

     6. John VERNON (1821-) [2099].

     6. Ellen VERNON (1817-) [2100].

     6. Betsy VERNON (1829-) [2101].

  5. Jenny BOSTOCK (1787-) [462].

  5. John BOSTOCK (1789-1823) [463].

  5. Fanny BOSTOCK (1799-) [468].

  5. Hannah BOSTOCK (1795-) [2041].

  5. John BOSTOCK (1803-) [2042].

Bostock Lineage

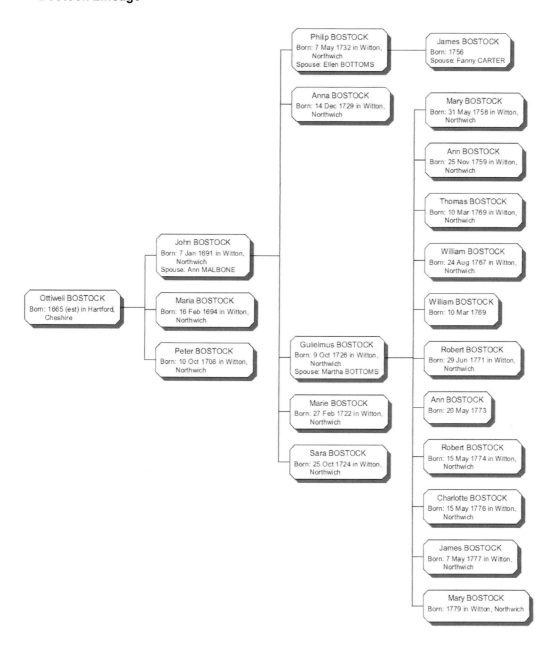

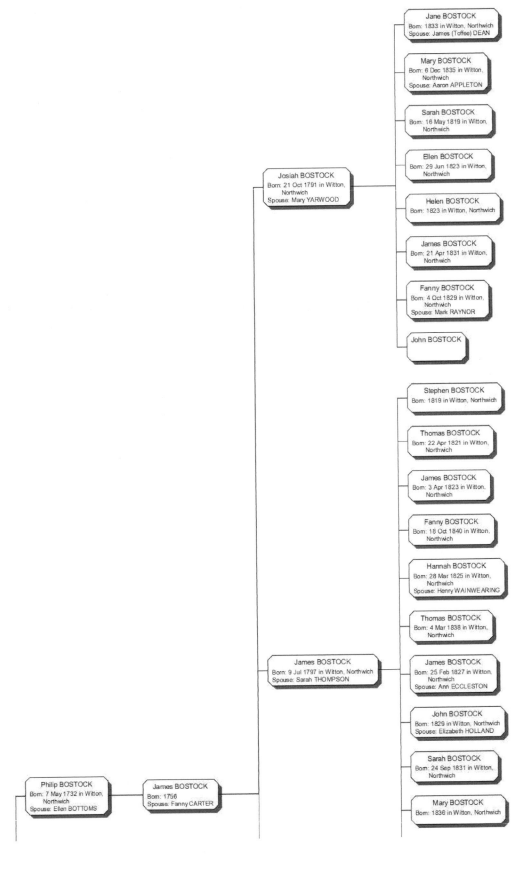

Jane BOSTOCK
Born: 1833 in Witton, Northwich
Spouse: James (Toffee) DEAN

Mary BOSTOCK
Born: 6 Dec 1835 in Witton, Northwich
Spouse: Aaron APPLETON

Sarah BOSTOCK
Born: 16 May 1819 in Witton, Northwich

Ellen BOSTOCK
Born: 29 Jun 1823 in Witton, Northwich

Helen BOSTOCK
Born: 1823 in Witton, Northwich

James BOSTOCK
Born: 21 Apr 1831 in Witton, Northwich

Fanny BOSTOCK
Born: 4 Oct 1829 in Witton, Northwich
Spouse: Mark RAYNOR

John BOSTOCK

Josiah BOSTOCK
Born: 21 Oct 1791 in Witton, Northwich
Spouse: Mary YARWOOD

Stephen BOSTOCK
Born: 1819 in Witton, Northwich

Thomas BOSTOCK
Born: 22 Apr 1821 in Witton, Northwich

James BOSTOCK
Born: 3 Apr 1823 in Witton, Northwich

Fanny BOSTOCK
Born: 18 Oct 1840 in Witton, Northwich

Hannah BOSTOCK
Born: 28 Mar 1825 in Witton, Northwich
Spouse: Henry WAINWEARING

Thomas BOSTOCK
Born: 4 Mar 1838 in Witton, Northwich

James BOSTOCK
Born: 25 Feb 1827 in Witton, Northwich
Spouse: Ann ECCLESTON

John BOSTOCK
Born: 1829 in Witton, Northwich
Spouse: Elizabeth HOLLAND

Sarah BOSTOCK
Born: 24 Sep 1831 in Witton, Northwich

Mary BOSTOCK
Born: 1836 in Witton, Northwich

James BOSTOCK
Born: 9 Jul 1797 in Witton, Northwich
Spouse: Sarah THOMPSON

Philip BOSTOCK
Born: 7 May 1732 in Witton, Northwich
Spouse: Ellen BOTTOMS

James BOSTOCK
Born: 1756
Spouse: Fanny CARTER

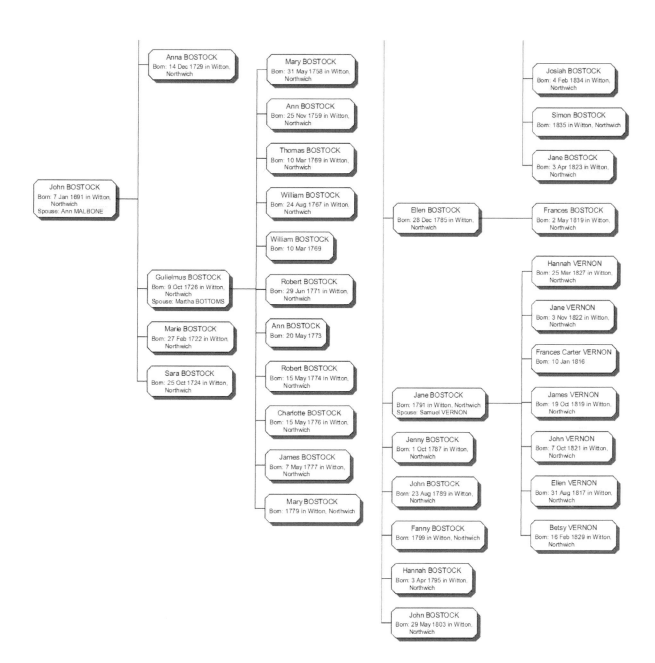

John BOSTOCK
Born: 7 Jan 1691 in Witton, Northwich
Spouse: Ann MALBONE

Anna BOSTOCK
Born: 14 Dec 1729 in Witton, Northwich

Gulielmus BOSTOCK
Born: 9 Oct 1726 in Witton, Northwich
Spouse: Martha BOTTOMS

Marie BOSTOCK
Born: 27 Feb 1722 in Witton, Northwich

Sara BOSTOCK
Born: 25 Oct 1724 in Witton, Northwich

Mary BOSTOCK
Born: 31 May 1758 in Witton, Northwich

Ann BOSTOCK
Born: 25 Nov 1759 in Witton, Northwich

Thomas BOSTOCK
Born: 10 Mar 1769 in Witton, Northwich

William BOSTOCK
Born: 24 Aug 1767 in Witton, Northwich

William BOSTOCK
Born: 10 Mar 1769

Robert BOSTOCK
Born: 29 Jun 1771 in Witton, Northwich

Ann BOSTOCK
Born: 20 May 1773

Robert BOSTOCK
Born: 15 May 1774 in Witton, Northwich

Charlotte BOSTOCK
Born: 15 May 1776 in Witton, Northwich

James BOSTOCK
Born: 7 May 1777 in Witton, Northwich

Mary BOSTOCK
Born: 1779 in Witton, Northwich

Ellen BOSTOCK
Born: 28 Dec 1785 in Witton, Northwich

Jane BOSTOCK
Born: 1791 in Witton, Northwich
Spouse: Samuel VERNON

Jenny BOSTOCK
Born: 1 Oct 1787 in Witton, Northwich

John BOSTOCK
Born: 23 Aug 1789 in Witton, Northwich

Fanny BOSTOCK
Born: 1799 in Witton, Northwich

Hannah BOSTOCK
Born: 3 Apr 1795 in Witton, Northwich

John BOSTOCK
Born: 29 May 1803 in Witton, Northwich

Josiah BOSTOCK
Born: 4 Feb 1834 in Witton, Northwich

Simon BOSTOCK
Born: 1835 in Witton, Northwich

Jane BOSTOCK
Born: 3 Apr 1823 in Witton, Northwich

Frances BOSTOCK
Born: 2 May 1819 in Witton, Northwich

Hannah VERNON
Born: 25 Mar 1827 in Witton, Northwich

Jane VERNON
Born: 3 Nov 1822 in Witton, Northwich

Frances Carter VERNON
Born: 10 Jan 1816

James VERNON
Born: 19 Oct 1819 in Witton, Northwich

John VERNON
Born: 7 Oct 1821 in Witton, Northwich

Ellen VERNON
Born: 31 Aug 1817 in Witton, Northwich

Betsy VERNON
Born: 16 Feb 1829 in Witton, Northwich

Carter Lineage

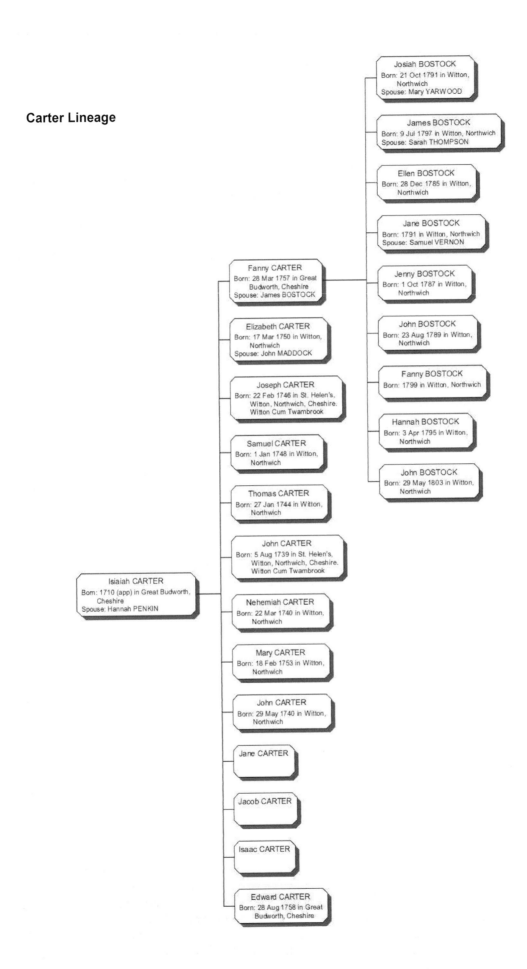

Josiah BOSTOCK
Born: 21 Oct 1791 in Witton, Northwich
Spouse: Mary YARWOOD

James BOSTOCK
Born: 9 Jul 1797 in Witton, Northwich
Spouse: Sarah THOMPSON

Ellen BOSTOCK
Born: 28 Dec 1785 in Witton, Northwich

Jane BOSTOCK
Born: 1791 in Witton, Northwich
Spouse: Samuel VERNON

Jenny BOSTOCK
Born: 1 Oct 1787 in Witton, Northwich

John BOSTOCK
Born: 23 Aug 1789 in Witton, Northwich

Fanny BOSTOCK
Born: 1799 in Witton, Northwich

Hannah BOSTOCK
Born: 3 Apr 1795 in Witton, Northwich

John BOSTOCK
Born: 29 May 1803 in Witton, Northwich

Fanny CARTER
Born: 28 Mar 1757 in Great Budworth, Cheshire
Spouse: James BOSTOCK

Elizabeth CARTER
Born: 17 Mar 1750 in Witton, Northwich
Spouse: John MADDOCK

Joseph CARTER
Born: 22 Feb 1746 in St. Helen's, Witton, Northwich, Cheshire. Witton Cum Twambrook

Samuel CARTER
Born: 1 Jan 1748 in Witton, Northwich

Thomas CARTER
Born: 27 Jan 1744 in Witton, Northwich

John CARTER
Born: 5 Aug 1739 in St. Helen's, Witton, Northwich, Cheshire. Witton Cum Twambrook

Isiaiah CARTER
Born: 1710 (app) in Great Budworth, Cheshire
Spouse: Hannah PENKIN

Nehemiah CARTER
Born: 22 Mar 1740 in Witton, Northwich

Mary CARTER
Born: 18 Feb 1753 in Witton, Northwich

John CARTER
Born: 29 May 1740 in Witton, Northwich

Jane CARTER

Jacob CARTER

Isaac CARTER

Edward CARTER
Born: 28 Aug 1758 in Great Budworth, Cheshire

Ottiwell BOSTOCK (circa 1665-)

1. Ottiwell BOSTOCK (circa 1665 -) [2065]. This Christian name has also been recorded as Attwell, Ottewell, Olliwell and Ottenwell.

Although it is reasonably certain that Ottiwell is the head of this family line there is another option which can be seen under **John BOSTOCK (1691-1771) [2040].**

Ottiwell was noted as residing in Hartford, Cheshire when his children were baptised at St. Helen's, Witton, Northwich. It is not known if Ottiwell was born in Hartford or whether he had moved from another area within Cheshire. It is worth mentioning that the Bostock's were registered at St. Helen's, Witton, Northwich as early as 1626 and mid 1600s in St. Wilfred's, Davenham, Northwich.

It has not been possible to identify the marriage record for Ottiwell. However, a marriage record at St. Helen's, Witton, Northwich has been found but the record was unreadable and the only information available was " ...O Bostock married 14 August 1697, to .... Tidsley, St. Helen's, Witton, Northwich". The birth of his children would fit with this marriage date.

Ollivelll's occupation has been recorded in Latin and has benn difficult to read. The following variations have been noted from the Latin script

fabric forrary = fabric –skilled work, stitcher, repairer
fabric ferrary = fabric, tailoring
fabric sorrary
fabric Serrary
Fabri ferrarri =iron worker, ie a blacksmith
Sautoris =patch or stitch
Fabric =working with silk

Therefore Ollivell's occupation could have had something to do with a tailor, someone working with silk or fabric, a repairer or a stitcher or a Blacksmith. It is worth noting that some of the Bostocks were tailors.

The following record was found for Ottiwell in Northwich which reads
"Ottiwell Bostoke £5 pa – 2.0
Book: Marriage Licences Granted within the Diocese of Chester (Marriage)
Collection: Cheshire: Northwich Hundred Poll Tax 1660 and Hearth Tax 1644".

Ollivell has noted three children all baptised at St. Helen's, Witton, Northwich. Marie baptised 16 Feb 1694, Peter baptised 10 Oct 1708 and Joannes 7 Jan 1691.
Sp. (unknown). Although likely to be Tidsley.

2. **Maria BOSTOCK (1694-) [2066].** Baptised 16 Feb 1694, St. Helen's, Witton, Northwich. Father Ottiwell, noted as a Fabri Ferrarry.
2. **Peter BOSTOCK (1708-) [2067].** Baptised 10 Oct 1708, St. Helen's, Witton, Northwich. No occupation was given for Peter's father Ottiwell.
2. **John BOSTOCK (1691-1771) [2040].** Baptised 7 Jan 1691, Witton, Northwich. Father noted as Ottiwell Bostock from Hartford, a Fabri Ferrarry John died 1771, buried St. Helen's, Witton, Northwich. John was noted as being a Lutoris (shoemaker) and a Tailor of Northwich.

There was another John baptised 19 Feb 1697, St. Wilfred's, Davenham, Northwich, son of Sarah and William Bostock of Leftwich, Northwich. It is possible that this John could be the line and not the line of John born to Ottiwell. William Bostock and Sarah married at St. Wilfred's, Davenham, Northwich and William was the son of Thomas Bostock. As this is a possibility the following information has been added.

William and Sarah Bostock had the following children
Philip baptised St. Wilfred's, Davenham, Northwich, 17 Nov 1707, parents of Bostock, Cheshire
Katherine baptised St. Wilfred's, Davenham, Northwich, 5 Oct 1712, parents of Bostock
William baptised St. Wilfred's, Davenham, Northwich, 18 Mar 1710, parents of Bostock
John baptised St. Wilfred's, Davenham, Northwich,19 Feb 1697, parents of Leftwich
William baptised St. Wilfred's, Davenham, Northwich, 26 Aug 1699, parents of Bostock
Sarah baptised St. Wilfred's, Davenham, Northwich, 3 Apr 1703, parents of Bostock

Thomas baptised St. Wilfred's, Davenham, Northwich, 26 Apr 1705, parents of Bostock

The reason which led to the theory that **John BOSTOCK (1691-1771) [2040]**, son of Ollivell is the correct line is because most of John's ancestors and descendants had and have been baptised and married at St. Helen's, Witton, Northwich and some of them were noted as tailors and shoemakers. William Bostock's family are noted as being from Bostock, Cheshire, although when their son John was born they were noted as being in Leftwich, Northwich.

Continuing with the theory, John was noted as a
- Lutoris of Northwich in 1722, 1724 and 1726 (Shoemaker)
- Alicnorum Sartor of Northwich in 1729 (patcher mender of cloth)
- Tailor in 1732

John Marr Ann MALBONE, 6 Jan 1721, St. Wilfred's, Davenham, Northwich, John was noted as being from this Parish and Ann was from the Parish of Great Budworth. Being of the Parish at the time does not necessarily mean he was baptised there. Additionally, John was buried at St. Helen's, Witton, Northwich and not at St. Wilfred's, Davenham, Northwich where he had been married.

John died in Nov 1771 and was buried 10 Nov 1771, St. Helen's, Witton, Northwich.

It is of course possible that the John baptised St. Wilfred's, Davenham, Northwich,19 Feb 1697, parents William and Sarah Bostock of Leftwich could have been the John who married Ann Malbone.
    Sp. Ann MALBONE (1702-1744) [2057], dau. of John MALBONE (-) [2102].

From here the lineage has been confirmed and the following descendants are from John Bostock and Ann Malbone.

3. **Anna BOSTOCK (1729-1787) [2061]**. Baptised 14 Dec 1729, St. Helen's, Witton, Northwich. Father John Bostock, a Lutoris (shoemaker). Anna died 19 Nov 1787, age 57. Buried 21 Nov 1787, St. Helen's, Witton, Northwich.

3. **William (Gulielmus) BOSTOCK (1726-1808) [2062]**. Baptised 9 Oct 1726, St. Helen's, Witton, Northwich, Father John Bostock of Northwich, Lutoris (shoemaker). William Marr Martha BOTTOMS, 10 Feb 1756, St. Helen's, Witton, Northwich. William's father was John Bostock, Lutoris (shoemaker) of Northwich. Martha's father was Robert Bottoms, Maltser of Northwich. Both resided in Witton Cum Twambrooks. Witnesses to the marriage were James Bagnley and William Milner. William signed his name. William died May 1808, buried 21 May 1808, age 81. St. Helen's, Witton, Northwich.

    Sp. Martha BOTTOMS (1737-1816) [2068], dau. of Robert BOTTOMS (1712-1777) [2058], Maltser of Northwich and Martha HIND (-) [2059]. Baptised 1737, St. Helen's, Witton, Northwich. Martha died sep 1816, buried 23 Sep 1816, Buried St. Helen's, Witton, Northwich.

SEE BOTTOMS FAMILY

4. **Mary BOSTOCK (1758-) [2069]**. Baptised 31 May 1758, St. Helen's, Witton, Northwich.
4. **Ann BOSTOCK (1759-) [2070]**. Baptised 25 Nov 1759, St. Helen's, Witton, Northwich.
4. **Thomas BOSTOCK (1769-) [2071]**. Baptised 10 Mar 1769, St. Helen's, Witton, Northwich.
4. **William BOSTOCK (1767-) [2072]**. Baptised 24 Aug 1767, St. Helen's, Witton, Northwich.
4. **William BOSTOCK (1769-) [2073]**. Baptised 10 Mar 1769, St. Helen's, Witton, Northwich.
4. **Robert BOSTOCK (1771-1772) [2074]**. Baptised 29 Jun 1771, St. Helen's, Witton, Northwich. Robert died Jan 1772, buried 4 Jan 1772,St. Helen's, Witton, Northwich.
4. **Ann BOSTOCK (1773-1773) [2075]**. Baptised 20 May 1773. Ann died Jul 1773, buried 14 Jul 1773, St. Helen's, Witton, Northwich.
4. **Robert BOSTOCK (1774-1781) [2076]**. Baptised 15 May 1774, St. Helen's, Witton, Northwich. Robert died Aug 1781, buried 20 Aug 1781, St. Helen's, Witton, Northwich.
4. **Charlotte BOSTOCK (1776-1776) [2077]**. Baptised 15 May 1776, St. Helen's, Witton, Northwich. Charlotte died 1776, buried St. Helen's, Witton, Northwich.
4. **James BOSTOCK (1777-) [2078]**. Baptised 7 May 1777, St. Helen's, Witton, Northwich.
4. **Mary BOSTOCK (1779-) [2079]**. Baptised 1779, St. Helen's, Witton, Northwich.

3. **Marie BOSTOCK (1722-) [2063].** Baptised 27 Feb 1722, St. Helen's, Witton, Northwich. Father John Bostock, a Lutoris (shoemaker).

3. **Sara BOSTOCK (1724-) [2064].** Baptised 25 Oct 1724, St. Helen's, Witton, Northwich. Father John Bostock, a Lutoris (shoemaker).

3. **Philip BOSTOCK (1732-1802) [412].** Baptised 7 May 1732, St. Helen's, Witton, Northwich, father John Bostock of Northwich, Taylor. Philip Marr Ellen BOTTOMS, 2 Dec 1755, St. Helen's, Witton, Northwich. Philip was noted as a Tailor of Northwich. Witnesses Mary Bottoms and Eliz ..tington. Both residing in Witton cum Twambrooks. Philip and Ellen signed their names. Philip died June 1802, buried 26 Jun 1802, age 70. St. Helen's, Witton, Northwich.

Sp. Ellen BOTTOMS (1732-1786) [461], dau. of Robertus BOTTOMS (1712-1777) [2058] and Martha HIND (-) [2059]. Baptised Hellon on 8 Jul 1734, St. Helen's, Witton, Northwich, father Robert Bottoms, Malster of Northwich. Ellen died 26 Sep 1786, age 54, buried St. Helen's, Witton, Northwich. Ellen's sister Martha married Gulielmus Bostock, brother to Philip Bostock.

SEE BOTTOMS FAMILY

4. **James BOSTOCK (1756-1827) [255].** Born 1756, according to his marriage certificate. No baptismal registration has been found. His existence and that of his parents are noted on the details of his children's baptismal details. James Marr Fanny CARTER, 29 Mar 1785, St. Helen's, Witton, Northwich. Witnesses John Hougkinson and James Swindall. Both of Witton Parish and both noted as being 29 years old. There was a note to say that Frances was the daughter of Isaiah Carter and Hannah Carter of Great Budworth, Cheshire.

During their lives they have been recorded as living in Leftwich, Witton and Northwich. James has been noted as a Flatman of Northwich, Leftwich and Witton. James died 25 Jan 1827, age 73, son of Philip Bostock of Northwich. Buried 28 Jan 1827, St. Helen's, Witton, Northwich. Cause of death: Jaundice.

Sp. Fanny CARTER (1757-1829) [262], dau. of Isaiah CARTER (circa 1710-) [413] and Hannah PENKIN (1718-) [414].

Isaiah CARTER (circa 1710-) [413] Marr Hannah PENKIN, 14 Oct 1738, Tarporley, Cheshire. The surname has sometimes been spelt Penkit. **Hannah PENKIN (1718-) [414],** dau. of Jonathan PENKIT (-) [2206] and Mary (-) [2207], baptised 31 Mar 1718, Little Budworth, Cheshire. Isaiah was living in Northwich in the 1750s.

Isaiah CARTER (circa 1710-) [413]. Born circa 1710, Great Budworth, Cheshire. Isaiah's baptismal details have not been confirmed. However, there is a reference for an Isaiah baptised 30 Dec 1711, St. Mary's and All Saints, Great Budworth born to Edward Carter, a Tailor and Jane Shawe. An Edward Carter and Jane Shaw married 26 Jan 1695, St. Helen's, Witton, Northwich. It is likely that Isaiah died 16 Jan 1797, age 85. Buried St. Helen's, Witton, Northwich. Once again it is not clear if this is the correct person.

Fanny Bostock nee Carter died 3 Apr 1829, buried 7 Apr 1829, age 73. Buried St. Helen's, Witton, Northwich, south side of the cemetery. Cause of death: Inflammation. Father Isaiah Carter.

However, a separate record states Fanny died Jul 1850, age 74, of Witton. Widow, parents: Isaiah and Hannah CARTER of Great Budworth, Cheshire. This would mean Fanny was nearly 100 when she died.

Fanny Bostock nee Carter's siblings were
- **Elizabeth CARTER (1750-1839) [2045].** Baptised 17 Mar 1750, St. Helen's, Witton, Northwich. Elizabeth Marr John MADDOCK. (-) [2046]. Elizabeth died 4 Feb 1839, age 88, buried St. Helen's, Witton, Northwich.
- **Joseph CARTER (1746-) [2047].** Baptised 22 Feb 1746, St. Helen's, Witton, Northwich.
- **Samuel CARTER (1748-1750) [2048].** Baptised 1 Jan 1748, St. Helen's, Witton, Northwich. Samuel died 6 Jan 1750, St. Helen's, Witton, Northwich.
- **Thomas CARTER (1744-1746) [2049].** Baptised 27 Jan 1744, St. Helen's, Witton, Northwich. Thomas died 11 Jul 1746, St. Helen's, Witton, Northwich.
- **John CARTER (1739-) [2050].** Baptised 5 Aug 1739, St. Helen's, Witton, Northwich.

- **Nehemiah CARTER (1740-1798) [2051].** Baptised 22 Mar 1740, St. Helen's, Witton, Northwich. Nehemiah died 20 Feb 1798, age 58, buried St. Helen's, Witton, Northwich.
- **Mary CARTER (1753-) [2052].** Baptised 18 Feb 1753, St. Helen's, Witton, Northwich.
- **John CARTER (1740-) [2053].** Baptised 29 May 1740, St. Helen's, Witton, Northwich.
- **Edward CARTER (1758-1744) [2378].** Baptised 28 Aug 1758, St. Mary's and All Saints, Great Budworth, Cheshire. Father Isiah Carter
- **Jane CARTER (-1771) [2054].** Died Jan 1771, buried 8 Jan 1771, St. Helen's, Witton, Northwich.
- **Jacob CARTER (-1746) [2055].** Died Jul 1746, buried 13 Jul 1746, St. Helen's, Witton, Northwich.
- **Isaac CARTER (-1744) [2056].** Died Jan 1744, buried 20 Jan 1744, St. Helen's, Witton, Northwich.

5. **Josiah BOSTOCK (1791-1838) [210].** Born 21 Oct 1791, Baptised Isaiah 13 Nov 1791, St. Helen's, Witton, Northwich. Son of James Bostock and Fanny Carter. Josiah Marr Mary YARWOOD, 10 May 1820, Great Budworth, Cheshire. Both were noted as being of the Parish. Mary the daughter of James Yarwood, Waller of Witton and Mary of Great Budworth. Josiah was recorded as being a Waterman. During their lives they lived at Great Budworth, Castle and Witton. Josiah was noted as being a Labourer, a Flatman and a Waterman.

In a record for baptisms at St. Helen's, Witton, Northwich, under the name of Josiah and Mary Bostock was
16 May 1819, Sarah, dau, Bostock, Witton, Flatman
29 June 1823, Ellen, dau, Bostock, Witton, Flatman
27 August 1826, Helen, dau, Bostock, Witton, Flatman
12 May 1831, James, son, Bostock, Witton, Flatman
12 May 1831, Fanny dau, Bostock, Witton, Flatman
6 Dec 1835, Mary, dau, Bostock, Witton, Flatman
(not all the births of their children were recorded in this note)

Josiah died 19 Oct 1838, age 45, Flatman, residence Witton, buried 22 Oct 1838, St. Helen's, Witton, Northwich. Buried the south side of cemetery. Cause of death: Derangement at Chester Lunatic Asylum. Also noted was Josiah had swelling of the brain.

Death Certificate
Death in the Sub-district of Cathedral Division in the County of Chester and in the City and County of the City of Chester18th of October 1838 at County Lunatic Asylum Upton, Josiah Bostock, male, age 37 years, occupation Bargeman, cause of death Inflammation of the brain.

Sp. **Mary YARWOOD (1794-) [211],** dau. of James YARWOOD (1760-1838) [263] and Mary DUTTON (1759-1840) [264]. Born 15 Jun 1794, Anderton, Cheshire, baptised 6 July 1794, St. Helen's, Witton, Northwich.

SEE YARWOOD FAMILY

When Josiah died Mary married George Fairhurst, Widower, 18 Jun 1840, Warrington, age 45. George was a Post Boy, son of Thomas Fairhurst. Mary Yarwood, Bostock's father was James Yarwood, deceased. George's first wife was Mary Dean. George died in 1845.

1841 English Census, Crown Inn Farm House, Witton Street, Witton, Great Budworth
George FAIRHURST, age 45, Publican. born Cheshire, Mary FAIRHURST, wife, age 40, born Cheshire, Fanny BOSTOCK, dau, age 12, born Cheshire, James BOSTOCK, son, age 10, born Cheshire, Jane BOSTOCK, dau, age 8, born Cheshire, Mary BOSTOCK, dau, age 6, born Cheshire.

1851 English Census, Kniky House, Davenham, Northwich
Mary FAIRHURST, Pauper, Widow, age 61, born 1790, Anderton, Cheshire, 'Service' was noted as her occupation.

By 1861 Mary was living with her daughter as the following census notes

1861 English Census, Witton, Street, Witton, Northwich
Mark RAYNOR. head, age 36, Tailor and Draper, born. Winchem, Cheshire, Fanny RAYNOR, wife, age 34, born Witton, Northwich, Joseph RAYNOR, son, age 13, born Witton, Tailor, Mary RAYNOR, dau, age 9, scholar, born Witton, John RAYNOR, son, age 7, born Witton, James RAYNOR, son, age 5, born Witton, Samuel RAYNOR, son age 3, born Witton, Elizabeth RAYNOR, dau, age 1, born Witton, Mary FAIRHURST, mother in law, widower, age 71, born Anderton, Cheshire, James FORSTER, age 20, Tailors Apprentice, born Weaverham, Cheshire, William WARBURTON, age 18, born Goostry. 1861.

> 6. **Jane BOSTOCK (1838-1870) [85].** Born Witton, Northwich. Dau of Josiah Bostock and Mary Yarwood. Baptismal details do not seem to be available. However, her existence is confirmed in other records. The records note several birth years as 1833, 1834 and 1838.

In the 1841 English Census, Crown Inn Farm House, Witton Street, Witton, Great Budworth, Jane was living with her mother and step father.

Jane Marr James (Toffee) DEAN, 14 Jun 1852, St. Mary's and All Saints, Great Budworth, Cheshire.

> **Sp. James (Toffee) DEAN (1834-1899) [44],** son of James (Senr) DEAN (1789-1871) [45] and Martha JACKSON (1794-1875) [46].

SEE DEAN FAMILY

> 6. **Mary BOSTOCK (1835-) [212].** Baptised 6 Dec 1835, St. Helen's, Witton, Northwich. Dau of Josiah Bostock and Mary Yarwood. Mary was a Witness to the marriage of her sister Jane Bostock to James (Toffee) Dean. Mary Marr Aaron APPLETON, 11 Apr 1859, St. Helen's, Witton, Northwich. In the 1841 English Census, Crown Inn Farm House, Witton Street, Witton, Great Budworth, Mary was living with her mother and step father.
> **Sp. Aaron APPLETON (-) [2080].**

> 6. **Sarah BOSTOCK (1819-) [242].** Baptised 16 May 1819, St. Helen's, Witton, Northwich. Dau of Josiah Bostock and Mary Yarwood.

1841 English Census, King Street, Drakelow, Davenham, Rudheath Lordship, Cheshire
Sarah BOSTOCK, age 21, born 1820, Cheshire. Farm Labourer.

Sarah Marr James RAYNOR.
> **Sp. James RAYNOR (-) [2399].**

> 6. **Ellen BOSTOCK (1823-1827) [243].** Baptised 29 Jun 1823, St. Helen's, Witton, Northwich. Dau of Josiah Bostock and Mary Yarwood. Ellen died April 1827, buried 2 May 1827, Buried St. Helen's, Witton, Northwich.
> 6. **Helen BOSTOCK (1823-1826) [244].** Born 1823, Baptised 27 Aug 1826, St. Helen's, Witton, Northwich. Dau of Josiah Bostock and Mary Yarwood. Helen died 4th May 1826, age 3, buried 6th May 1826, St. Helen's, Witton, Northwich on the south side of the cemetery. Cause of death croup.
> 6. **James BOSTOCK (1831-1852) [245].** Born 21 Apr 1831, Witton, baptised 15 May 1831, St. Helen's, Witton, Northwich. James was baptised the same day as his sister Fanny. Son of Josiah Bostock and Mary Yarwood. In the 1841 English Census, Crown Inn Farm House, Witton Street, Witton, Great Budworth, James was living with his mother and step father. James died 4 Mar 1852, age 21, Waterman, buried 17 Mar 1852, St. Helen's, Witton, Northwich. Cause of death: Consumption.
> 6. **Fanny BOSTOCK (1829-1883) [246].** Born 4 Oct 1829, baptised 15 May 1831, St. Helen's, Witton, Northwich. Dau of Josiah Bostock and Mary Yarwood. Fanny died 28 Jun 1883, Bolton, Lancashire, age 54. In the 1841 English Census, Crown Inn Farm House, Witton Street, Witton, Great Budworth, Fanny was living with her mother and step father. Fanny Marr Mark RAYNER, 4 May 1845, St. Helen's, Witton, Northwich.
> **Sp. Mark RAYNOR (1826-) [379].** Raynor also spelt Reynor and Rognor. Son of Samuel Raynor, Shoemaker.

1851 English Census, Dane Bridge, Leftwich, Northwich
Mark REYNOR, head, age 25, Tailor, born Wincham Cheshire, Fanny REYNOR, wife age 23, born Witton, Northwich, Joseph RAYNOR, son, age 5, born Leftwich, Cheshire.

1861 English Census, Witton, Street, Witton, Northwich
Mark RAYNOR. head, age 36, Tailor and Draper, born. Winchem, Cheshire, Fanny RAYNOR, wife, age 34, born Witton, Northwich, Joseph RAYNOR, son, age 13, born Witton, Tailor, Mary RAYNOR, dau, age 9, scholar, born Witton, John RAYNOR, son, age 7, born Witton, James RAYNOR, son, age 5, born Witton, Samuel RAYNOR, son age 3, born Witton, Elizabeth RAYNOR, dau, age 1, born Witton, Mary FAIRHURST, mother in law, widower, age 71, born Anderton, Cheshire, James FORSTER, age 20, Tailors Apprentice, born Weaverham, Cheshire, William WARBURTON, age 18, born Goostry. 1861.

1881 English Census, 83 York Street, Hulme, Manchester, Lancashire
Mark RAYNOR, head, age 55, Tailor, born Wincham, Fanny RAYNOR, wife, age 54, born Northwich, Mark RAYNOR, son age 12, born Manchester, Eleanor SIDDIS, dau, married, age 19, born Witton, John RAYNOR, son, married, age 25, born Witton, Tailor.

> 7. **Mark RAYNOR (1869-) [380].** Born 1869, Manchester. Mark was living with his parents in 1881 English Census, 83 York Street, Hulme, Manchester, Lancashire.
>
> 7. **Eleanor RAYNOR (1862-) [381].** Born 1862, Witton, Northwich. Eleanor was living with her parents in 1881 English Census, 83 York Street, Hulme, Manchester, Lancashire. Eleanor married a SIDDIS. Eleanor Marr Albert Siddis, spelt Sidders, 1880, St. Paul's Hulme, Manchester.
>
> **Sp. Albert SIDDIS (-) [383].** Surname also spelt Sidders.
>
> 7. **John RAYNOR (1854-) [382].** Born 1854, Witton, Northwich. Tailor. John was living with his parents in 1861 English Census, Witton, Street, Witton, Northwich and in 1881 English Census, 83 York Street, Hulme, Manchester, Lancashire.
>
> 7. **Joseph RAYNOR (1846-) [384].** Born 1846, Leftwich, Cheshire. Joseph was living with his parents in 1851 Census Dane Bridge Leftwich, Northwich and in 1861 English Census, Witton, Street, Witton, Northwich.
>
> 7. **Mary RAYNOR (1852-) [391].** Born 1852, Witton, Northwich. Mary was living with her parents in 1861 English Census, Witton, Street, Witton, Northwich.
>
> 7. **James RAYNOR (1856-) [392].** Born 1856, Witton, Northwich. James was living with his parents in 1861 English Census, Witton, Street, Witton, Northwich.
>
> 7. **Samuel RAYNOR (1858-) [393].** Born 1858, Witton, Northwich. Living with parents in 1861 English Census, Witton, Street, Witton, Northwich.
>
> 7. **Elizabeth RAYNOR (1860-) [394].** Born 1860. Witton, Northwich. Elizabeth was living with her parents in 1861 English Census, Witton, Street, Witton, Northwich.

> 6. **John BOSTOCK (-) [415].** Son of Josiah Bostock and Mary Yarwood.

5. **James BOSTOCK (1797-1872) [256].** Baptised 9 Jul 1797, St. Helen's, Witton, Northwich. Son of James Bostock and Fanny Carter. James Marr Sarah THOMSON, 4 May 1820, St. Mary's and All Saints, Great Budworth. James died 4 Jun 1872, age 68, West Point, buried St. Helen's Witton, Northwich. Known as James Junior.
Sp. Sarah THOMSON (1799-1872) [257], dau. of John Thompson and Hannah.

> 6. **Stephen BOSTOCK (1819-) [2084].** Born 1819, Witton, Northwich. Son of James Bostock and Sarah Thompson.
> **Sp. (unknown).**

> > 7. **William BOSTOCK (1838-1891) [354].** Born 1838, Witton, Northwich. William Marr Jane .... William died Sep 1891, age 44. buried St. Helen's Witton, Northwich. William was living with Samuel Vernon in 1841.
> > **Sp. Jane (1847-1922) [2105].**

1841 English Census, Great Budworth, Witton Street, Witton, Northwich
Samuel VERNON, age 45, born 1796, Cheshire, Jane VERNON, age 50, born 1791, Cheshire, Hannah VERNON, age 15, born 1826, Cheshire, William BOSTOCK, age 3, born 1838, Cheshire, Jane BOSTOCK, age 1, born 1840, Cheshire.

6. **Thomas BOSTOCK (1821-) [2085].** Baptised 22 Apr 1821, St. Helen's, Witton, Northwich. Son of James Bostock and Sarah Thompson.

6. **James BOSTOCK (1823-) [2086].** Born 3 Apr 1823, baptised 10 Apr 1825, St. Helen's, Witton, Northwich. Son of James Bostock and Sarah Thompson.

6. **Fanny BOSTOCK (1840-) [2087].** Baptised 18 Oct 1840, St. Helen's, Witton, Northwich. Dau of James Bostock and Sarah Thompson.

6. **Hannah BOSTOCK (1825-) [2088].** Born 28 Mar 1825, baptised 10 Apr 1825, St. Helen's, Witton, Northwich. Dau of James Bostock and Sarah Thompson. Hannah Marr Henry WAINWEARING, 22 Jul 1843, St. Mary and All Saints, Great Budworth.

Sp. **Henry WAINWEARING (-) [2089].**

6. **Thomas BOSTOCK (1838-) [2090].** Baptised 4 Mar 1838, St Helen's, Witton, Northwich. Son of James Bostock and Sarah Thompson.

6. **James BOSTOCK (1827-) [2091].** Baptised 25 Feb 1827,St Helen's, Witton, Northwich. Son of James Bostock and Sarah Thompson. James Marr Ann ECCLESTON.

Sp. **Ann ECCLESTON (1825-) [2092].**

6. **John BOSTOCK (1829-) [2093].** Born 1829, Witton, Northwich. Waterman. Son of James Bostock and Sarah Thompson. John was living with his parents in 1861 English Census, Winnington Yard, Witton Street, Witton cum Twambrooks. John Marr Elizabeth HOLLAND, 20 Oct 1851, St. Mary and All Saints, Great Budworth.

Sp. **Elizabeth HOLLAND (1833-) [2094].**

7. **James BOSTOCK (1852-) [2111].** Born 1 Mar 1852, Born Liverpool. James was living with his parents in 1861 English Census, Winnington Yard, Witton Street, Witton cum Twambrooks.

7. **Joseph BOSTOCK (1855-) [2112].** Born 1855, Born Runcorn, Cheshire. Joseph was living with his parents in 1861 English Census, Winnington Yard, Witton Street, Witton cum Twambrooks.

6. **Sarah BOSTOCK (1831-) [2095].** Born 24 Sep 1831, baptised 30 Mar 1834, St Helen's, Witton, Northwich. Dau of James Bostock and Sarah Thompson.

6. **Mary BOSTOCK (1836-) [2096].** Born 1836, Witton, Northwich. Dau of James Bostock and Sarah Thompson.

6. **Josiah BOSTOCK (1834-) [2097].** Born 4 Feb 1834, baptised 30 Mar 1834, St Helen's, Witton, Northwich. Son of James Bostock and Sarah Thompson.

6. **Simon BOSTOCK (1835-) [2098].** Born 1835, Witton, Northwich. Son of James Bostock and Sarah Thompson.

6. **Jane BOSTOCK (1823-) [2109].** Baptised 3 Apr 1823, St. Helen's, Witton, Northwich. Dau of James Bostock and Sarah Thompson.

5. **Ellen BOSTOCK (1785-) [258].** Born 28 Dec 1785, baptised 22 Jan 1786, St Helen's, Witton, Northwich. Dau of James Bostock and Fanny Carter.

6. **Frances BOSTOCK (1819-) [2083].** Baptised 2 May 1819, St. Helen's, Witton, Northwich.

5. **Jane BOSTOCK (circa 1791-1856) [342].** Born circa 1791, Witton, Northwich. Dau of James Bostock and Fanny Carter. Jane Marr Samuel VERNON, 27 Sep 1815, Lancashire. Jane died 1856, age 63, buried St. Helen's, Witton, Northwich.

1841 English Census, Great Budworth, Witton Street, Witton, Northwich
Samuel VERNON, age 45, born 1796, Cheshire, Jane VERNON, age 50, born 1791, Cheshire, Hannah VERNON, age 15, born 1826, Cheshire, William BOSTOCK, age 3, born 1838, Cheshire, Jane BOSTOCK, age 1, born 1840, Cheshire.

Sp. **Samuel VERNON (1796-) [343],** son of John Vernon and Fanny.

6. **Hannah VERNON (1827-) [344].** Baptised 25 Mar 1827, St Helen's, Witton, Northwich. Hannah was living with her parents in 1841 English Census, Great Budworth, Witton Street, Witton, Northwich.

6. **Jane VERNON (1822-) [345].** Baptised 3 Nov 1822, St Helen's, Witton, Northwich. Jane was living with her parents in the 1841 English Census, Great Budworth, Witton Street, Witton, Northwich.

6. **Francis Carter VERNON (1816-1850) [348].** Born 10 Jan 1816. Baptised 21 Jan 1816, St. Helen's, Witton, Northwich. Francis Carter, son of Samuel Vernon. Samuel Vernon's parents were John and Fanny Vernon. Mother, Jane's, parents were James and Fanny Bostock of Witton. Frances died Jul 1850, age 74 of Witton.

6. **James VERNON (1819-) [470].** Baptised 19 Oct 1819, St. Helen's, Northwich. Waterman of Witton.

6. **John VERNON (1821-) [2099].** Baptised 7 Oct 1821, St Helen's, Witton, Northwich.

6. **Ellen VERNON (1817-) [2100].** Baptised 31 Aug 1817, St Helen's, Witton, Northwich.

6. **Betsy VERNON (1829-) [2101].** Born 16 Feb 1829, Baptised 8 Mar 1829, St Helen's, Witton, Northwich.

5. **Jenny BOSTOCK (1787-) [462].** Born 1 Oct 1787, baptised 20 Oct 1787, St. Helen's, Witton, Northwich. Dau of James Bostock and Fanny Carter.

5. **John BOSTOCK (1789-1823) [463].** Born 23 Aug 1789, baptised 21 Sept 1789, St. Helen's, Witton, Northwich. Son of James Bostock and Fanny Carter. John died 6 Oct 1823, age 34. Parents were James and Fanny Bostock, buried 9 Oct 1823, Flatman, lived at Witton. Cause of death: Consumption.

5. **Fanny BOSTOCK (1799-) [468].** Born 1799, Baptised 4 Jan 1800, St. Helen's, Witton, Northwich. Dau of James Bostock and Fanny Carter.

5. **Hannah BOSTOCK (1795-) [2041].** Baptised 3 Apr 1795, St. Helen's, Witton, Northwich. Dau of James Bostock and Fanny Carter.

5. **John BOSTOCK (1803-) [2042].** Baptised 29 May 1803, St. Helen's, Witton, Northwich. Son of James Bostock and Fanny Carter.

Wombwell's Bostock Menagerie, Hull Fair 1919. Courtesy of National Fairground Archive, University of Sheffield Library.

Chapter Five

THE BOTTOMS FAMILY

Bottoms Family Outline

Roberti BOTTOMS (circa 1680 -1739)

---

1. Roberti BOTTOMS (circa 1680-1739) [2172].
Sp. Frances WATERWORTH (circa 1690-1729) [2175].
    2. Robert BOTTOMS (1712-1777) [2058].
   Sp. Martha HIND (-) [2059].
       3. Ellen BOTTOMS (1732-1786) [461].
      Sp. Philip BOSTOCK (1732-1802) [412], son of John BOSTOCK (1691-1771) [2040] and Ann
          MALBONE (1702-1744) [2057].
SEE BOSTOCK FAMILY
       3. Martha BOTTOMS (1737-1816) [2068].
      Sp. Gulielmus BOSTOCK (1726-1808) [2062], son of John BOSTOCK (1691-1771) [2040] and Ann
          MALBONE (1702-1744) [2057].
SEE BOSTOCK FAMILY
       3. Mary BOTTOMS (1736-1808) [2103].
      Sp. Samuel HALL (-) [2182].
      Sp. Wharton GRAYNOW (-) [2190].
       3. Elizabeth BOTTOMS (1735-) [2168].
       3. Robert BOTTOMS (-1733) [2186].
       3. John BOTTOMS (1733-) [2233].
    2. Anna BOTTOMS (1716-) [2173].
    2. Thomas BOTTOMS (1719-) [2174].
   Sp. Martha (-) [2193].
       3. Betty BOTTOMS (1734-1812) [2191].
      Sp. Thomas BEBBINGTON (-) [2192].

Bottoms Lineage

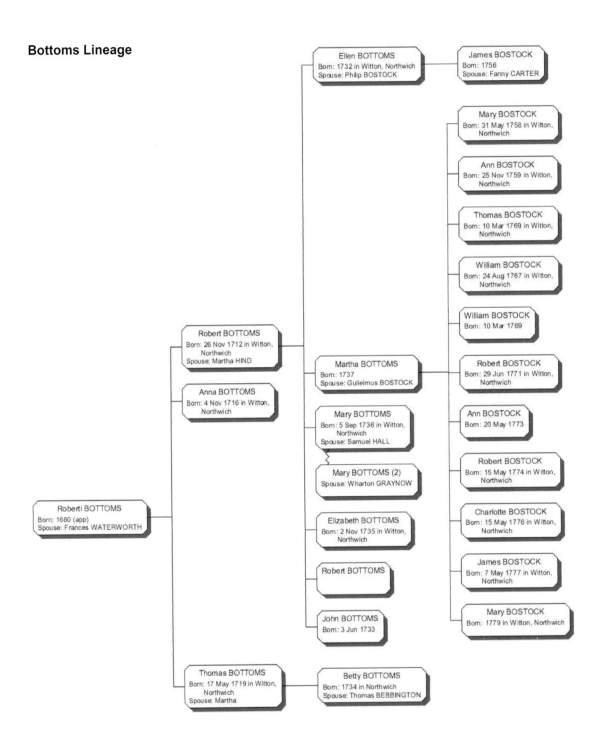

Ellen BOTTOMS
Born: 1732 in Witton, Northwich
Spouse: Philip BOSTOCK

James BOSTOCK
Born: 1756
Spouse: Fanny CARTER

Mary BOSTOCK
Born: 31 May 1758 in Witton, Northwich

Ann BOSTOCK
Born: 25 Nov 1759 in Witton, Northwich

Thomas BOSTOCK
Born: 10 Mar 1769 in Witton, Northwich

William BOSTOCK
Born: 24 Aug 1767 in Witton, Northwich

William BOSTOCK
Born: 10 Mar 1769

Robert BOSTOCK
Born: 29 Jun 1771 in Witton, Northwich

Ann BOSTOCK
Born: 20 May 1773

Robert BOSTOCK
Born: 15 May 1774 in Witton, Northwich

Charlotte BOSTOCK
Born: 15 May 1776 in Witton, Northwich

James BOSTOCK
Born: 7 May 1777 in Witton, Northwich

Mary BOSTOCK
Born: 1779 in Witton, Northwich

Robert BOTTOMS
Born: 26 Nov 1712 in Witton, Northwich
Spouse: Martha HIND

Anna BOTTOMS
Born: 4 Nov 1716 in Witton, Northwich

Martha BOTTOMS
Born: 1737
Spouse: Gulielmus BOSTOCK

Mary BOTTOMS
Born: 5 Sep 1736 in Witton, Northwich
Spouse: Samuel HALL

Mary BOTTOMS (2)
Spouse: Wharton GRAYNOW

Elizabeth BOTTOMS
Born: 2 Nov 1735 in Witton, Northwich

Robert BOTTOMS

John BOTTOMS
Born: 3 Jun 1733

Roberti BOTTOMS
Born: 1680 (app)
Spouse: Frances WATERWORTH

Thomas BOTTOMS
Born: 17 May 1719 in Witton, Northwich
Spouse: Martha

Betty BOTTOMS
Born: 1734 in Northwich
Spouse: Thomas BEBBINGTON

Roberti BOTTOMS (circa 1680 -1739)

1. Roberti BOTTOMS (circa 1680-1739) [2172]. Born circa 1680. Roberti was a Malster of Northwich. A Malster was someone who brewed beer or prepared malt for brewing purposes – a Manufacturer of malt.

Roberti Marr Frances WATERWORTH, 24 Dec 1711, St. Helen's, Witton, Northwich.

Robert died Jun 1739, buried 22 Jun 1739, St. Helen's, Witton, Northwich, no age given. Malstser of Northwich.

The following details have been added for interest as they may well be relations of this family.

Robert Bottoms married 7 Oct, 1742 St. Helen's, Witton, Northwich, Elizabeth Minshall
Elizabeth Bottoms, buried 16 Jul 1763, St. Helen's, Witton, Northwich, spouse Robert Bottoms
Robert Bottoms died 8 Sept 1733, Witton, Northwich, Cheshire, son of Robert Bottoms of Witton
Robert Bottom married 9 Sept 1740, St. Helen's, Witton, Northwich, Esther Oldfield

Sp. Frances WATERWORTH (circa 1690-1729) [2175]. Frances was of Witton Cum Twambrook, Northwich. Francisca died 1729, buried 8 Sept 1729, St. Helen's, Witton, Northwich, spouse Roberti Bottoms.

    2. Robert BOTTOMS (1712-1777) [2058]. Baptised 26 Nov 1712, Witton, Northwich, father noted as Roberti Botham. Malster of Northwich. Robert was also a Malster of Northwich and when he died he was noted as an Inn Keeper.

Robert Botham Marr 19 Jul 1730, St. Mary and St. Helen, Neston, Chester, Martha Hind. Robert was noted as a Malster. Both being resident in Neston, Chester. Robert died Feb 1777, Witton, Northwich, age 64, buried 9 Feb 1777, St. Helen's, Witton, Northwich, Inn Keeper.

    Sp. Martha HIND (-) [2059]. There is a death reference for Martha Bottoms, Widow of Northwich, died 1755, buried 22 Apr 1755, St. Helen's, Witton. This is unlikely to refer to Martha Hind as Roberti was still alive.

        3. Ellen BOTTOMS (1732-1786) [461]. Baptised Hellon on 8 Jul 1734, St. Helen's, Witton, Northwich, father Robert Bottoms, Malster of Northwich. Ellen Marr Philip BOSTOCK, 2 Dec 1755, Witton, Northwich. Witnesses Mary Bottoms and Eliz ..tington. Philip and Ellen signed their names. Both resided at Witton cum Twambrooks, Northwich. Ellen died Sep 1786, Witton, Northwich, buried 26 Sep 1786, age 54, buried St. Helen's, Witton, Northwich. Ellen's sister Martha married Gulielmus Bostock, brother to Philip Bostock.

        Sp. Philip BOSTOCK (1732-1802) [412], son of John BOSTOCK (1691-1771) [2040] and Ann MALBONE (1702-1744) [2057]. Baptised 7 May 1732, St. Helen's, Witton, Northwich, Cheshire.

SEE BOSTOCK FAMILY

        3. Martha BOTTOMS (1737-1816) [2068]. Born 1737, father Robert Bottoms, Maltser of Northwich. Martha Marr Gulielmus BOSTOCK, 10 Feb 1756, Witton, Northwich. Both resided at Witton Cum Twambrooks. Witnesses James Bagnley and William Milner. William signed his name. Martha died Sept 1816, buried 23 Sep 1816, St. Helen's, Witton, Northwich.

        Sp. Gulielmus BOSTOCK (1726-1808) [2062], son of John BOSTOCK (1691-1771) [2040] and Ann MALBONE (1702-1744) [2057].

SEE BOSTOCK FAMILY

        3. Mary BOTTOMS (1736-1808) [2103]. Baptised 5 Sept 1736, St. Hellen's, Witton, born to Robert and Martha, Malster of Northwich, residence Northwich. Mary Marr Samuel HALL, 20 Jun 1758, St. Helen's, Witton, Northwich. Both of Witton Cum Twambrook. Mary later married Wharton Graynow. Mary Graynow died Jan 1808, buried 19 Jan 1808, St. Helen's, Witton, Northwich, age 74, father Robert Bottoms, mother Martha Bottoms, spouse Wharton Graynow.

        Sp. Samuel HALL (-) [2182].

        Sp. Wharton GRAYNOW (-) [2190].

3. **Elizabeth BOTTOMS (1735-) [2168].** Baptised 2 Nov 1735, St. Helen's, Witton, Northwich, father Robert Bottoms.
3. **Robert BOTTOMS (-1733) [2186].** Died Sep 1733, Witton, Northwich, buried 8 Sept 1733, St. Helen's, Witton, Northwich, Cheshire, son of Robert Bottoms, Inn keeper of Witton.
3. **John BOTTOMS (1733-) [2233].** Baptised 3 Jun 1733. Father Robert Bottoms of Northwich, Malster.

2. **Anna BOTTOMS (1716-) [2173].** Baptised 4 Nov 1716, St. Helen's, Witton, Northwich, father Roberti Bottoms.
2. **Thomas BOTTOMS (1719-) [2174].** Baptised 17 May 1719, St. Helen's, Witton, Northwich, Roberti Bottomes. Thomas Marr Martha.
Sp. Martha (-) [2193].

3. **Betty BOTTOMS (1734-1812) [2191].** Born 1734, Northwich. Betty died Apr 1812, buried 20 Apr 1812, St. Helen's, Witton, Northwich, age 78, born 1734, father Thomas Bottoms, mother Martha Bottoms, spouse Thomas Bebbington.
Sp. Thomas BEBBINGTON (-) [2192].

Chapter Six

THE YARWOOD FAMILY

Yarwood Family Outline

James YARWOOD (circa 1660-)

---

1. James YARWOOD (circa 1660 -) [454].
Sp. (unknown).
   2. Timothy YARWOOD (circa 1698-1738) [452].
   Sp. Ann EDGERTON (circa 1698-) [453].
      3. Elizabeth YARWOOD (1720-) [455].
      3. Mary YARWOOD (1726-) [456].
      3. Hannah YARWOOD (1729-1730) [457].
      3. Ann YARWOOD (1726-) [458].
      3. John YARWOOD (1723-) [418].
      Sp. Elizabeth SWAN (1726-1819) [417], dau of Stephen SWAN (circa 1700-) [471].
         4. Elizabeth YARWOOD (1756-) [449].
         4. John YARWOOD Junior (1754-) [450].
         4. Mary YARWOOD (1752-) [451].
         4. James YARWOOD (1760-1838) [263].
         Sp. Mary DUTTON (1756-1840) [264], dau. of Peter DUTTON (-) [447] and Martha (-)
            [448].
            5. Mary YARWOOD (1794-1838) [211].
            Sp. Josiah BOSTOCK (1792-1838) [210], son of James BOSTOCK (1756-) and [255] and
               Fanny CARTER (1765-1850) [262]. Fanny CARTER dau of Isaiah CARTER (circa
               1725-) [413] and Hannah PENKIN (-) [414].

SEE BOSTOCK FAMILY
            5. Child YARWOOD (1803-) [472].
            5. Joseph YARWOOD (1797-) [387].
            5. James YARWOOD (1797-) [388].
            Sp. Betty JOHNSON (-) [390].
            5. Hugh YARWOOD (1799-) [389].
            5. William YARWOOD (1788-1813) [416].
            5. James YARWOOD (1782-) [443].
            5. Sally YARWOOD (1802-) [444].
            5. Betty YARWOOD (1874-) [445].
            5. Hannah YARWOOD (1792-) [446].
            5. Nancy YARWOOD (1789-) [459].
            5. John YARWOOD (1779-1832 [909]

Yarwood Lineage

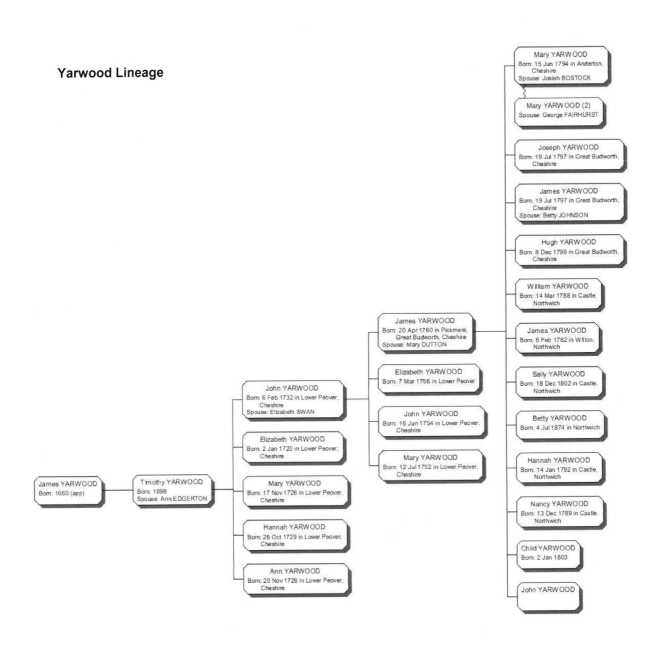

Mary YARWOOD
Born: 15 Jun 1794 in Anderton, Cheshire
Spouse: Josiah BOSTOCK

Mary YARWOOD (2)
Spouse: George FAIRHURST

Joseph YARWOOD
Born: 19 Jul 1797 in Great Budworth, Cheshire

James YARWOOD
Born: 19 Jul 1797 in Great Budworth, Cheshire
Spouse: Betty JOHNSON

Hugh YARWOOD
Born: 8 Dec 1799 in Great Budworth, Cheshire

William YARWOOD
Born: 14 Mar 1788 in Castle, Northwich

James YARWOOD
Born: 6 Feb 1782 in Witton, Northwich

Sally YARWOOD
Born: 18 Dec 1802 in Castle, Northwich

Betty YARWOOD
Born: 4 Jul 1874 in Northwich

Hannah YARWOOD
Born: 14 Jan 1792 in Castle, Northwich

Nancy YARWOOD
Born: 13 Dec 1789 in Castle, Northwich

Child YARWOOD
Born: 2 Jan 1803

John YARWOOD

James YARWOOD
Born: 20 Apr 1760 in Pickmere, Great Budworth, Cheshire
Spouse: Mary DUTTON

Elizabeth YARWOOD
Born: 7 Mar 1756 in Lower Peover

John YARWOOD
Born: 16 Jun 1754 in Lower Peover, Cheshire

Mary YARWOOD
Born: 12 Jul 1752 in Lower Peover, Cheshire

John YARWOOD
Born: 6 Feb 1732 in Lower Peover, Cheshire
Spouse: Elizabeth SWAN

Elizabeth YARWOOD
Born: 2 Jan 1720 in Lower Peover, Cheshire

Mary YARWOOD
Born: 17 Nov 1726 in Lower Peover, Cheshire

Hannah YARWOOD
Born: 26 Oct 1729 in Lower Peover, Cheshire

Ann YARWOOD
Born: 20 Nov 1726 in Lower Peover, Cheshire

James YARWOOD
Born: 1660 (app)

Timothy YARWOOD
Born: 1698
Spouse: Ann EDGERTON

James YARWOOD (circa 1660-)

1. **James YARWOOD (circa 1660-) [454].**
Sp. (unknown).

   2. **Timothy YARWOOD (circa 1698-1738) [452].** Born circa 1698, to James Yarwood. Timothy Marr Ann EDGERTON, 19 Apr 1719, St. Mary's and All Saints, Great Budworth, Cheshire. Both noted as residing at Peover, Great Budworth. Timothy died 20 Oct 1738, buried Over Peover, the son of James Yarwood.
   Sp. Ann EDGERTON (circa 1698 -) [453]. Of Peover, Great Budworth.

      3. **Elizabeth YARWOOD (1720-) [455].** Baptised 2 Jan 1720, St. Mary's and All Saints, Lower Peover, Great Budworth. Dau of Timothy Yarwood and Ann Edgerton.
      3. **Mary YARWOOD (1726-) [456].** Born 17 Nov 1726, Lower Peover. Baptised 20 Nov 1726, St. Mary's and All Saints, Lower Peover, Great Budworth. Dau of Timothy Yarwood and Ann Edgerton.
      3. **Hannah YARWOOD (1729-1730) [457].** Baptised 26 Oct 1729, St. Mary's and All Saints, Lower Peover, Great Budworth. Dau of Timothy Yarwood and Ann Edgerton. Hannah died 12 Oct 1730, buried 12 Oct 1730, Lower Peover, Cheshire.
      3. **Ann YARWOOD (1726-) [458].** Born 17 Nov 1726, Lower Peover. Baptised 20 Nov 1726, St. Mary's and All Saints, Lower Peover, Great Budworth. Dau of Timothy Yarwood and Ann Edgerton.
      3. **John YARWOOD (1723-) [418].** Born 6 Feb 1723, Lostock, Lower Peover. Baptised 9 Feb 1723, Lover Peover. Son of Timothy Yarwood and Ann Edgerton. There was also a John Yarwood baptised 8 Sept 1723, St. Mary's and All Saints, Great Budworth, parent John Yarwood. Thought to be a cousin of John.

         John Marr Elizabeth SWAN, 11 Feb 1751 Lower Peover. One reference states Elizabeth was a Widow of Moulton, parents unknown when she married.
      Sp. Elizabeth SWAN (1726-1819) [417]. Baptised 10 July 1726, St. Mary's and All Saints, Great Budworth, dau of Stephen Swan (-) [471] of Great Budworth.

There was a **Stephen Swan** baptised 21 Jun 1706, St. Mary's and All Saints, Great Budworth, son of Joseph Swan, residence Pickmere. Stephen could have been Elizabeth's father and Joseph Swan her grandfather although not confirmed.

The following are the siblings of the above mentioned Stephen baptised 21 Jun 1706
*   Child baptised April 1679, St. Mary's and All Saints, Great Budworth, born to Stephen Swan (name of the child unreadable)
*   Mary baptised 5 Sept 1708, St. Mary's and All Saints, Great Budworth, born to Joseph Swan
*   Mary baptised 8 Jul 1703, St. Mary's and All Saints, Great Budworth, born to Joseph Swan
*   Sarah baptised 22 Oct 1704, St. Mary's and All Saints, Great Budworth, born to Joseph Swan
*   Thomas baptised 13 Aug 1710, St. Mary's and All Saints, Great Budworth, born to Joseph Swan. Thomas died 14 Oct 1716, buried St. Mary's and All Saints, Great Budworth

The following was the only reference to a Joseph Swan
*   Josephus Swan baptised 30 May 1672, St. Mary's and All Saints, Great Budworth, born to Thomas Swan of Alderley.

A further record was found but unfortunately the name of the child was unreadable
*   Child baptised 14 Dec 1623, St. Mary and All Saints, Great Budworth, born to John Swan

         Elizabeth Yarwood died 8 Sep 1819, age 86, buried 13 Sep 1819. Natural Decay was the cause of death.

         In 1782 John and Elizabeth were listed as living in Hulse, which is just west of Lostock Gralam and near to Lower Peover. By 1794 John and Elizabeth had moved to Pickmere.

4. **Elizabeth YARWOOD (1756-) [449].** Baptised 7 Mar 1756, St. Mary's and All Saints, Lower Peover, Great Budworth. Dau of John Yarward and Elizabeth Swan.

4. **John YARWOOD Junior (1754-) [450].** Baptised 16 Jan 1754, St. Mary's and All Saints, Lower Peover, Great Budworth. Son of John Yarwood and Elizabeth Swan.

4. **Mary YARWOOD (1752-) [451].** Baptised 12 Jul 1752, St. Mary's and All Saints, Lower Peover, Great Budworth. Dau of John Yarwood and Elizabeth Swan.

4. **James YARWOOD (1760-1838) [263].** Baptised 20 Apr 1760, St. Mary's and All Saints, Lower Peover, Great Budworth. Son of John Yarwood and Elizabeth Swan. Residence noted as Pickmere.

James Marr Mary DUTTON, 15 Mar 1779, St. Helen's, Witton, Northwich. Both age 19 and both resident at Witton cum Twambrooks, Northwich. James was noted as a Waller, residing in Witton. Witnesses John Page and James Swindell. James died 21 Jan 1838, age 80, buried St. Helen's, Witton, Northwich, south side of the cemetery. An accident is noted as the cause of his death.

Sp. Mary DUTTON (1756-1840) [264], dau. of Peter DUTTON (-) [447] and Martha (-) [448] of Shipbrook, near Shurlach, (south east of Lostock Gralam). Mary died 24 Aug 1840, age 84. Buried 28 Aug 1840, St. Helen's, Witton, Northwich. Mary's burial record states, Widow of James Yarwood. Cause of death old Age.

Although not confirmed it is likely Mary 's mother was Martha Millington. Peter Dutton Marr Martha MILLINGTON, 16 June 1755, Witton cum Twanbrooks, Northwich. Witnesses William Milner and William Forster. Peter was noted as a Labourer of Davenham and both were of the Parish of Great Budworth.

From 1782 to 1792, James and Mary are listed as living at Castle, Northwich and from 1794 to 1799, the family are listed as living in Anderton, Cheshire. Witton Township, St. Helen's, Witton, Castle and Anderton are all in the Chapelry of Great Budworth.

5. **Mary YARWOOD (1794-) [211].** Born 15 Jun 1794, Anderton. Baptised 6 July 1794, St. Helen's, Witton, Northwich. Dau of James Yarwood and Mary Dutton. Mary Marr Josiah BOSTOCK, Waterman, 10 May 1820, St. Mary's and All Saints, Great Budworth. Parents listed as James Yarwood, Waller of Witton and Mary Dutton of Great Budworth. Josiah's parents were listed as James Bostock and mother, Fanny Carter of Witton, Northwich.

Sp. Josiah BOSTOCK (1792-1838) [210], son of James BOSTOCK (1756-) [255], Flatman and Fanny CARTER (1765-850) [262]. Josiah died 18 Oct 1838, age 45, buried 22 Oct 1838, St. Helen's, Witton, Northwich.

SEE BOSTOCK FAMILY

5. **Child YARWOOD (1803-) [472].** Baptised 2 Jan 1803, St. Mary's and All Saints, Great Budworth. Child of James Yarwood and Mary Dutton. The name of the child is unreadable.

5. **Joseph YARWOOD (1797-) [387].** Born 1797, Anderton. Baptised 9 Jul 1797, St. Mary's and All Saints, Great Budworth. Twin to James. Son of James Yarwood and Mary Dutton.

5. **James YARWOOD (1797-) [388].** Born 1797, Anderton. Baptised 9 Jul 1797, St. Mary's and All Saints, Great Budworth. Twin to Joseph. Son of James Yarwood and Mary Dutton. James Marr Betty JOHNSON, 20 Dec 1824.

Sp. Betty JOHNSON (-) [390]. Of Great Budworth

5. **Hugh YARWOOD (1799-) [389].** Baptised 8 Dec 1799, St. Mary's and All Saints, Great Budworth. Son of James Yarwood and Mary Dutton.

5. **William YARWOOD (1788-1813) [416].** Born 14 Mar 1788 Castle, Northwich. Another record states Davenham. Baptised 30 Mar 1788, St Helen's, Witton, Northwich. Son of James Yarwood and Mary Dutton. William died 26 Jun 1813, age 25, Flatman of Castle, Northwich. Buried 28 Jun 1813, age 25, St. Helen's, Witton, Northwich. Stated to be son of James and Mary Yarwood of Anderton. Cause of death Executed for Rape.

Cheshire Quarter Sessions records - death warrants (ref QAB 5/8/13) Name: "John Burgess, Wm. Yarwood, Wm. Wilkinson; Crime: Rape".

In further quarter session records (ref QAB 5/8/14) Name:
"John Burgess, Wm. Yarwood, Wm. Wilkinson; Crime: Rape; Remarks: Executed 26 June 1813 persisting their innocence to using force".

Public execution in Chester on the 26 June 1813
"William Wilkinson, James Yarwood (probably a misprint and should read William Yarwood) and William Burgess executed for a rape on Mary Porter near Weston Point, Cheshire".

> **5. James YARWOOD (1782-) [443].** Born 6 Feb 1782, Castle, Witton, Northwich. Baptised 3 Mar 1782, St. Helen's, Witton, Northwich. Son of James Yarwood and Mary Dutton. James died Dec 1840.
>
> **5. Sally YARWOOD (1802-) [444].** Born 18 Dec 1802, Castle, Northwich, baptised 2 Jan 1803, St. Helen's, Witton, Northwich. Dau of James Yarwood and Mary Dutton.
>
> **5. Betty YARWOOD (1874-) [445].** Born Castle, baptised 4 Jul 1874, St. Helen's, Witton, Northwich. Dau of James Yarwood and Mary Dutton.
>
> **5. Hannah YARWOOD (1792-) [446].** Born 12 Feb 1792, Castle. Baptised 14 Jan 1792, St. Helen's, Witton, Northwich. Dau of James Yarwood and Mary Dutton.
>
> **5. Nancy YARWOOD (1789-) [459].** Born 13 Dec 1789, Castle. Baptised 25 Dec 1789, St. Helen's, Witton, Northwich. Dau of James Yarwood and Mary Dutton.
>
> **5. John YARWOOD (1779-1832 [909].** Born 1779. Son of James Yarwood and Mary Dutton. John died 3 June 1832, buried 4 June 1832, age 53, St. Helen's, Witton, Northwich, south side of the cemetery. Died of Cholera Asphyea.

Chapter Seven

THE DIXON FAMILY

Dixon Family Outline

Richard / Pat DIXON (-)

---

1. Richard / Pat DIXON (-) [248].
Sp. (unknown).
   2. Philip DIXON (1819-) [42].
   Sp. Elizabeth DUTTON (1822-) [209], dau of James DUTTON (1792-) [247] and Elizabeth WILLIAMS
       (1787-) [643].
SEE DUTTON FAMILY
      3. Philip DIXON (1845-) [374].
      3. Charles DIXON (1839-) [375].
      3. James DIXON (1840-) [376].
      3. Hannah DIXON (1847-) [377].
      3. Mary DIXON (1843-) [378].
      3. George HEALING (1840-) [2277] son of Thomas HEALING (1813-) [2278] and Ann (1815-)
        [2279].
      3. Robert DIXON (1849-1916) [34].
      Sp. Betsy DEAN (1852-1911) [33], dau of James (Toffee) DEAN (1834-1899) [44] and Jane
        BOSTOCK (1838-1870) [85].
SEE DEAN AND BOSTOCK FAMILY
        4. Gilbert DIXON (1885-1956) [16].
        Sp. Margaret Ellen CLOUGH (1886-1986) [17], dau of Edward CLOUGH (1861-1937) [63] and
          Sarah Ellen CORDWELL (1866-1933) [64].
SEE CLOUGH AND CORDWELL FAMILY
         5. Betsy DIXON (1908-1983) [9].
         Sp. Robert HINES (1901-1951) [8], son of Robert W HINES (1875-1956) [224] and Mary
           Elizabeth STOCKDALE (1880-1952) [225].
SEE HINES AND SCOTT /STOCKDALE FAMILY
         Sp. William ROBERTS (-) [213].
         5. Alice DIXON (1910-1916) [18].
         5. Gilbert Verdin Junior DIXON (-1971) [19].
         Sp. Daisy MANDERS (-) [20].
          5. Billy DIXON (-) [28].
         Sp. Sally (-) [29].
          5. Edward (Teddy) DIXON (-) [41].
       4. Charlie DIXON (1884-) [35]
       Sp. Charlotte LOCKE(-) [915].
         5. Charlie (Chuck) DIXON (1908 -) [200].
         Sp. Agnes BELL (-) [916].
          5. Bob DIXON (1903-) [201].
          5. Alice DIXON (1911-) [917].
         Sp. Joe MULHEARN (-) [918].
          3. Aggie DIXON (-) [1723].
      4. Jane DIXON (1872-1927) [36].
       Sp. Martin HAYES (-) [37].
         5. Bernard HAYES (-) [196].
         5. Charlie HAYES (-) [197].
         5. Jimmy HAYES (-) [198].
         5. Laura HAYES (-) [199].
      4. Jim DIXON (1870-) [38].
      4. Lizy DIXON (1873-) [39].
       Sp. Herbert SHAW (1866-) [128].
         5. Herbert SHAW (1898-) [129].
         Sp. Kathy WALKER (-) [136].

5. Robert SHAW (-) [130].
Sp. Alice INGHAM (-) [139].
5. William Jarrow SHAW (circa 1907-) [131].
Sp. Alice GILL (-) [142].
5. Betsy SHAW (1900-1987) [132].
Sp. Tommy EDWARDS (-) [146].
5. Loretta SHAW (1909-1996) [133].
Sp. William SMITH (-) [154].
5. Connie SHAW (1905-1985) [134].
Sp. William CRADDOCK (-) [151].
5. Lily SHAW (1896-) [135].
Sp. Patrick MULHEARN (-) [158].
4. Alice DIXON (1892 -) [40].
Sp. Francis Christopher MATTHEWS (-) [161].
     5. Mary MATTHEWS (1919-1920) [207].
4. Hannah DIXON (1877-1903) [47].
Sp. James FEARNS (1873-1939) [48].
     5. Gilbert FEARNS (1902-1976) [49].
     Sp. Elizabeth REAY (-) [50].
     5. Margaret Alice FEARNS (1897-1953) [162].
     Sp. Davie LITLIERNHURNEST (-) [163].
4. John DIXON (1895-1895) [194].
4. Thomas DIXON (1890-1896) [195].

Dixon Lineage

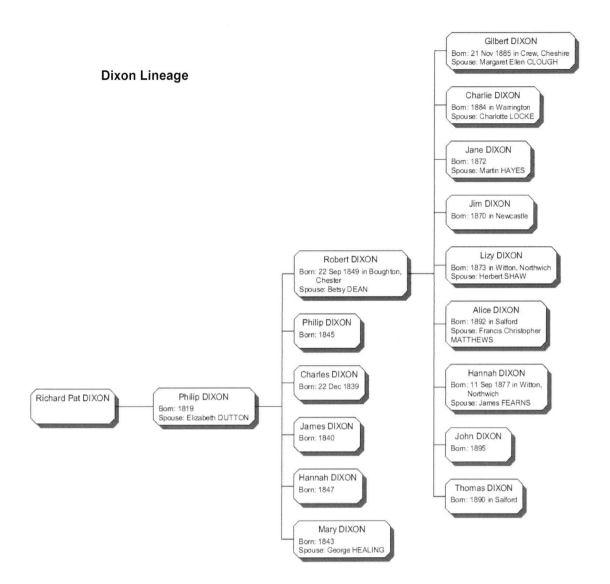

Richard Pat DIXON

Philip DIXON
Born: 1819
Spouse: Elizabeth DUTTON

Robert DIXON
Born: 22 Sep 1849 in Boughton, Chester
Spouse: Betsy DEAN

Philip DIXON
Born: 1845

Charles DIXON
Born: 22 Dec 1839

James DIXON
Born: 1840

Hannah DIXON
Born: 1847

Mary DIXON
Born: 1843
Spouse: George HEALING

Gilbert DIXON
Born: 21 Nov 1885 in Crew, Cheshire
Spouse: Margaret Ellen CLOUGH

Charlie DIXON
Born: 1884 in Warrington
Spouse: Charlotte LOCKE

Jane DIXON
Born: 1872
Spouse: Martin HAYES

Jim DIXON
Born: 1870 in Newcastle

Lizy DIXON
Born: 1873 in Witton, Northwich
Spouse: Herbert SHAW

Alice DIXON
Born: 1892 in Salford
Spouse: Francis Christopher MATTHEWS

Hannah DIXON
Born: 11 Sep 1877 in Witton, Northwich
Spouse: James FEARNS

John DIXON
Born: 1895

Thomas DIXON
Born: 1890 in Salford

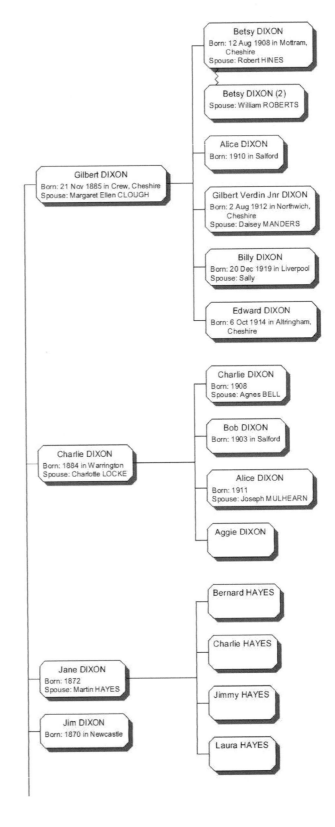

Gilbert DIXON
Born: 21 Nov 1885 in Crew, Cheshire
Spouse: Margaret Ellen CLOUGH

Betsy DIXON
Born: 12 Aug 1908 in Mottram, Cheshire
Spouse: Robert HINES

Betsy DIXON (2)
Spouse: William ROBERTS

Alice DIXON
Born: 1910 in Salford

Gilbert Verdin Jnr DIXON
Born: 2 Aug 1912 in Northwich, Cheshire
Spouse: Daisey MANDERS

Billy DIXON
Born: 20 Dec 1919 in Liverpool
Spouse: Sally

Edward DIXON
Born: 6 Oct 1914 in Altringham, Cheshire

Charlie DIXON
Born: 1884 in Warrington
Spouse: Charlotte LOCKE

Charlie DIXON
Born: 1908
Spouse: Agnes BELL

Bob DIXON
Born: 1903 in Salford

Alice DIXON
Born: 1911
Spouse: Joseph MULHEARN

Aggie DIXON

Jane DIXON
Born: 1872
Spouse: Martin HAYES

Bernard HAYES

Charlie HAYES

Jimmy HAYES

Laura HAYES

Jim DIXON
Born: 1870 in Newcastle

74

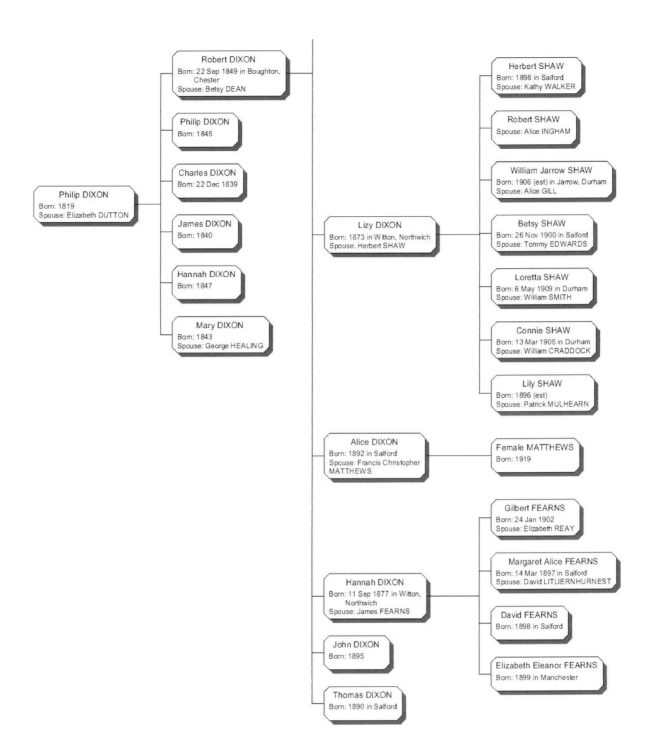

Philip DIXON
Born: 1819
Spouse: Elizabeth DUTTON

Robert DIXON
Born: 22 Sep 1849 in Boughton, Chester
Spouse: Betsy DEAN

Philip DIXON
Born: 1845

Charles DIXON
Born: 22 Dec 1839

James DIXON
Born: 1840

Hannah DIXON
Born: 1847

Mary DIXON
Born: 1843
Spouse: George HEALING

Lizy DIXON
Born: 1873 in Witton, Northwich
Spouse: Herbert SHAW

Herbert SHAW
Born: 1898 in Salford
Spouse: Kathy WALKER

Robert SHAW
Spouse: Alice INGHAM

William Jarrow SHAW
Born: 1906 (est) in Jarrow, Durham
Spouse: Alice GILL

Betsy SHAW
Born: 26 Nov 1900 in Salford
Spouse: Tommy EDWARDS

Loretta SHAW
Born: 6 May 1909 in Durham
Spouse: William SMITH

Connie SHAW
Born: 13 Mar 1905 in Durham
Spouse: William CRADDOCK

Lily SHAW
Born: 1896 (est)
Spouse: Patrick MULHEARN

Alice DIXON
Born: 1892 in Salford
Spouse: Francis Christopher MATTHEWS

Female MATTHEWS
Born: 1919

Hannah DIXON
Born: 11 Sep 1877 in Witton, Northwich
Spouse: James FEARNS

Gilbert FEARNS
Born: 24 Jan 1902
Spouse: Elizabeth REAY

Margaret Alice FEARNS
Born: 14 Mar 1897 in Salford
Spouse: David LITLIERNHURNEST

David FEARNS
Born: 1898 in Salford

Elizabeth Eleanor FEARNS
Born: 1899 in Manchester

John DIXON
Born: 1895

Thomas DIXON
Born: 1890 in Salford

1. Richard / Pat DIXON (-) [248]. The spelling of the surname has also been recorded as Dickson.

There is evidence to support the fact that the above name is Richard and Pat.

- When his son Philip was in court in 1830, his father was referred to as Pat Dixon
- Philip noted his father as Richard Dixon on his marriage certificate

The following illustrates the evidence

11 June 1830, from The Chester Chronicle, "Philip Dixon and three other boys, none of them were age 14 years old were in court for steeling rabbits. Pat Dixon father of one of the lads took hold of his son and with all the characteristic warmth of his countrymen, addressing him saying "Till de gintlemen de trut, you spalpeen, or I'll put the life out o'ye – The lad hesitated upon which Pat with still greater energy (pulling a halter out of his pocket, ready noosed) said "see here, my honey, Ye'll come to be hung yet, if ye go on in this line; and the divil fly away wid me, if I won't just be after hanging ye, if ye don't till the trut".

This would clearly suggest that Philip's father was called Pat Dixon and judging by the accent from the above report it is likely his father was Irish.

Philip Marr Elizabeth DUTTON, 6 Dec 1838, St. Mary's Parish Church in the County of the City of Chester, father, Richard Dixon, Labourer. Elizabeth Dutton's father, William Dutton, Labourer.

The name of Elizabeth's father was James Dutton and not William. It is not clear why Elizabeth gave an alternative name for her father but it looks like Philip did the same.

It is possible Richard had two names and or was also known as Pat.

According to a newspaper article, dictated by Philip Dixon while in the prison at Chester Castle, his father became a Catholic when he married Philip's mother and Philip and his siblings were brought up as Catholics. Therefore, his parents may have married at St. Werburgh's, Chester.

Unfortunately, there appears to be only one reference found in St. Werburgh's Roman Catholic Church for a Jacobus Dixon born 26 Jan 1822, baptised 29 Jan 1822, St. Werburgh's, Chester, parents Richardi Dixon and Maria Smith Dixon. Jacobus Dixon is buried St. Werburgh's, Chester 1884. It has not been confirmed Jacobus or his family refer to this particular family.

Sp. (unknown).

2. Philip DIXON (1819-) [42]. Born 1819. Presumed son of Richard Dixon according to Philip's marriage certificate, or Pat Dixon according to the newspaper report noted above..

Although Philip states he was born in Chester no birth details have been found.

As detailed above in 1830, Philip and three other boys were in court for steeling rabbits.

Philip Marr Elizabeth DUTTON, 6 Dec 1838, St. Mary's Parish Church in the County of the City of Chester.

Marriage certificate
Married at St. Mary's Parish Church in the County of Chester, 6 Dec 1838, Philip Dixon of full age, bachelor, Labourer, residence Handbridge, Chester, father, Richard Dixon, Labourer, married Elizabeth Dutton of full age, spinster, no profession given, residence, Handbridge, Chester, father, William Dutton, Labourer. Philip Dixon signed his name, Elizabeth made an X as her mark. The witness, who also made an X as their marks were Mary Prescott and Stephen Jones.

It is not clear why Elizabeth gave her father's name as William as the records show her father's name was definitely James.

The Parish Church of St. Mary in the County of the City of Chester was known as St. Mary's on the Hill and also St. Mary's within the Walls. Most of the residents of Handbridge, although living across the River Dee, attended this church. At a later date a church was built in Handbridge and became known as St. Mary's without the Walls.

In 1839, when their son Charles was born Philip and Elizabeth were living at Foregate Street, Chester and Philip was noted as a Labourer. By 1841, Philip was in prison as confirmed by the 1841 English Census, Knutsford, Cheshire, House of Correction Nether Knutsford (Prison), Philip DIXON, inmate, age 22, Paper Maker, born Cheshire.

By 1849, Philip and Elizabeth were living at Machine Bank, Boughton, Chester. Machine Bank, Boughton, Chester, became extinct as an area after 1851. However, up until 1851 this area was in the Parish of St. John's and situated close to the old waterworks on the road between Chester City centre and Vicars Cross. Machine Bank was connected in some way to the waterworks. There was an old pub close by called 'The Engine'. This pub is likely to have served the waterworks workers.

Travelling along the canal in Boughton there are some houses along the bank opposite what use to be the old waterworks. Although the original cottages would have been replaced by new houses within the last century, some of these cottages are called 'bank' and would have been for the employees of the waterworks.

The following information provides an excellent account of Philip's life. Created with the assistance of Gilbert and Julie Dixon.

Courtesy of the Cheshire and Flint Assizes and Cheshire Archives and Local Studies, the following is a list of court cases mentioning Philip in his early years leading up to and before he was transported to Australia.

"1841 Philip Dixon, age 21, Larceny, Cheshire, Chester Assizes, 17 May 1841, sentence, 1 month".

1841 English Census, Knutsford, Cheshire, House of Correction
Philip Dixon, inmate, age 22, paper maker, born Cheshire.

"1844, Philip Dixon, age 24, Larceny, Flintshire, Flint, 17 Oct 1844, - Acquittal".

"1847, Elizabeth Dixon, age 24, House Breaking, Cheshire, Chester Assizes, 11 Jan 1847, - Acquittal".

"1847, Philip Dixon, House Breaking, Cheshire, Chester Assizes, 11 Jan 1847, sentence - 15 years, Transportation". There is a reference in a newspaper relating to a jewellery robbery for which he received a sentence of 15 years, transportation.

After this sentence Philip was detained in the Hulks at Portsmouth waiting to be deported. However, Philip escaped and made his way home where he was recaptured – "Philip Dixon, Feloniously Returning Home after 1 month, Cheshire, Chester Assizes, 4 August 1849, sentence -15 years, Transportation".

Philip was held for a while at Chester Castle where he befriended a priest. This is a short auto-biography of his exploits (appears as dictated). This was published in the Chester Courant in 1849.

Life and Times of Philip Dixon
Article courtesy of the Cheshire Archives and Local Studies and The Chester Courant Newspaper.

"THE LIFE OF THE NOTORIOUS "PHIL DIXON" - Dictated by himself. (Extracts)

The subject of the following auto-biography was convicted at the last Chester Assizes, of having returned from transportation before the period of his sentence had expired, and now awaits at Knutsford, for his removal to a penal settlement.

Chester Castle, August 10 1849.

I was born in the year 1820. My parents were poor people, and lived in Chester, of which place I am a native. When I was seven years of age I was sent to the Rev. Mr Briggs` School in Queen Street. My father was for a time a Protestant, but through my mother's influence became a Roman Catholic, and in this faith I was brought up. I continued at this school until I was about twelve years of age, and soon after this I lost my mother. There were five of us in the family, three of whom were living at home at Boughton. My father was given to drink and left us all in a destitute condition, so that from 12 years of age I was left to get my living in the best way I could. One day I was in the Market, and Miss Currie sent me home with some flower pots; this was on a Saturday. She told me to come again to my dinner on the following day---Sunday. She wished me to go to Church, and I went. She then told me to come the next day. She appeared to be interested in me, and shortly after she brought me a suit of livery, and engaged me as her servant. After I had lived with her nearly 12 months, she told me not to go into town, as the cholera was very bad. Against her will, and unknown to her, I went in my livery; this was at Boughton wakes, and the commencement of my bad career. I did not return to my situation, but after I had spent all my money drinking and debauchery, I went home to my father's house, who was also a great drunkard. Had it not been for the common small ale houses, I should never have been brought to these troubles; in these I spent my money in card playing, dice, and gambling of every description, and was associated with a number of bad women of the town. After I had spent my money, I went and slept in any outbuildings or stables wherever I could get until I became filthy, and as black as a sweep. Mr Hassall from Abby Court knew I was in service at Miss Curries, and seeing me in such a filthy condition, he called me to him and said---if he promised to get me back again to my situation, would I go and conduct myself as a good boy. I said I would. He took me to Miss Curries, and went in and spoke to her, whilst I remained outside, and shortly after they both came out, and ordered me to get my supper. I continued with her a month or two longer; she was an excellent good lady and was more than a mother to me, she would have made a man of me had I taken her advice. I always went to Church with her every Sunday, as my mistress was very particular in this, and we had prayers in the family. One Saturday when returning from the market, I met with one of my old companions, who wished me to meet him at the Coach and Horses in Boughton, as there was a raffle for a copper tea kettle that evening. I left my place again, got drunk, and never returned to my situation. Miss Currie frequently saw me and asked me whether I was in work, I always said yes; at the same time I was not. I had now pawned my livery, sold my boots, hat and shirt, and spent all my money with bad women.

Shortly after this I was enticed away by some gipsies and went tramping about the country. The first night I stayed with them was in Hoole lane. They put me to lie on some straw under the cart; and before I went to bed the woman came home with plenty of broken victuals of all sorts---such as beef, mutton, &c. &c. which they got by telling fortunes. They spoke a language to each other which I did not understand. I used to put their horse and ass in a field at night and was called up about three o'clock in the morning to bring them back again. If any hay was seen in the field I was always sent to bring it to the camp. I was always frequently sent to pilfer beans, potatoes, turnips, fowls, and anything else I could meet with. I travelled with them into Wales and into Warwickshire; we then returned again to Shocklach, near Malpas, when one night they all got drunk and had a regular fight amongst themselves and I ran away off to Chester. I went to Birkenhead, and had about 4s or 5s in my pocket. I started over to Liverpool, and got with a regular gang of thieves in Bannister Street at a lodging house. After I had been there a night or two, one of the lads asked me if I would purchase a pocket handkerchief; he showed it to me; I said it was the wrong sort. He then pulled out several others, and asked me if any of them would do. I told him he had better pawn them; I knew he had stolen them, he did so, and on the following day (Saturday) I went into the market with several of them to see what we could pilfer. We had not been in long before we went and bought some fruit at a stall and the woman that kept it shouted and fainted; the others left me and ran off to the lodging house, and I followed them and found they had picked her pocket and stolen from her £6 18s. Of which I received 20s. I then returned to Chester the following day and went to live with Mr Sneade, the butcher, in Flookerbrook. I did not remain with him more than about three months. I then went to live with Mr Snelson, in Bridge Street, as ostler. I was angry with my master and after I had lived with him about three months I left him. I was then about 15 years of age. Shortly after this I lived with Mr Cope, in Boughton and bought old iron and stores. I was with him on and off, for about three years, when I became acquainted with my wife. I was very fond of drink which induced me to commit many small robberies such as picking pockets, stealing from shops, going into confectioners` and stealing cakes &c.

Going down John street one day I went into the yard of Mr Harrison, surgeon, and there saw a large brass mortar I bought from him, as it was too heavy for me to carry, otherwise I should have stolen it as I had many opportunities of doing so and often tried but I could not lift it. I gave him 5s for it but it was worth £1 11s. 8p. which sum I got for it from Mr Cope. After this I went to work on the Birkenhead Railway. I then saved about £5, a good suit of clothes, and a watch.

When I was 18 years of age I got married. After this I bought a barrow and dogs and went to fairs and races. I then commenced gambling and everything that was bad such as fighting, drinking, and stealing. I was a good boxer and often got well treated for fighting by rich and poor. I had often been in Chester prison for fighting and getting drunk. I was convicted once at Knutsford, and got one month for stealing two sovereigns from a man that was drinking with me at Tarvin.

When I was at Wrexham fair I got acquainted with Connolly. We came to Chester and went to the brew house near the Walls. It is just close Mr Huxley's brewery. We unlocked the door of a private house with a false key. We searched the house but could not find anything that we wished to take. Then we broke into Mrs Rutter`s house, for which we were both convicted. We stole about £252 2s. in money and plate, the night we took it, we went and hid the plate. The jewellery we stole I threw away. We hid the plate in Garden lane near to the College. The third night after the robbery was committed the servant girl was taken up. She had informed Connolly where everything was to be found in the house. Connolly was courting her. They lived in Handbridge but not in the same house and she gave him all the information about Mrs Rutter`s house. For this we were both tried and sentenced to 15 years transportation, but we cleared the girl before the Magistrates. I was so dreadfully distressed in my mind on account of my poor wife and children, that I was quite tired of my life and attempted to commit suicide in the dock at the Town Hall during the time of my trial. It was with a razor which I picked up in the City Gaol and which I believe belonged to one of the prisoners. I feel now that it was through the mercy of God that I was not permitted to do so. I am thankful that I am spared as it would have been an awful thing to have committed suicide. I do not say I will not attempt my escape again as I am willing to suffer anything-- any hardship-- so that I may be with my wife and family again. I will lead a different life for the future for my own sake and for the sake of my dear wife and children. I am quite convinced if it were more generally know what hardships a transport has to endure there would be less crime committed. The two years that I have already suffered convinces me that no greater trials can possibly be endured by a human being. Death is far more preferable!

I was removed from here shortly after my trial to Millbank prison where I was kept in solitary confinement but had plenty of good books to read, which were the means of bringing me to think seriously of my past life and what I had brought myself to. In consequence of my good conduct I was removed with nine more out of about 1.400 prisoners to Portsmouth to the York hulk. Here I remained for a nearly 20 months. During this time I saw 14 convicts so severely flogged that the flesh came from the back bone and were immediately sent out to work again with the rest of the convicts, all for bad behaviour. On one occasion I was present when a convict of the name of Hatter murdered our guard, James Connor. I seized the mallet out of his hand at the time but it was to late-- the poor guard was dead! For this Hatter was tried at the Winchester assizes, condemned and hung.

I was still very unhappy and whilst many of my fellow suffers were fast asleep in their hammocks I was thinking of my poor wife and children and contriving in my mind how I could make my escape from that place. I was in the daytime working on the gun-wharf and there I picked up a file. I concealed it under my sleeve and brought it in. The following night when all was still and quite I began filing the bars of the port window of the ship but dare not do much at a time lest I should be heard. The next night I did the same. I generally embraced the opportunity of working at this when the tide might be coming in and the wind made a noise so that the guard should not hear me from the quarter deck. When I had finished a certain portion of my filing I filled it up with brown soap which was the colour of the paint on the bars. I found I could not get on so well as I wished that night so I concealed myself under the hammock on the Thursday evening when all the prisoners went to chapel. During this time I did a great deal of work towards getting the iron bars from my window. I had them all finished on the ninth night. I got up about twelve o'clock to get through the window and jump into the sea but the tide was going out at a very rapid pace and the wind was so very high that I was obliged to give it up for that night. I was as I suppose seen by some of the prisoners putting in the soap the next morning and I came up on deck I was stopped by one of the officers. One of them went down into my ward and found the iron bars had been out. They brought me before the captain. They put a pair of cross irons upon me. I kept them on and worked in them and slept in them for three months. They then shipped me into the Dockyard where they thought I should be more secure but I knew better for after my irons were taken off I resolved a second time to make my escape. I could not forget my poor wife and children. They were constantly before my mind. I was determined to get some clothing out of the men of war ships which were in the dockyards. In this I succeeded and got a shirt, a cap, a handkerchief, and an old pair of trousers. I concealed them in my own cell one by one at different times and kept them in my hammock until I could find an opportunity of making my escape. I got up one morning about three o'clock and dressed myself with the clothes I had stolen and put my convict's dress over them, at the time we mustered, which was always about seven o'clock in the morning during the winter, the guard searched me, and I passed. I got into the boat and was again detected, was called on the quarter deck and was stripped naked. I was again ironed and put into the black hole and was kept there fourteen days and nights, upon a pound of bread a day and plenty of water. Seven of these days I did not see daylight but the other seven days I was allowed to exercise an hour in the day. After the expiration of these fourteen days I was brought out of the black hole and when I got on deck, I, for the first time of my life fainted. The irons were kept on me. I was then under the Doctor's care for about three weeks. After this I went to work as usual with about 20lbs weight of iron upon me for a full three months. During this time my wife came to see me. I was cut to my heart, on account of her great distress of mind. She wept bitterly when she saw the heavy irons upon me and told me that both her and her children were almost in a state of starvation as the parish would not allow them sufficient to support them. I thought to myself when I saw her I will try again to make my escape for her sake and for the sake of my dear children. I could not rest night nor day on their account after having seen her. I became more determined and desperate than ever. I was again set to work in the Dockyard with light irons. I considered a plan one night when in my hammock and which I was resolved to try the next day although I had several guards to pass and a very long way to swim. I prayed that God would assist me through it for my family's sake. Consequently, on the following night when we had left off work to go into the small boat, which always took us from our work to the ship the York, which was on the 25th of November, instead of going into the boat I ran up to the piles, under the jetty, up to my middle in water, where I remained for about an hour and a half. When the boat was pushed off to return to thee hulks I heard the guard say-" where is Dixon"? I heard one of them say, "he has done us at last, for he is not here". When they came on shore they were over my head and again exclaimed "he has done us". They asked one of the soldiers whether he had seen one of their men and he answered no. All this time I was in the water. I was afraid to use my file to take off my irons lest the soldier above me should hear me. Presently the drum on board the Victory was beaten as is usual. I then began to use my file and got my iron off. As soon as it became dusk (it was very foggy) I began to strip. I uttered up a few words in prayer and cast myself into the water. The tide was coming in very strongly. I went at a rapid rate and had to pass by a guard on the Illustrious and several other guards higher up the harbour. After I had been in the water about a quarter of an hour I heard a gunshot. After this several more had been fired. I thought they were all coming to me. Then I thought it was all up with me. I was alarmed but I believe it was only in consequence of the Queen having visited Portsmouth that day and they were taking down the standard. I was so much terrified shooting that when I passed by the King George's Yacht I fastened myself to one of the buoys. It was, however, so very cold that I was obliged to let go and plunge again into the great deep. I ultimately landed at Polchester Castle a distance of about five miles from the Dockyard. When I got out of the water I was almost exhausted and was forced to lie down for a considerable time as I had nearly lost the use of my arms. I then started off naked. I think it was about nine o'clock, p.m. and travelled on some distance when I heard the footsteps of someone and it struck me it was one of the guards on Portdown Bridge where a file of soldiers are always kept. I returned back again and went over a small hill, at the bottom of which was a small river, about as wide as the Dee. I swam across this river which I found much more cold than the sea. I went over hedges and ditches quite naked until came in daylight. I then got into a pig-stye and covered myself over with straw and remained there until night without food or drink and several thorns in my feet. I then started off again and travelled all night until I got to a farmhouse and made my way into one of the stables where I found an old smock frock, which I gladly put on me. Here I remained all day. This was the third day I had had no food. Going over Epsom race-course I saw a policeman. I turned down a lane before he could see me and got into a cottage where I found an old woman. I begged for mercy and pardon. She took me to the fire, she gave me a pair of stockings, a cap, and an old pair of shoes. I travelled on but was so much fatigued then I was obliged to go to a house and beg for a bit of bread. I got some, with some cheese. On my way onwards I saw a man with some cattle going to London. I helped him to drive the cattle and he gave me 4 ½ d. being all he had. I wanted a nights rest and went to a lodging-house on the road. I asked the woman how much my lodgings would be. She said 4d. I had only then one halfpenny left, with this I bought some apples. I went to bed and had a good nights rest and started off early next morning for London. When within a mile of the town I stopped at some common and there was a load of coals brought to a house. I got the coals in for them and received sixpence and something to eat. I then went into London and found out a man who's brother was a convict and who had told me where he lived. He gave me clothing, plenty to eat, and 10s. to start me off. I started off the day after and went by the way of the Canal until I reached Oxford. I stayed one night on the road. I travelled on to Banbury and from there I went to Warwick. H ere I got 2s. for taking charge of some cattle in the fair. Next day I got 3s 6d. to take some cattle to Birmingham. I had now 7s 6d. and laid it all out in steel pens. I then wrote to my wife and informed her where I was and I went out hawking my pens, and cleared 3s the first day. I travelled on to Wolverhampton and earned about 4s more and got rid of all my pens. I wrote to my wife to meet me at Wolverhampton. In the mean time I bought three umbrellas. I sold them and was able to purchase five more the next day. At night, my wife not having yet arrived, I became very unhappy and almost mad as I found I was as badly off as ever. The following day I went out again on the turnpike road and there met my wife coming to meet me from Chester. It was indeed a happy meeting. We travelled on together to Newport, where I carried on my

hawking umbrellas. My wife soon returned to Chester. She endeavoured to get my children sent off by the parish at Boughton but did not succeed. I received a letter to that effect from her. I then left the town where I understand about half an hour after Mr Hill, Superintendent of Police, arrived there in search of me. Eager to get my poor children I got nearer and nearer to Chester, within 20 miles, at Whitchurch, where I again met with my wife. Soon after we had got our supper the policemen came into the house one through the front door and one through the back. I saw them both they took hold of my wife. I heard her shout out "let me alone, what have I done," at this I leaped over the garden wall and went off to Wem. Here I remained for about a week and made my way to Shrewsbury, from thence to Welshpool it being market day. I was in the market-place when one of the police of the town came and asked me whether I knew Phil Dixon as he heard he was in town. I referred him to a man at an orange stand and told him that he came from Chester and no doubt would tell him all about him. I then made off again and went to Newtown. Here I remained for a for a few days hawking umbrellas and found that I was known by some persons that kept stalls in the market, so I soon left there and went to Machynlleth. Shortly after breakfast I saw two policemen, one from Newtown. I was afraid they were after me. I went out and shook hands with the Newtown policeman. He spoke to me and appeared very much afraid of me. I got into the back yard and started off to Aberystwyth. I afterwards heard that five officers came down and took up another man in mistake of me. At night I arrived at a house on the road where none of the family could speak English. I had to show them my money and put my hand to my mouth to say I wanted something to eat. Next morning I arrived at Aberystwyth. I went on to the steelworks at Merthyr where I got work at a Mr Crushar`s and earned 15s. a week. I remained here two weeks and got leave to go and get my wife and children. I started off and on my way met with a man who hawked cloth, with him I went to Bala, on my way towards my wife. I happened to go with this man to an ale house where I met with a man who had robbed this hawker. That I was with of £5. I struck him for doing this. He said "very well, Dixon, you will remember this". I was shortly after this followed by about 200 men and was taken into custody and was very ill treated and beaten. I was asked my name. I told them it was James Edwards. Next morning I was brought before the magistrates and this man that I had beaten was there and he told them who and what I was. When I heard it I fainted as I had not been able to see my poor children. All my anxiety was about them. I was immediately put into heavy irons. Mr Hill was sent for and I was brought to Chester. I did not rob Sir Edward Walker but I think I know who did, I may tell some day but not now.
PHILIP DIXON. Signed in my presence this 11th day of August, 1849.
H.S. JOSEPH, Chaplain. Chester Castle".

Article courtesy of the Cheshire Archives and Local Studies and The Chester Courant Newspaper. The following article was published on Wednesday, 29th August 1849, in the Chester Courant.

"PHILIP DIXON AGAIN.
To the Editor of the Chester Courant.
Sir,---however great the inconvenience of intruding into the Columns of a public journal, I feel compelled to do so in the resent instance, owing to the report of this prosecution, contained in your widely-circulated paper of the 8th inst, in which I am represented to have acted in a manner unworthy of my professional character, or of the position I am anxious to retain in society. I trust, therefore, I may be allowed to state the circumstances of this case, which, without vindicating the part I took in the matter, shall speak for themselves, and that, with your wonted courtesy, you will give insertion to this letter.

This unfortunate but daring convict was apprehended at Bala, on the 5th of April last, for an assault in the street and stated his name to be "James Edwards". He was, however, identified by Thomas, Thomas, the constable, as being the celebrated "Phil. Dixon," an escaped convict, which Thomas communicated to me as magistrates` clerk; and when before the magistrates on the following day for the assault, the prisoner was positively sworn to by Thomas from a scar upon his neck, when the prisoner admitted he was the escaped convict. Thomas's information and deposition were then taken in the ordinary way, and the magistrates bound him over to prosecute, and remanded the Prisoner for the purpose of having his previous conviction proved. Mr Hill was therefore written to by direction of the magistrates, who arrived in Bala on the 10th April, being five days after the Prisoner had been identified, and produced a certificate of the previous conviction; and on the 11th, he, accompanied by Thomas, took the prisoner to Chester where he had before been tried.

The Act of Parliament, by which escaped prisoners are rendered amenable to punishment, directs that-- "Whoever shall discover and prosecute to conviction any such offender, shall be entitled to a reward of £20 for every such offender so convicted." Thomas, therefore, having "discovered" the offender, and having been bound over by the magistrates in his recognizance to prosecute, had no other course left, in order to entitle himself to the reward, than to prosecute the offender "to conviction," which he did effectually. How Mr Hill or his attorney could, under these circumstances, take upon themselves to prosecute I am at a loss to conceive, particularly when Mr Hill was not prepared at the Assizes with the necessary evidence to convict the prisoner, supposing him to have pleaded "not guilty" inasmuch as the prisoner was not "at large" when Mr Hill saw him at Bala, being then actually in the custody of the law and in chains, under the charge of being an escaped convict. Besides which, the indictment which your report states the prisoner to have been arraigned upon, "in which Mr Hill was prosecutor," charged the prisoner with being at large on the "first of April," which was not the fact, and therefore being a date prior to the commission of the offence, the prisoner, if defended, would have been acquitted upon this indictment. The result of this question of title to the reward having been decided by the learned judge, after Mr Hill had had an opportunity of filing affidavits, and Amended affidavits prepared by counsel, is a sufficient answer to any question upon this head. But with regard to your report Of my "having made acquaintance with the prisoner during his imprisonment in Bala lock-up," and subsequently turning round upon my new acquaintance, the convicted felon, I have only to say briefly that my poor client Thomas naturally retained me to conduct the prosecution for him, in return for the means of living, which my employment and purse has afforded him for some years; and I rejoice that by this sacrifice of a week of my time, rendered necessary by unavoidable circumstances, I have succeeded in procuring for my poor client that reward, which the learned judge, who heard all the facts, has decided, after mature deliberation, he is justly entitled to. Apologizing for this trespass upon your columns, I trust you will give insertion to this statement of facts; and that your numerous readers will see I am not the "prison acquaintance" of the convicted felon, and that my conduct in this matter has been that of determined perseverance only, on behalf of a poor man, whom I have served effectually, but at considerable sacrifice to myself.

I am Sir, your subscriber and obedient servant.

ISSACC GILBERTSON. Brynygoes, Bala, 18th August 1849".

Philip Dixon was eventually transported from Portsmouth, aboard the convict ship the 'Mermaid', to the Swan River Colony Western Australia.

There appear to be a number of conflicting reports on the actual voyage date, one account states the voyage date from Portsmouth was 30 December 1850, a further accounts states the voyage date was on 9 January 1851, and after 123 days the Mermaid arrived in Freemantle 13th May 1851. A further conflicting report stated on the 7th May 1851 Philip Dixon arrived in Western Australia, bound for The Swan River Colony". What is clear is that Philip Dixon was on the convict ship the Mermaid and he did leave from Portsmouth for the Swan River Colony in Western Australia.

Philip's recorded details from reference (Piece; HO 11/6) are

"Philip Dixon, age 29 years old, height 5' 8", dark hair, hazel eyes, face long with a fresh complexion and sandy whiskers, Cut on knuckle of 3rd Finger of right hand, one on little finger; cut over the left eye, married with six children, occupation noted as a groom, convict registration number 313, transportation on the Convict Ship the Mermaid, 4th August 1849 was the date of conviction at Chester, Cheshire, England, offence was returning from transportation, voyage date 30th December 1850, bound for the Colony in Western Australia". (Piece; HO 11/6).

Philip became quite a character during his time in Australia, and whilst there is some confusion as to the exact dates and the number of times he was convicted the records do confirm he spent some time in the following prisons before he was finally transported to the Andaman Islands, Bay of Bengal, India.

- **The Swan River Penal Colony Western Australia**
  In 1828 the British Government established The Swan River Colony. Between 1850 and 1868 nearly 10,000 convicts had been transported there. Records show that most convicts did not spend much time locked up but were put to work. In 1868 transporting convicts to Western Australia ceased.

- **Van Diemen's Land**
  In 1803 Van Diemen's Land, re named Tasmania in 1853, was colonised by the British as a penal colony. Records show that approximately 40% (75,000) of convicts sent to Australia were sent to the Tasmanian Peninsula Prison, known as Port Arthur Prison. Again, in the main, male convicts were assigned to labour. Transportation to Van Diemen's Land ceased in 1853.

- **Rottnest Island**

  Rottnest Island became a penal establishment for Aboriginals in 1839. This prison was mainly used for Aboriginal prisoners. There is an Aboriginal cemetery within the Thompson Bay Settlement. This penal establishment was officially closed in 1904.

- **Andaman Islands, Bay of Bengal, India**

  The Andaman Islands are a group of islands in the Bay of Bengal. In 1789 a penal colony was established on Chatham Island in the south east bay of Great Andaman, now known as Port Blair. After a few years the colony moved to the north east of the Great Andaman, named Port Cornwallis. However, after much disease and death in 1796, this ceased as a prison.

  However, in 1857, the British had many prisoners as a result of the Indian Rebellion and construction began on a new penal settlement at Port Blair. This was said to be the second concentration camp in the world. The first being in South Africa, as a result of the Boar War.

On the 12th April 1853, approximately three years after Philip's arrival in the Penal Colony of Western Australia, Philip was granted a ticket of leave. A ticket of leave meant a prisoner could move around more freely. During this period Philip was employed by John and Bridget Hurford.

By October 1855, Philip had been a witness in the murder case of John Hurford. John Hurford was murdered by his wife Bridget Hurford and William Enoch Dodd, also a man who had been granted a ticket of leave. Bridget and William were hung. Bridget Hurford was the first women to be hung in Australia. During the period of the trial and perhaps just after Philip spent some time at Rottnest Island. It is understood that Philip requested this transfer to Rottnest Island, which he was granted, because he was in fear of his life from prisoners who would have seen him as a 'grass'. Being in an all Aboriginal prison would have been a safer option for him.

Also on trial was Philip Dixon for having conspired with Bridget Hurford and William Enoch Dodd by forging a Will in Bridget's favour. Philip was found guilty and was sentenced to transportation to Van Diemen's Land for the rest of his natural life. However, accounts also state he was given a free pardon for turning King's evidence.

There are many newspaper articles on the life and times of Philip Dixon following his transportation from England to Australia then to the Bay of Bengal, India.

The following newspaper article references and brief extracts note his life and times and have been recorded below with the courtesy of

The National Library of Australia and with -

The State Library of Western Australia, The Inquirer & Commercial News (Perth, WA 1855-1901), Wednesday 18 February 1852, page 2 – "Philip Dixon, a prisoner in the convict establishment, charged with being drunk".

The State Library of Western Australia, The Perth Gazette and Independent Journal of Politics and News (WA 1848-1864), Friday 14 September 1855, pages 3, 4, 5 - "Trial of the murder of John Hurford".

The State Library of Western Australia, The Perth Gazette and Independent Journal of Politics and News (WA 1848-1864), Friday 5 October 1855, page 2 - "Witness at the trial in the murder of Hurford. Philip Dixon and T Larkin charged with forging Will".

The State Library of Western Australia, The Perth Gazette and Independent Journal of Politics and News (WA 1848-1864), Friday 12 October 1855 page 3, 4 - "Witness at the trial of prisoner Morris. Philip Dixon knows Morris, the prisoner".

The State Library of Western Australia, The Perth Gazette and Independent Journal of Politics and News (WA 1848-1864), Friday 19 October 1855, page 3 - "Philip Dixon went to Rottnest Isle".

Philip Dixon was convicted of forgery of a Will at the Oct 1855 Quarter Sessions in Perth, Australia.

The State Library of South Australia, The *South Australian Register (Adelaide, SA 1839-1900), Tuesday 20 November 1855, page 2 – "Philip Dixon sentenced to transportation for life for forging the will of John Hurford has had his sentence remitted".*

The State Library of New South Wales (BN445) and The *Sydney Morning Herald (NSW 1842-1954), Thursday 6 December 1855, page 5 -- "Murder in Western Australia - case trial of Bridget Hurford and W Dodd. Bridget was the first woman hung in Australia. Philip Dixon was found guilty of forging the Will of John Hurford".*

The State Library of Western Australia, The *Perth Gazette and Independent Journal of Politics and News (WA 1848-1864), Friday 25 January 1856, page 5 - References an article in the Chester Courant - "Philip Dixon now lies in Chester Castle awaiting his removal to a penal settlement". The Chester Courant gives an autobiography.*

The State Library of Western Australia, The *Inquirer & Commercial News (Perth, WA 1855-1901), Wednesday 30 January 1856, page 2 – "Mr Dixon's Exploits at Rockingham".*

The State Library of Western Australia, The *Inquirer & Commercial News (Perth, WA 1855-1901), Wednesday 20 February 1856, page 2 – "Philip Dixon been found guilty of gross misconduct and for his last offence been sentenced to three years imprisonment in irons, shortly after his release walking about in Perth claiming to be a police officer, later to be apprehended and taken to Rottnest Island".*

The State Library of Western Australia, The Perth Gazette and Independent Journal of Politics and News (WA 1848-1864), Friday 22 February 1856, page 2 - "Philip Dixon was a most mischievous character".

On the 14 Feb 1856 Philip was convicted before the Bench of Magistrates at Rottnest "on the 12th inst for having wilfully advised and convened the escape of some native prisoners from Rottnest prison and sentenced to 3 years hard labour in the convict establishment".

According to the convict database Philip Dixon left the colony in 1856.

The records show that there are number of letters referring to Philip's pardon for having turned King's evidence. On the 30 June 1857, Petition of reg. no 313, "P Dixon prepared to sign, appears to record an agreement to sign Philip's pardon in consideration of his evidence in the Hurford Murder if Philip can find some means of leaving the Colony".

Philip was still in Western Australia in 1858, as in this year he was escorted onboard the Firefly bound for Southern Australia. His passage appears to have been paid for by a policeman named Sergeant Snook. Whether this payment was made by the authorities is not clear.

The State Library of South Australia, *South Australian Register (Adelaide, SA 1839-1900), Monday 26 July, 1858, page 3 - "John Smith, alias Philip Dixon, committed 23 July 1858 for obtaining goods".*

The State Library of South Australia, *South Australian Register (Adelaide, SA 1839-1900), Tuesday 27 July, 1858, page 2 – "Philip Dixon obtaining goods from several tradesmen by false pretences"*

The State Library of South Australia, *South Australian Register (Adelaide, SA 1839-1900), Monday 31 July 1858, page 2 – "Philip Dixon of Swan River notoriety in February 1856 sentenced to three years hard labour".*

The State Library of South Australia, The *South Australian Advertiser (Adelaide, SA 1858-1889), Monday 2 August 1858, page 4 - "John Smith alias Phil Dixon obtaining goods under false pretences".*

The State Library of South Australia, The *South Australian Advertiser (Adelaide, SA 1858-1889), Thursday 5 August 1858, page 3 - "John Smith alias Phil Dixon obtaining goods under false pretences".*

The State Library of South Australia, The *South Australian Advertiser (Adelaide, SA 1858-1889), Thursday 12 August 1858, page 3 -"Adjourned case - John Smith alias Phil Dixon appeared to answer a charge of being an escaped convict from Fremantle, Western Australia. Police Constable Harris of the Port deposed that he knew the prisoner at the Swan as a re convicted felon. The last time he saw him was in September*

1857 knew that he received a sentence of three years hard labour in February or March. The bench observed this witness could not give evidence as to the sentence. By prisoner - remembered prisoner speaking to him about the penal establishment. By the bench - he came up to witness and said Good morning Mr Harris". Witness did not recognise him and asked him his name. He said it was John Smith. He said Superintendent Dixon, of the Convict Establishment had gone to India. By the prisoner -heard nothing about the Governor having given him a free pardon. Heard this prisoner had petitioned but his petition had been rejected. Alexander Duncan, Water Police, Port, confirmed the testimony of the last witness. By the prisoner - heard the prisoner was trying to obtain a free pardon. The witness prior to giving his evidence requested to be paid his expenses. The bench remarked that is was every person duty to attend and give evidence in such cases whether paid or not. By prisoner -Snook paid him the passage money at King George's Sound. Snook in Sergeant of the Water Police there. He accompanied the prisoner and sailed three or four miles with the vessel. Asked him who and what prisoner was but did not make any answer. It was the 22nd May the prisoner was put on board. Bail was allowed".

The State Library of South Australia, South Australian Register (Adelaide, SA 1839-1900),) Tuesday 10 August 1858, page 4 – "Swan River celebrity, on a charge of obtaining goods from several tradesmen by false pretences, witness claimed the goods belonged to the prisoner".

The State Library of South Australia, The South Australian Advertiser (Adelaide SA 1858-1889), Thursday 12 August 1858, page 2, 3 – "Philip Dixon charged for being at large in the colony prior to the expiration of the term for which he was sentenced" and "John Smith alias Philip Dixon appeared to answer a charge of being an escaped convict from Freemantle, Western Australia and the issues as to whether or not he had received a free pardon".

The State Library of Western Australia, The Perth Gazette and Independent Journal of Politics and News (WA 1848-1864), Friday 3 September 1858, page 2 - "The notorious Philip Dixon has been arrested in Southern Australia for robbery, he was sent to that colony by the Government of this".

The State Library of Western Australia, The Perth Gazette and Independent Journal of Politics and News (WA 1848-1864), Friday 17 September 1858, page 4 - "Swan River Celebrity - a man described as John Smith, alias Phil Dixon has been sent out of the colony to bless some other part of the globe with his presence".

The State Library of Western Australia, The Inquirer & Commercial News (Perth, WA 1855-1901), Wednesday 8 September 1858, page 2 – "reporting on how enthusiastically received Philip Dixon was in South Australia".

The State Library of Western Australia, The Inquirer & Commercial News (Perth, WA 1855-1901), Wednesday 15 September 1858, page 4 - "Swan River Celebrity, a man described as John Smith, alias Philip Dixon, on a charge of receiving goods under false pretences"

The State Library of Western Australia, The Perth Gazette and Independent Journal of Politics and News (WA 1848-1864), Friday 17 September 1858, page 4 - reporting on the Commercial News of May 26th reference states "Philip Dixon has been sent out of the colony to bless some other part of the globe".

The State Library of South Australia, The South Australian Advertiser (Adelaide, SA 1858-1889), Wednesday 22 September 1858, page 2 -- "Appearing from the police reports of the 11th and 12th August last that John Smith alias Phil Dixon a convicted felon had been sent to this colony free by the Western Australian government".

The South Australian Parliament Legislation Council, Wednesday 29 September 1858, page 2 - "The Chief Secretary has written a despatch to the colonial secretary of Western Australia requesting information as to the circumstances under which Phil Dixon, alias Smith received, as alleged a free pardon and passage at the hands of that Government so as to enable him to land in this colony".

The State Library of South Australia, The South Australian Advertiser (Adelaide, SA 1858-1889), Wednesday 29 September 1858, page 2 – "Secretary of Western Australia requesting information on the circumstances on why Philip Dixon, alias Smith received a free pardon".

The State Library of South Australia, The South Australian Register (Adelaide, SA 1839-1900), Monday 22 November 1858, page 2 – "reprinted articles on the Government deporting Philip to South Australia".

The State Library of Western Australia, The Perth Gazette and Independent Journal of Politics and News (WA 1848-1864), Friday 26 October 1860, page 2- letter to the newspaper asking what happened to a number of prisoners, one of which was Philip Dixon".

According to the Southern Australian Parliament Philip was to be transported to the Isle of Andaman in the Bay of Bengal. Philip Dixon never made it back to his wife and children and presumably died in Andaman Islands, Bay of Bengal, India. Many resources have been explored to try and locate the place and date of his death but without success.

> **Sp. Elizabeth DUTTON (1822-) [209],** dau of James DUTTON (1792-) [247] and Elizabeth WILLIAMS (1787-) [643]. Born 22 Jan 1822, Chester.

SEE DUTTON FAMILY

During Philip's time in Knutsford Prison Elizabeth was living with her parents as the following census confirms

1841 English Census, Great Boughton, St. John the Baptist, Chester
James DUTTON, age 49, Agricultural Labourer, born 1792, Cheshire, Elizabeth DUTTON, wife, age 54, born Cheshire, Hannah DUTTON, dau, age 15, born Cheshire, William DUTTON, son, age 13, born Cheshire, Elizabeth DICKSON, dau, age 20, born Cheshire, James DICKSON, grandson, age 1, born Cheshire, Charles DICKSON, grandson, age 3, born Cheshire, Boughton.

By the 1851 census Elizabeth and her children were in the workhouse
1851 English Census, Chester House of Industry (Cathedral Division), Chester
Elizabeth DIXON, married, pauper, age 28, born Chester, Charles DIXON, son, pauper age 11, scholar, born Chester, James DIXON, son, pauper, age 10, scholar, born Chester, Mary DIXON, dau, pauper, age 8, born Chester, Philip DIXON, son, pauper, age 5, born Chester, Hannah DIXON, dau, pauper, age 4 scholar, born Chester, Robert DIXON, son, pauper, age 18 months, born Chester.

With the exception of Robert, Mary and Philip, no further references have been found for Elizabeth and the rest of her family after the 1851 English Census.

> 3. **Philip DIXON (1845-) [374].** Born 1845. Son of Philip Dixon and Elizabeth Dutton. Unfortunately, Philip appears to have followed in his father's footsteps in terms of crime. On a number of occasions Philip was in court in Chester. The newspaper reports found so far are dated 1866 and 1867. An earlier newspaper report on the 6 August 1864 in the Cheshire Observer, note "Philip Dixon charged with desertion from The Royal Artillery at Shoeburyness". It was also reported he stole a shawl from his sister who lived in Saughall, Chester.
> 3. **Charles DIXON (1839-) [375].** Born 22 Dec 1839, Foregate Street, Chester. Son of Philip Dixon and Elizabeth Dutton. Philip was noted as a Labourer.
> 3. **James DIXON (1840-) [376].** Born 1840. Son of Philip Dixon and Elizabeth Dutton. Although not confirmed the following reference could refer to James.

1861 English Census, 18 Pool Street, Birkenhead
James Dickenson, age 20, born 1841, Chester. Lodger

> 3. **Hannah DIXON (1847-) [377].** Born 1847, Chester. Dau of Philip Dixon and Elizabeth Dutton.
> 3. **Mary Ann DIXON (1843-) [378].** Born 1843, Chester. Dau of Philip Dixon and Elizabeth Dutton. Unfortunately, as with the other siblings no baptismal reference has been found for Mary.

Mary Ann Dixon Marr George HEALING, 17 Dec 1860, St. Mary on the Hill, Chester, both of Potter's Court, Chester. Mary was age 19 and her father was Philip Dixon, Labourer. George was 18 years old and his father was Thomas Healing of Potter's Court. Witnesses Sarah Dutton and George Dutton. Sarah and George Dutton would likely be close relatives and may provide a clue as to which Dutton family this Dixon family links with.

Sp. George HEALING (1840-) [2277] son of Thomas HEALING (1813-) [2278] and Ann (1815-) [2279]. Thomas HEALING (1813-) [2278]. Born 1813, Saughall, Cheshire. Shoemaker.

George lived with his family until he married Mary Ann Dixon
1841 English Census, Saughall, Great, Shotwick, Saughall
Thomas HEALING, age 28, born 1813, Cheshire, Assistant Labourer, Ann HEALING, age 25, born 1815, Cheshire, Elizabeth HEALING, dau, age 2, born 1839, Cheshire, George HEALING, son, age 1, born 1840, Cheshire

1851 English Census, Sea Hill, Great Saughall
Thomas HEALING, married, age 39, born 1812, Shotwich, Cheshire, Shoemaker, Ann HEALING, wife, age 36, born 1815, St. Oswald's, Chester, George HEALING, son, age 11, born 1840, Shotwick, Cheshire, Thomas HEALING, son, age 9, born 1842, Shotwick, Cheshire, Sarah HEALING, dau, age 6, born 1845, Shotwick, Cheshire, Hannah HEALING, dau, age 1, born 1850, Shotwick, Cheshire

1861 English Census, 10 Milton Street, St. John, Chester
George HEALING, married, age 19, born 1842, Cheshire, Bricklayor, Mary HEALING, wife, age 18, born 1843, Chester

Unfortunately, Mary has not been found in any of the census' after 1861

1871 English Census, Greenside, Everton, Liverpool
George HEALING, lodger, age 26, born 1845, Cheshire

1881 English Census, The Village, Great Saughall
Thomas HEALING, head, married, age 69, born 1812, Saughall, Postman (C S Mess), Ann HEALING, wife, age 66, born 1815, Chester, Postman's Wife, George HEALING, son, married, age 41, born 1840, Saughall, Bricklayer, John HEALING, son, married, age 40, born 1841, Saughall, Engine Driver, Catherine HEALING, dau, single, age 24, born 1857, Saughall, Sarah Ann ROWLANDS, granddaughter, age 9, born 1872, Padeswood, Flintshire.

George Healing's Siblings were
Elizabeth HEALING (1839-) [2280]. Born 1839, Shotwick, Saughall.
Thomas HEALING (1842-) [2281]. Born 1842, Shotwick, Saughall.
Sarah HEALING (1845-) [2282]. Born 1845, Shotwick, Saughall.
Hannah HEALING (1850-) [2283]. Born 1850, Shotwick, Saughall.
John HEALING (1841-) [2284]. Born 1841, Shotwick, Saughall.
Catherine HEALING (1857-) [2285]. Born 1857, Shotwick, Saughall.

3. **Robert DIXON (1849-1916) [34].** Born 22 Sep 1849, 2h 30m a.m. near Machine, Boughton, Chester, St. John's. Son of Philip Dixon and Elizabeth Dutton. A time noted on this birth reference would suggest Robert was a twin. A birth certificate for the twin has not been found.

Birth certificate
Registration District Great Boughton, in the district of the Castle Division in the County of Chester and City and County of the City, 22nd September 1849, 2h30m a.m. near Machine, Boughton, St. John's Parish, Chester. Robert, a boy, father, Philip Dickson, Labourer, mother, Elizabeth Dickson formerly Dutton. Elizabeth made an X as her mark, resident near Machine, Boughton, St John's Parish, Chester. Registered 9 October 1849.

St. John the Baptist was Chester's first Cathedral and situated within the City of Chester. Courtesy of St. John The Baptist Church " the church was a Saxon church founded in 689 A D by King Etheired and Bishop Wulfryce. The present building begun in 1066, by Bishop Peter".

It is not known when Elizabeth, Robert's mother, died but in 1861, Robert was living with his mother's brother, William Dutton.

Robert DIXON 1849-1916. Courtesy of National Fairground Archive, University of Sheffield Library.

1861 English Census, 112 Potters Court, Bunce Street, St. Mary's, Chester
William DUTTON, head, age 32, Widower, Butcher, born Chester, Robert DIXON, nephew, age 11.

1861 English Census, 7 Furlong Passage, Burslem, Staffordshire
Robert DICKSON, age 11, nephew, born Chester, William DUTTON, age 32, born Chester.

Robert Marr Betsy DEAN, 9 Feb 1869, The Parish Church, Parish of Burslem, County of Staffordshire.

Marriage Certificate
9 Feb 1869, The Parish Church in the Parish of Burslem in the County of Stafford, Robert Dixon, age 19, bachelor, Labourer, residence Burslem, father, Philip Dixon, Labourer, married Elizabeth Dean, age 17, spinster, no profession given, residence Burslem, father, James Dean, Cabinet Maker. Witnesses Alexander Taylor and Emily Howland. Both Robert and Elizabeth made an X each as their mark.

1871 English Census, Furlong Passage, Burslem, Staffordshire
Robert DIXON, head, married, age 21, Butcher, born Northwich, Betsy DIXON, wife, married, age 18, born Northwich, Jim (James) DIXON, son, age 1, born Burslem, Staffordshire.

1881 English Census, 66 Greenall Road, Witton, Northwich, Cheshire
Robert DIXON, age 31, Hawker of Cutlery, born Chester, Betsy DIXON, wife, age 28, Hawker's wife, born Northwich, Jim (James) DIXON, son, age 11, scholar, born Newcastle, Jane DIXON, dau, age 9, scholar, born Burslem, Lizy DIXON, dau, age 8, scholar, born Northwich, Hannah DIXON, dau, age 3, born Northwich.

1891 English Census, Caravan, Blackfriars St, Salford, Greengate, Lancashire
Robert DIXON, age 41, Travelling Showman, born Chester, Betsy DIXON, wife, age 37, born Northwich, Hannah DIXON, dau, age 10, born Northwich, Thomas (Tom) DIXON, son, age 1, born Salford, Lancashire.

1901 English Census, Salford, Trinity Ward, Blackfriars Road Fairground (caravan), Lancashire
Robert DIXON, head, age 51, EXIB Showman, born Chester, Betsy DIXON, wife, age 48, born Northwich, Charlie DIXON, son, single, age 17, worker, born Warrington, Gilbert DIXON, son, single, age 15, worker, born Crew, Alice DIXON, dau, age 9, born Salford.

1911 English Census, Salford, Trinity Market, Blackfriars Road (Caravan), Lancashire
Robert DIXON, head, Widower, age 58, born 1853, Chester, Showman, Alice DIXON, dau, age 19, born 1892, Salford.

As part of the fairground attractions, Robert had a 14 foot set of swings (very large swing boats of 6 boats in a set), an 'emma' (popular game around Lancashire and Cheshire at this time) and a 'pan am'. Robert leased out plots/spaces to stall holders on the Flat Iron Market in Salford on behalf of Major Hardcastle. Robert was in the Lancashire, Cheshire and North Wales Section of The Showmen's Guild. During his time he was President and Honorary Secretary.

Robert Dixon's Panam.
Courtesy of National Fairground Archive. University of Sheffield Library

Robert Dixon's Stall.
Courtesy of National Fairground Archive. University of Sheffield Library

Swing Boats. Courtesy of National
Fairground Archive, University of
Sheffield Library.

Robert purchased the grave at Weaste Cemetery, Salford - Grave No. 2336, Plot F. At the time of purchase his address was Blackfriars, Salford. The following eight family members are in this grave

Date of interment
21 March 1895, John Dixon, 17 months
27 January 1896, Toni Dixon, 6 years
11 February 1896, Cornelia Shaw, 2 years
5 August 1896, Alice Shaw, 6 months
16 January 1911, Elizabeth Dixon, 54 years
5 May 1916, Robert Dixon, 63 years
7 June 1924, Georgette Lloyd, 3 years
9 March 1927, Jane Hayes, 56 years.

Robert died 5 May 1916. Buried Weaste Cemetery, Salford. Grave No. 2336 Plot F.

The following newspaper report is from the Salford City Reporter Newspaper, 13th May 1916
"The late Robert Dixon, a Showman. By the death of Mr Robert Dixon, Salford has lost a man who was well known and respected. Born at Chester he came to Salford as a young man. He became manager for Mr John Hancock, who had rented the open space, off Blackfriars Road, from Major Hardcastle and had allowed shows and stalls to be erected thereon. The land is known as 'Trinity Market' and is opposite the Flat Iron Market, which belongs to Salford Corporation. On the death of Mr Hancock thirty eight years ago Mr Dixon became the leasee and had remained so since. He had lived for thirty eight years in vans on the Trinity Market and although he had a residence at Holmes Chapel known as Cherry Tree Cottage, he preferred to make his home in the van. Since he was leasee many shows of note had exhibited there. Mr Dixon had acted for some years as agent for Mr J Collins, amusement caterer-a position which had taken him to fairs all over Lancashire and Cheshire. His duty was to provide land and let out spaces for stalls and shows. He was known by showmen all over England. Mr Dixon's death was sudden and was explained at the inquest reported below. Mr A E Ferns, the Stockport and District coroner, held an inquiry at the Stockport Infirmary touching the death of Mr R Dixon on Wednesday week. Mr Dixon died whilst travelling in a train between Manchester and Stockport on Monday afternoon-Gilbert Dixon, a showman of Salford said the deceased, who was his father, had always been a healthy man and had never been under the doctor. He was 63 years of age and agent for John Collins, amusement caterer of Liverpool. - Allen Cooper, a rubber tyre manufacturer, residing at Charles Street, Stockport said that on Monday afternoon he got into a compartment of a train at London Road Station, Manchester, with a gentleman from Hazel Grove the deceased also got into the carriage and taking a newspaper from his pocket placed it on his knee. He commenced to snore, but witnesses thought he was asleep. Just before reaching Longsight Station the deceased began to snore very loudly and witness drew the attention of the other passengers to him and said he thought he must be ill. At Stockport an inspector was called and on examination it was found that the deceased was dead. Dr Conway arriving later pronounced life extinct-further evidence was given then the body was removed to the mortuary and a post mortem examination was held by Dr Ratchie, the house surgeon at Stockport Infirmary, who discovered that he was suffering from valvular disease of the heart-a verdict of death from natural causes was recorded. The internment took place on Friday afternoon at Weaste Cemetery. A service was held at Sacred Trinity Church, Salford. The church was crowded, showmen being present from all parts of the country. It was an impressive service which was taken by the Rev A E Cranbeer (Rector) and the Rev T Horne (Chaplin to the Showmen). At the graveside the service was conducted by Mr Horne. The ten coaches were occupied as follows: First carriage Mrs Dixon (widow), Mrs Cooper (mother in law), Mrs Hayes (daughter), Mr Dixon (son), the Rev T Horne. Second carriage Mrs Shaw (daughter), Mr G Dixon (son), Mrs Matthews (daughter), Mr R Cooper (brother in law). Third carriage Mrs C Dixon (daughter in law), Mrs G Dixon (daughter in law), Mr & Mrs Dean (nephew and niece), Mr & Mrs Darlington. Fourth carriage Mr & Mrs Cooper (brother in law and wife), Mr & Mrs H Cooper (brother in law and wife). Fifth carriage Mr R Cooper (brother in law), Mrs H Cooper (cousin), Mr John Collins, Mrs Matthews. Sixth carriage Mrs Clough, Mr & Mrs J Matthews, Mr & Mrs J H Royle. Seventh carriage Mr & Mrs Matthews, Mrs Britland, Mr J Matthews, Mrs A Jewell. Eighth carriage Mr & Mrs W Bradbury, Mrs J Norman, Mr & Mrs Peters, Mr J Lennard. Ninth carriage Mr & Mrs Rogerson, Mrs Holmes, Mrs Beasley, Mrs Jones. Tenth carriage Mr & Mrs J Foster, Mr F Mellor, Mr T Fitzpartick, Mr T White and Mr Marco Seretti. The bearers were:-F Matthews, T White, J Darlington, J Lennard, Marco Seretti and J Foster. Wreaths came from:- the widow, mother in law and brothers in law, Mrs Hayes (daughter), Mr & Mrs Shaw (daughter and son in law), Mr & Mrs G Dixon (son and daughter in law), Mr & Mrs D Dixon (son and daughter in law), Mr & Mrs Matthews (daughter and son in law), Mr & Mrs T Dean (nephew and niece), Laura (granddaughter), Mr & Mrs H Cooper (brother in law and wife), Annie, Frank and Francis, Mr John

Collins, Mr Marco Serritte, Mr J Pessango, Mr & Mrs G Chadwick, Mr & Mrs Brennan, Mr & Mrs Mercer, Mr & Mrs J H Royle, Mr & Mrs Darlington and family, Mr & Mrs Ingham, Mr & Mrs H Hibbert, Lancashire & Cheshire Stallholders Association, Mr &Mrs Southward, Mr & Mrs T White, Dr & Mrs Picton, Mrs J Norman and family, Mr & Mrs Testo, Mr & Mrs J Thwaites, Mr & Mrs Peters, Mr & Mrs Clough, Mr & Mrs Rogerson, Mr & Mrs Foster, Mr & Mrs Bradbury, Mr & Mrs F Matthews, Mrs A Jewell, Mr & Mrs P Mitchell, Mr & Mrs J Cooke, Mr & Mrs Brady and Mary Ann, P T Fitzpatrick, Mrs Burton and family, Mr J E Kirkham of Lower Broughton Road, Broughton conducted the funeral".

Robert Dixon's Estate notes
"Be it known that Robert Dixon of Cherry Tree Cottage, Holmes Chapel near Crew in the County of Chester, who at the time of his death had a fixed place of abode at Cherry Tree Cottage aforesaid within the District of the County of Chester, died on the 5th day of May 1916 at Edgeley Station, Stockport in the said County intestate a widower and be it further known that at the date hereunder written letters of administration of all the estate which by law devolves to and vests in the personal representative of the said intestate were granted by His Majesty's High Court of Justice at the District Probate Registry thereof at Chester to Jane Hayes of Living Carriage, Flat Iron, Blackfriars Road, Salford in the County of Lancashire, widow, the natural and lawful daughter and one of the next of kin. The gross value of estate is £158.5.4. Will dated and stamped the 29th May 1916. The sureties of the Will were William Lennon of No 10 Saint Stephen Street, Salford aforesaid Greengrocer and James Goodwin of No 38 Crescent, Salford aforesaid Confectioner".

Sp. Betsy DEAN (1852-1911) [33], dau of James (Toffee) DEAN (1834-1899) [44] and Jane BOSTOCK (1838-1870) [85]. Born 14 Jul 1852, Witton, Northwich.

SEE DEAN AND BOSTOCK FAMILY

4. **John DIXON (1895-1895) [194].** Born 1895. Son of Robert Dixon and Besty Dean. John died 1895, buried 21 Mar 1895, Weaste Cemetery, Salford.
4. **Thomas DIXON (1890-1896) [195].** Born 1890. Son of Robert Dixon and Betsy Dean. Thomas died 27 Jan 1896. Buried 27 Jan 1896, Weaste Cemetery, Salford, age 6.
4. **Gilbert DIXON (1885-1956) [16].** Born 21 Nov 1885, Crew, baptised 4 Dec 1885, Parish of Christ Church, Crew. Son of Robert Dixon and Betsy Dean.

Gilbert Dixon 1885-1956

Birth certificate

Registration District Nantwich in the sub-district of Crew in the County of Chester, 21 Nov 1885, Upper Mill (or Upper Hill) Street, Monks, Coppenhall, UD. Gilbert, boy, father, Robert Dixon, mother, Elizabeth Dixon formerly Dean, occupation of father was Travelling Hawker. Elizabeth Dixon of Upper Mill (or Upper Hill) Street, Monks Coppenhall made an X as her mark. Registered 1st January 1886.

In the 1901 English Census, Salford, Trinity Ward, Blackfriars Road Fairground (caravan), Lancashire, Gilbert was living with his parents.

Gilbert Marr Margaret Ellen CLOUGH, 4 Sep 1907, Trinity Church, Salford. The wedding reception was held at the Black Lion Pub on the corner of Blackfriars and Chapel Street, Salford. This was also where the inauguration took place, of what is now known as The Showman's Guild, in the rooms upstairs.

Gilbert attended Sacred Trinity School, Blackfriars, Salford. Three times swimming winner of the Swimming Shield. Gilbert and his son Gilbert junior during their careers were sign writers.

Gilbert's family had very strong ties with the Church of England and one of Gilbert's relatives was a Bishop in the Church of England. The condition of Margaret Clough's marriage to Gilbert Dixon was that she had to give up her Catholic religion. However, when Margaret died her rosary beads were found in her drawer by her bedside cabinet.

1911 English Census, Trinity Market, Salford

Gilbert DIXON, age 25, born Crewe, Cheshire, Showman, Margaret Ellen DIXON (nee CLOUGH), age 23, born Blakley Lancashire, Betsy DIXON, age 2, born Mottram, Cheshire, Alice DIXON, age 1, born Salford.

Gilbert was in the Lancashire, Cheshire and North Wales Section and the Midlands Section of the Showman's Guild. Gilbert served in the war and he was said to be the Groom to General Charles in World War I. After the war he returned but his career as a Travelling Showman ended. Gilbert and his family settled in the Midlands.

Gilbert died 9 May 1956, age 73, Coventry Hospital, buried 14 May 1956, London Road Cemetery,Coventry.

The World's Fair newspaper 26 May 1956

"Funeral of Mr Gilbert Dixon Snr. The funeral of Mr Gilbert Dixon, Snr. of the Midland Section-whose death in hospital at Coventry, was reported in The World's Fair of May 12 - took place at London Road Cemetery, Coventry, on Monday 14 May. The service was conducted by the Rev W A Williams, M.A. Vicar of Westwood, Tile Hill. The mourners included: Mrs Gilbert Dixon Snr. (wife), Mr & Mrs Gilbert Jnr. (son & daughter in law), Mr Edward Dixon (son), Mr & Mrs W Dixon (son & Daughter in law), Mrs W Roberts (daughter), Mr Charles Hayes (nephew), Mr Sam Clough (brother in law), Mrs James Manders (sister in law), Mrs Arthur Jones (sister in law), Mrs Harry Cooper, Mrs S A Jones, Mrs Joan Meakin, Mrs Coulter, Mr & Mrs Billy Roberts, Mr Joe Proverbs, Mr Lionel Barnett, Mr Jack Jones (Tile Hill), Mr Eric Barnes (Bell Inn, Tile Hill) John (a friend) Tile Hill, Mr Johnson (Coventry). F loral tributes were from: Mrs Gilbert Dixon Snr. (wife), Mr & Mrs Gilbert Dixon Jnr. (son & daughter in law), Mr Edward Dixon (son), Mr & Mrs W Dixon (son & daughter in law), Mr & Mrs W Roberts (daughter and son in law), Mr & Mrs Charles Hayes (nephew & niece), Mr & Mrs Sam Clough & family, Mr & Mrs James Manders & family, Mr & Mrs Arthur Jones, Mr & Mrs F Matthews Snr. (sister & brother in law), Mr & Mrs F Matthews Jnr. (nephew & niece), Mr & Mrs Robert Hines (grandchildren), Mr & Mrs Patrick Green (grandchildren), Margaret, John, Janet & Gilbert (grandchildren), Rosemary, Joyce & Billy (grandchildren), Kathleen (great grand daughter), Christine & Maureen (great grand daughters), Mr & Mrs Geoff Burroughs, Mr & Mrs Warmington, Mr & Mrs W Courts, Mr & Mrs Bert Hayden, his friends at the club, Mrs Clara Collins, Mr & Mrs John Powell & family, friends from the Horse & Jockey (Coventry), Mr & Mrs Tommy Crick & family, Mr & Mrs H Cooper, Mr & Mrs Allcock, Mrs S A Jones & Harry, friends from The Bell Inn, Tile Hill, Mr & Mrs Lionel Barnett, Mr & Mrs Billy Roberts, Mrs Meakin & family, Mr J Humphreys and daughters, Mr & Mrs Mo Harris & family, Mr & Mrs H Chaplin & family, Mr & Mrs G Furborough. I apologise for any names that may have been omitted- W.D".

Sp. Margaret Ellen CLOUGH (1886-1986) [17], dau of Edward CLOUGH (1861-1937) [63] and Sarah Ellen CORDWELL (1866-1933) [64]. Baptised 1887, Parish Church, Blakely Wakes, Manchester.

SEE CLOUGH AND CORDWELL FAMILY

5. Betsy DIXON (1908-1983) [9]. Born 12 Aug 1908, Mottram, Cheshire. Dau of Gilbert Dixon and Margaret Ellen Clough. Betsy was named after her grandmother Betsy (Elizabeth) Dixon, nee Dean.

Betsy Dixon 1908-1983

Betsy Marr Robert HINES Feb 1928, St. Werburgh's Church, Grange Road, Birkenhead. Betsy Converted to the Roman Catholic religion when she married Robert Hines. After the death of Robert Betsy married William Roberts.

Betsy died 29 Nov 1983, 45 Christleton Drive, Overpool, Ellesmere Port, South Wirral, Cheshire. Buried 5 Dec 1983, Chester Crematorium.

The funeral mass was held at Our Lady's Roman Catholic Church, Ellesmere Port, Cheshire, on the 5 Dec 1983. A further service was held at Blacon Crematorium, Chester, where her ashes were buried along with her second husband William Roberts.

> **Sp. Robert HINES (1901-1951) [8].** Born 5 Sep 1901, Youdle Street, Workington, Whitehaven, Cumbria. Son of Robert W HINES (1875-1956) [224] and Mary Elizabeth STOCKDALE (1880-1952) [225].

SEE HINES, SCOTT AND STOCKDALE FAMILY

> **Sp. William ROBERTS (-) [213].**

5. **Alice DIXON (1910 -1916) [18].** Dau of Gilbert Dixon and Margaret Ellen Clough. Alice died when she was 6 years old, buried at St. Helen's, Witton, Northwich in the Barber's grave.

5. **Gilbert Verdin (junior) DIXON (-1971) [19**]. Son of Gilbert Dixon and Margaret Ellen Clough. Gilbert Verdin died 25 Jan 1971. Gilbert Marr Daisy MANDERS.

Gilbert Dixon 1885-1956 and His son Gilbert Verdin Dixon

Sp. Daisy MANDERS (-) [20]. Dau of George Arthur MANDERS (-) [2379] and Margaret BUCKLEY (-) [2380]. George MANDERS was brother to James Henry MANDERS who married Louise NAIL

Daisy Manders Courtesy of Gilbert Dixon

Daisy Manders and friends. Courtesy of Gilbert Dixon

Daisy and Nancy Manders. Courtesy of Gilbert Dixon

5. Billy DIXON (-) [28]. Son of Gilbert Dixon and Margaret Ellen Clough. Gilbert Marr Sally..
Sp. Sally (-) [29].

5. Edward (Teddy) DIXON (-) [41]. Born Altringham, Cheshire. Son of Gilbert Dixon and Margaret Ellen Clough.

Edward (Teddy) Dixon

Betsy Price nee Manders, Magaret Ellen Dixon nee Clough and Edward (Teddy) Dixon

4. Charlie DIXON (1884-) [35]. Born 1884, Warrington. Son of Robert Dixon and Betsy Dean. Charlie had what is known in the fairground world as a 'Penalty'. Charlie Marr Charlotte LOCKE, 1902

Sp. Charlotte LOCKE(-) [915].

In the 1901 and 1911 English Census, Salford, Trinity Ward, Blackfriars Road Fairground (caravan), Lancashire, Charlie was living with his parents.

      5. Bob DIXON (1903 -) [201]. Born 1903, Salford. Son of Charlie Dixon and Charlotte.

      5. Charlie (Chuck) DIXON (1908 -) [200]. Born 1908, Salford. Son of Charlie Dixon and Charlotte. Charlie Marr Agnes BELL.

      Sp. Agnes BELL (-) [916].

      5. Alice DIXON (1911-) [917]. Dau of Charlie Dixon and Charlotte. Alice Marr Joe MULHEARN.

      Sp. Joe MULHEARN (-) [918]. A Lancashire Showman

      5. Aggie DIXON (-) [1723]. Dau of Charlie Dixon and Charlotte.

4. Jane DIXON (1872-1927) [36]. Born 1872, Wolstanton, Staffordshire. Dau of Robert Dixon and Betsy Dean. Jane Marr Martin HAYES. Jane died 9 Mar 1927, age 56, buried Weaste Cemetery, Salford.

Sp. Martin HAYES (-) [37].

      5. Bernard HAYES (-) [196]. Son of Martin Hayes and Jane Dixon.

      5. Charlie HAYES (-) [197]. Son of Martin Hayes and Jane Dixon.

      5. Jimmy HAYES (-) [198]. Son of Martin Hayes and Jane Dixon.

      5. Laura HAYES (-) [199]. Dau of Martin Hayes and Jane Dixon.

4. Jim DIXON (1870-) [38]. Born 1870. Son of Robert Dixon and Betsy Dean.

4. Lizy DIXON (1873-) [39]. Born 1873, Northwich. Dau of Robert Dixon and Betsy Dean. Lizy Marr Herbert SHAW, 14 Oct 1890, Chorlton, Manchester.

Sp. Herbert SHAW (1866 -) [128]. Born 1866, Sheffield.

      5. Herbert SHAW (1898 -) [129]. Born Salford. Son of Herbert Shaw and Lizy Dixon. Herbert Marr Kathy WALKER.

      Sp. Kathy WALKER (-) [136].

      5. Robert SHAW (-) [130]. Son of Herbert Shaw and Lizy Dixon. Robert Marr Alice INGHAM.

      Sp. Alice INGHAM (-) [139].

      5. William Jarrow SHAW (circa 1907 -) [131]. Born circa 1907, Jarrow, Durham. Son of Herbert Shaw and Lizy Dixon. William Jarrow Marr Alice GILL.

      Sp. Alice GILL (-) [142].

      5. Betsy SHAW (1900 -1987) [132]. Born 1900, Salford. Dau of Herbert Shaw and Lizy Dixon. Betsy Marr Tommy EDWARDS, 21 Sept 1920. Betsy died July 1987, Manchester.

      Sp. Tommy EDWARDS (-) [146].

      5. Loretta SHAW (1909 -) [133]. Born 6 May 1909, Hebburn, Durham. Dau of Herbert Shaw and Lizy Dixon. Loretta Marr William SMITH, 1928, Salford. Loretta buried 11 Jan 1996, Blackley Cemetery, Manchester.

      Sp. William SMITH (1905-) [154].

      5. Connie SHAW (1905-1985) [134]. Born 13 Mar 1905, Burnhope, Durham. Dau of Herbert Shaw and Lizy Dixon. Connie Marr William CRADDOCK,1927 Connie died 1985, Salford

      Sp. William CRADDOCK (-) [151].

      5. Lily SHAW (1896 -) [135]. Born 1896, Salford. Dau of Herbert Shaw and Lizy Dixon. Lily Marr Patrick MULHEARN.

      Sp. Patrick MULHEARN (-) [158].

4. Alice DIXON (1892-) [40]. Born 1892, Trinity Market Fairground, The Flat Iron Market, Salford. Dau of Robert Dixon and Betsy Dean. Alice Marr Francis Chrsitopher MATTHEWS, 1911.

Sp. Francis Christopher MATTHEWS (-) [161]. Known as a 'pot man' (a market trader selling crockery). Francis Christopher came from Wigan, Lancashire.

      5. Mary MATTHEWS (1919-1920) [207]. Born 1919. Died 1920, aged 20 months. Buried Weaste Cemetery, Salford.

4. Hannah DIXON (1877-1903) [47]. Born 11 Sept 1877, Witton, Northwich. Dau of Robert Dixon and Betsy Dean. Hannah Marr James FEARNS, 12 Feb 1895, Sacred Trinity Church, Salford. Hannah died 1895. 26 Apr 1903, Salford.

Sp. James FEARNS (1873-1939) [48]. Born 25 May 1873,10 Water Street, Blackburn, Lancashire. James Marr Hannah DIXON 12 Feb 1895, Sacred Trinity Church, Salford. James died 7 Jan 1939, Manchester.

James Fearns circa 1910.
Courtesy of John Fearns

Fearns Family Outline

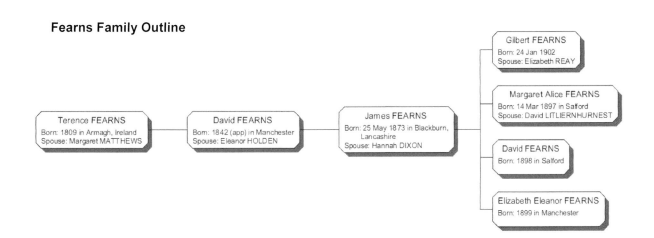

1. Terence FEARNS (1809-1871) [805]. Born 1809, Armagh, Ireland. Terence Marr Margaret MATTHEWS, 10 Apr 1831, Manchester Cathedral. Terence died 4 Nov 1871, Shaw Street, Manchester.

The following information has been taken from Richard Griffiths' Primary Valuation of Ireland 1848-1864, for Armagh. Although the exact link and lineage of Terence is unclear, evidence suggests that there is a close link with the following families

Surname	First Name	Townland	Parish	County
Fearns	Thomas	Duburren	Killevy	Armagh
Fearns	Patrick	Duburren	Killevy	Armagh
Fearns	John	Drumilly	Killevy	Armagh
Fearns	Grace	Ballintemple	Killevy	Armagh
Fearns	Byran	Ballintemple	Killevy	Armagh
Fearns	Francis	Duburren	Killevy	Armagh

Sp. Margaret MATTHEWS (1810-1891) [806]. Born Kilkenny, Ireland.

2. David FEARNS (circa 1842-1891) [803]. Born circa 1842, 6 Thornley Brow, Manchester. David Marr Eleanor HOLDEN, 25 May 1869, St Nichols Church, Liverpool. David died 19 May 1891, Earlstown, Lancashire.

Sp. Eleanor HOLDEN (-) [804], dau. of Joseph Holden Noblet and Ellen Mayor. Ellen Mayor was the dau of Thomas Mayor and Ellen.

Parents of Eleanor HOLDEN
Joseph Holden Noblet, born 27 Jan 1825, Blackburn, Lancashire. During his life noted as a Cotton Weaver, Hawker, Fruiterer and Fish Seller. Joseph used the surname of his mother . Joseph's parents, James Noblet and Jane Holden never married. Joseph Marr Ellen MAYOR, 27 May 1844, Preston Yard, Lancashire, dau of Thomas Mayor and Ellen.

Joseph's brother was Leonard Noblet, Confectioner and Sweet Manufacturers in Liverpool, Manchester, Whitehaven and Dublin. The shops were known as 'Noblets' – 'for the Purest Confectionery'. The shops would use paper bags with the logo of 'Old Mother Noblet's Toffee' and also a picture of old mother Noblet wearing her apron and carrying a basket, with a further brand mark "sweets bearing this mark are the best of their kind'. Leonard Marr Bridget Mary DEWHURST. One of their children was Stephen Noblet who became the Manager of Noblet's Sweets and Confectionery. Two other children became Priests and two other children became Nuns.

Siblings of Eleanor HOLDEN
Alice Holden Marr Benjamin FENTON and emigrated to America in the late 1870s.
Lucy Hannah Holden Marr John GRAHAM.
Jane Holden Marr William MITCHELL, 1867.
Elizabeth Ann Holden Marr James Henry SLATER.
Thomas Holden Marr Susan WILSON.
There were a further 9 siblings, 7 died young.

5. Margaret Alice FEARNS (1897-1953) [162]. Born 14 Mar 1897, Salford. Dau of James Fearns and Hannah Dixon. Margaret Alice Marr Davie LITLIERNHURNEST, 1923. Margaret Alice died 1953.
Sp. Davie LITLIERNHURNEST (-) [163].

5. Gilbert FEARNS (1902 -1976) [49]. Born 26 Jan 1902, Salford. Son of James Fearns and Hannah Dixon. Gilbert Marr Elizabeth REAY. GIbert died 23 Jun 1976, Manchester.
Sp. Elizabeth REAY (-) [50]. Daughter of John Reay and Elizabeth Cardwell.

Gilbert Fearns and the Silcock
Brothers. Courtesy of John Fearns

Reay Family Outline

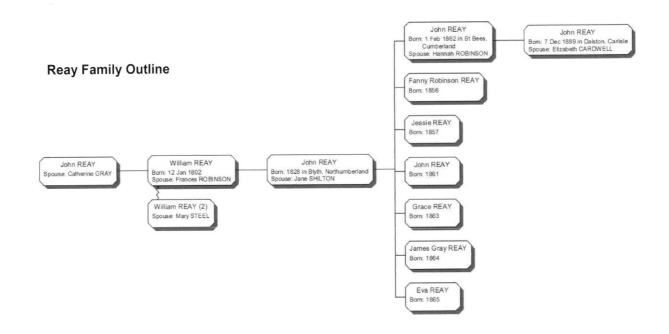

1. **John REAY (-) [861].** John Marr Catherine GRAY 12 Mar 1796.
Sp. Catherine GRAY (-) [862].

   2. **William REAY (1802-1855) [859].** Born 12 Jan 1802. William Marr firstly Frances ROBINSON, 7 Feb
      1828, Tanfield, Durham and secondly Marr Mary STEEL, 7 Feb 1842, Parish Church, Hepworth,
      Jarrow, Durham. William was a Widower when he married Mary. William died 1855, Whitehaven,
      Cumberland.
   Sp. Frances ROBINSON (-) [860].

      3. **John REAY (1828-1883) [857].** Born 1828, Blyth, Northumberland. John Marr Jane SHILTON, 18
         Apr 1852, St Bees, Whitehaven, Cumberland. Although born in Co. Durham John had settled
         in St. Bees, Whitehaven by the 1840s. John become a Druggist/Chemist, owning his own
         premises/shop and was a well known and respected person in St. Bees, and Whitehaven.
         Sometime in 1882/3, he had the misfortune to fall into an open `sewerage` trench, this resulted
         in ill health causing his death on 2 April 1883, Main Street, St. Bees, Whitehaven.
      Sp. Jane SHILTON (1828-1915) [858]. Born 1828, St Bees, Whitehaven, Cumberland. Jane died 12
         Jan 1915, 36 Fortune Green Road, London.

      Jane was the dau of Daniel Shilton and Elizabeth Fisher. Daniel Marr Elizabeth FISHER, 1883.
      Elizabeth Fisher, born 1797, the dau of James Fisher and Nancy Bone. Daniel Shilton, born
      1793, died 1850, Whitehaven, Cumberland and he was the son of Joseph Shilton and Elizabeth
      Dansan. Joseph Shilton Marr Elizabeth DANSAN 4 Mar 1790.

         4. **John REAY (1862-1920) [855].** Born 1 Feb 1862, St Bees, Cumberland. Son of John Reay and
            Jane Shilton. John Marr Hannah MARTIN nee ROBINSON, Widow, 18 Jul 1889, St
            James, Cumberland. John died 19 Apr 1920, 11 Miller Street, Leigh. For reasons unknown
            John left the family business and moved, with Hannah to Warrington, Lancashire, where he
            became a railway porter.
         Sp. Hannah MARTIN nee ROBINSON (1854-1894) [856]. Born 1854, Whitehaven, Cumberland.
            (Hannah had previously been married to William Martin) Hannah dau of John Robinson and
            Mary Bowerbank (married 1849, Penrith, Cumberland). Mary Bowerbank, born circa 1820,
            Ousby, Cumberland, was the dau of Joseph Bowerbank, born 1772, Berrier, Westmorland,

the son of John Bowerbank and Dinah Jacques. John Marr Dinah JACQUES, 13 Aug 1763. Joseph Bowerbank Marr Ann TEASDALE, 23 Jul 1809, Greystoke, Cumberland. Ann Teasdale, born 20 May 1787, Berrier, Westmorland, was the dau of John Teasdale and Ann.

Hannah Died 19 Dec 1894, Factory Row, Leigh, Lancashire.

Bowerbank Family Outline

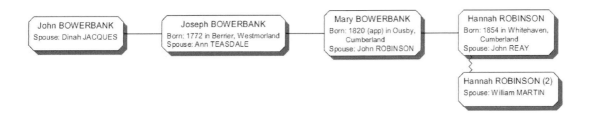

5. **John REAY (1889-1961) [853].** Born 7 Dec 1889, Dalston, Near Carlisle. John Marr Elizabeth CARDWELL, 11 Apr 1914, St Thomas Parish, Golborne, Wigan. John died 15 Nov 1961, 15 West Avenue, Golborne, Wigan.

    Sp. Elizabeth CARDWELL (1895-1940) [854], dau. of William Cardwell, born 1852 and Mary J Anderton, born 1868.

6. **Elizabeth REAY (-) [50].** Elizabeth Marr Gilbert FEARNS, 4 Aug 1935.
    Sp. Gilbert FEARNS (1902-1976) [49], son of James Fearns and Hannah Dixon.

4. **Fanny Robinson REAY (1856-) [898].** Born 1856. Dau of John Reay and Jane Shilton.
4. **Jessie REAY (1857-) [899].** Born 1857. Dau of John Reay and Jane Shilton.
4. **John REAY (1861-) [900].** Born 1861. Son of John Reay and Jane Shilton.
4. **Grace REAY (1863-) [901].** Born 1863. Dau of John Reay and Jane Shilton.
4. **James Gray REAY (1864-) [902].** Born 1864. Son of John Reay and Jane Shilton.
4. **Eva REAY (1865-) [903].** Born 1865. Dau of John Reay and Jane Shilton.

Anderton Family Outline

1. **William ANDERTON (circa 1764- circa 1850) [891].** Born circa 1764 and died circa 1850.
Sp. Sarah (-) [892].
>   2. **Joseph ANDERTON (1816-1887) [889].** Born 1 Mar 1816, Newton-in-Makerfield, Lancashire. Joseph Marr Mary MAINES, 14 Jul 1844, Winwick, Lancashire. Joseph died 23 Jun 1887, Golborne, Wigan, Lancashire.
>   **Sp. Mary MAINES (1821-1891) [890],** dau of Samuel Maines and Jane Mather. Samuel Marr Jane MATHER, 1818.
>>   3. **Samuel ANDERTON (1845-) [887].** Born 1845, 100 Rylance Foundry, Lancashire. Samuel Marr Margaret E ALLEN, 6 Jan 1866, Parish Church, Golborne, Wigan, Lancashire.
>>   **Sp. Margaret E ALLEN (circa 1845-1884) [888],** dau. of Augustus Allen born circa 1798 and Alice Higson. Alice Higson dau of Peter Higson and Ann Basset. Margaret E died 1884, Golborne, Wigan, Lancshire.
>>>   4. **Mary J ANDERTON (1868- circa 1914) [879].** Born 1868, Golborne, Wigan. dau of Samuel Anderton and Margaret E Allen. Mary J Marr William CARDWELL, 15 Feb 1890, Leigh, Lancashire. Mary J died circa 1914, Golborne, Wigan, Lancashire.
>>>   **Sp. William CARDWELL (1852- circa 1913) [878],** son of Thomas Cardwell born 1814 and Ann Wilding born circa 1818. William died circa 1913, Golborne, Wigan.

Thomas Cardwell born 1814, Peel, Blackpool, Lancashire, son of James Cardwell born circa 1798, Lancashire and Ann Wilding born circa 1818, dau of Joseph Wilding born circa 1792 and Jane /Joan Jackson. Joseph Wilding son of John Wilding and Jane Sherrington.

Chapter Eight

THE DUTTON FAMILY

Dutton Family Outline

James DUTTON (1792-)

---

1. James DUTTON (1792-) [247].
Sp. Elizabeth WILLIAMS (circa 1787-) [643].
      2. Elizabeth DUTTON (1822-) [209].
      Sp. Philip DIXON (1819-) [42], son of Richard or Pat DIXON (-) [248].
SEE THE DIXON FAMILY
      2. William DUTTON (1828-) [593].
      2. Hannah DUTTON (1826-) [644].
      2. Margaret DUTTON (1824-) [645].
      2. Mary DUTTON (1818-) [1190].

Dutton Lineage

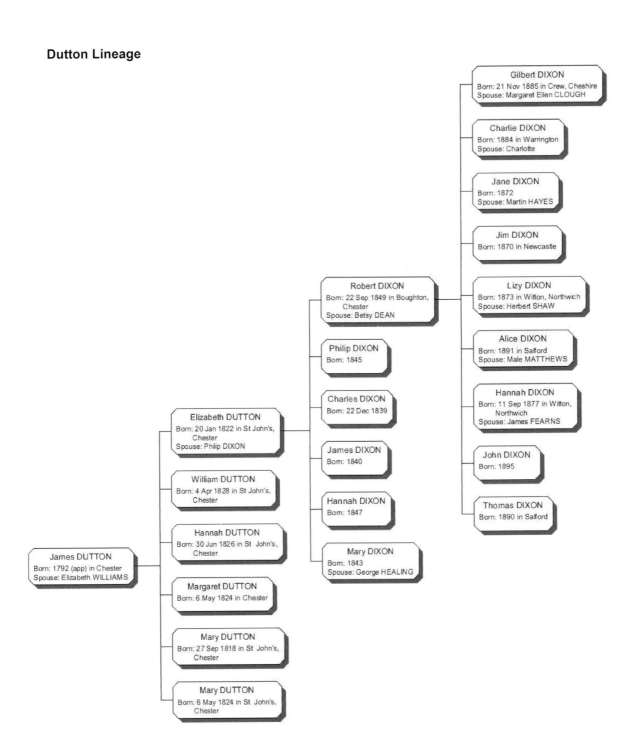

Gilbert DIXON
Born: 21 Nov 1885 in Crew, Cheshire
Spouse: Margaret Ellen CLOUGH

Charlie DIXON
Born: 1884 in Warrington
Spouse: Charlotte

Jane DIXON
Born: 1872
Spouse: Martin HAYES

Jim DIXON
Born: 1870 in Newcastle

Lizy DIXON
Born: 1873 in Witton, Northwich
Spouse: Herbert SHAW

Alice DIXON
Born: 1891 in Salford
Spouse: Male MATTHEWS

Hannah DIXON
Born: 11 Sep 1877 in Witton, Northwich
Spouse: James FEARNS

John DIXON
Born: 1895

Thomas DIXON
Born: 1890 in Salford

Robert DIXON
Born: 22 Sep 1849 in Boughton, Chester
Spouse: Betsy DEAN

Philip DIXON
Born: 1845

Charles DIXON
Born: 22 Dec 1839

James DIXON
Born: 1840

Hannah DIXON
Born: 1847

Mary DIXON
Born: 1843
Spouse: George HEALING

Elizabeth DUTTON
Born: 20 Jan 1822 in St John's, Chester
Spouse: Philip DIXON

William DUTTON
Born: 4 Apr 1828 in St John's, Chester

Hannah DUTTON
Born: 30 Jun 1826 in St John's, Chester

Margaret DUTTON
Born: 6 May 1824 in Chester

Mary DUTTON
Born: 27 Sep 1818 in St John's, Chester

Mary DUTTON
Born: 6 May 1824 in St John's, Chester

James DUTTON
Born: 1792 (app) in Chester
Spouse: Elizabeth WILLIAMS

James DUTTON (circa 1792-)

1. James DUTTON (circa 1792-) [247]. Born circa 1792

James' marriage details did not provide any information on his age or the names of his parents. It is clear he was born in Chester, therefore, the following possible family groups have been added as one of them may refer to James. Additionally, on a marriage certificate of a close relation was a Sarah and George Dutton. These names also appear in the following groups.

St Oswald's, Chester

1. *John DUTTON (circa 1755-) [1696]. Born circa 1755, Chester*
Sp. (unknown).
    2. *William DUTTON (1777-) [1695]. Baptised 26 Oct 1777, St Oswald's, Chester. Father, John Dutton.*
    2. *James DUTTON (1772-) [1692]. Baptised 1772, St. Oswald's, Chester. Chandler.*

In the 1841 English Census a James appears in the Chester House of Industry and his occupation recorded as a Chandler. Although not confirmed it is likely James is the son of John Dutton.

    Sp. (unknown). It is possible James Marr Martha ELLIS, 1797, St. Oswald's, Chester, both aged 22. At the time of his marriage he was noted as a Yeoman, residence Holton, Denbigh, Chester.
      3. James DUTTON (1792-) [1691]. *Baptised 16 Sep 1792, St Oswald's, Chester. Father, James Dutton, Chandler.*
      3. *Joseph James DUTTON (1791-) [1693]. Baptised 17 Jul 1791, St Oswald's, Chester. Father, James Dutton, Chandler.*
      3. *William DUTTON (1794-) [1674]. Baptised 18 Oct 1794, St Oswald's, Chester. Father, James Dutton, Chandler. It has been assumed this is the William who married Ellen and together they had the following children.*
    Sp. Ellen (-) [1675].
        4. *Elizabeth DUTTON (1814-) [1676]. Baptised 19 Jul 1814, St. Oswald's, Cathedral, Chester.*
        4. *Elizabeth DUTTON (1816-) [1677]. Baptised 17 Feb 1816, St. Oswald's, Cathedral, Chester.*
        4. *William DUTTON (1818-) [2018]. Baptised 6 Jun 1818, St. Oswald's, Chester. Father noted as a Bargeman of Northgate Street, Chester.*
        4. *John DUTTON (1822-) [2019]. Born 16 Oct 1822, baptised 5 Nov 1822, St. Oswald's, Chester. Father noted as a Flatman of Northgate Street, Chester.*

The following reference has been added as there may be a connection as this family were also Chandlers

St Mary's, Chester

1. *Thomas DUTTON (circa 1660-) [1407]. Born circa 1660. Chandler.*
Sp. (unknown).
    2. *George DUTTON (1685-) [1408]. Baptised 18 Mar 1685, St Mary's, Chester.*
    2. *Joseph DUTTON (1686-) [1409]. Baptised 28 Nov 1686, St Mary's, Chester.*

St Mary, Chester

1. *Thomas DUTTON (circa 1760-) [1385]. Born circa 1760. Plasterer.*
Sp. Mary (-) [1386].
    2. *Martha DUTTON (1787-) [1387]. Born 22 Jul 1787, baptised St Mary's, Chester.*
    2. *James DUTTON (1779-) [1388]. Born 21 Aug 1779, baptised St Mary's, Chester.*
    2. *John DUTTON (1791-) [1389]. Born 24 Aug 1791, baptised St Mary's, Chester.*
    2. James DUTTON (1789-) [1678]. *Baptised 21 Aug 1789, St. Mary's, Chester.*

The following family groups were Butchers and for this reason have been included as James and Elizabeth's son William became a Butcher. It is not know if this particular branch of the Dutton family were closely related to the Dutton Butcher's of Chester, or just a coincidence, given the background of William's father.

St John's, Chester

1. *Robert DUTTON (1708-1794) [998]. Born 1708. Of St John's, Chester. Butcher. Robert died 22 Dec 1794, Age 86. Cause of death Decay. St John's, Chester.*
Sp. *Catherine (-) [999].*
  2. *Jacob DUTTON (1741-) [1000]. Baptised 20 Jul 1741, St John's, Chester. Butcher.*
  Sp. *Sarah (-) [1001].*
    3. *Martha DUTTON (1780-) [1003]. Baptised 28 May 1780, St John's, Chester. Twin.*
    3. *Mary DUTTON (1780-) [1004]. Baptised 28 May 1780, St John's, Chester. Twin.*
    3. *Joseph DUTTON (1784-) [1005]. Baptised 5 Sep 1784, St John's, Chester.*
    3. **Jacob DUTTON (1782-) [1006]. Born 10 Nov 1782, baptised 27 Jan 1783 St John's, Chester.**
    3. *Roger DUTTON (1785-) [1007]. Born 16 Aug 1785, baptised 10 Feb 1786 St John's, Chester.*
    3. *Catherine DUTTON (1787-) [1008]. Born 15 Feb 1787, baptised 11 June 1787 St John's, Chester.*
    3. *William DUTTON (1791-) [1009]. Born 11 Mar 1791, baptised 12 Aug 1791 St John's, Chester.*
    3. *Frances DUTTON (1778-) [1140]. Baptised 11 Oct 1778, St John's Chester*
    3. *William DUTTON (1771- circa 1791) [1698]. Baptised 19 May 1771, St Oswald's, Chester.*
    3. *Sarah DUTTON (1772-) [1699]. Baptised 12 Jul 1772, St Oswald's, Chester.*
    3. *DUTTON (1791-) [1706]. Baptised 17 Aug 1791, St John's, Chester.*
  2. *Catherine DUTTON (1744-) [1213]. Baptised 2 May 1744, St John's, Chester.*
  2. *Thomas DUTTON (1747-) [1214]. Baptised 10 May 1747, St John's, Chester. Twin.*
  2. *Catherine DUTTON (1747-) [1215]. Baptised 10 May 1747, St John's, Chester. Twin.*
  2. *Thomas DUTTON (1749-) [1216]. Baptised 25 Jun 1749, St John's, Chester. Twin.*
  2. *Robert DUTTON (circa 1736-1780) [1185]. Born circa 1736. Butcher. A Robert died 8 Sep 1780, age 44. St John's, Chester. If his age at death is incorrect then he may have been the Robert born in 1728.*
  Sp. *Martha (-) [1186].*
    3. *Elizabeth DUTTON (1768-) [1187]. Baptised 6 Apr 1768, St. John's, Chester.*
    3. *Catherine DUTTON (1770-) [1188]. Baptised 4 Mar 1770, St. John's, Chester.*
    3. *Robert DUTTON (1772-) [1189]. Baptised 15 Mar 1772, St John's, Chester. Robert died 22 Mar 1772, St John's Chester.*
    3. *William DUTTON (-1773) [1125]. Died 22 Apr 1773, St John's Chester.*

St John's, Chester

1. *John DUTTON (circa 1760-) [1010]. Born circa 1760. Butcher.*
Sp. *Mary (-) [1011].*
  2. *Robert DUTTON (1792-1798) [1012]. Born 1792. Robert died 16 Feb 1798, age 6. Registered 19 Feb 1798. St John's, Chester. Another record states age 1.*
  2. *Robert DUTTON (1797-1798) [1013]. Born 3 Jul 1797. Robert died 19 Feb 1798, Age 1.*
  2. *William DUTTON (1798-) [1014]. Born 22 Nov 1798, baptised 12 May 1799. St John's, Chester.*
  2. *Mary DUTTON (1800-) [1192]. Born 20 Sep 1800, baptised 14 Dec 1800 St John's, Chester.*
  2. *Martha DUTTON (1796-) [1193]. Born 29 Feb 1796, baptised 4 May 1796 St John's, Chester.*
  2. *Catherine DUTTON (1806-) [1194]. Born 16 Aug 1806, baptised 10 Sept 1806 St John's, Chester. Twin.*
  2. *Sarah DUTTON (1804-) [1195]. Born 1 Aug 1804, baptised 10 Sept 1806 St John's, Chester. Twin.*
  2. *Ann DUTTON (1810-) [1196]. Born 9 Oct 1810, baptised 31 Oct 1810 St John's, Chester. Twin.*
  2. *Ann DUTTON (1812-) [1197]. Born 28 May 1812, baptised 12 June 1812 St John's, Chester. Twin.*
  2. *Robert DUTTON (1808-) [1224]. Born 22 Jun 1808, baptised 7 June 1808 St John's, Chester.*
  2. *John DUTTON (1802-) [1225]. Born 30 Jul 1802, baptised 3 Oct 1802 St John's, Chester.*
  2. *Mary DUTTON (1813-) [1243]. Born 25 Dec 1813, baptised St John's, Chester.*

It is thought that James had a brother Charles, therefore, the following references have been included.

St. Oswald's, Chester

1. *Charles DUTTON (circa 1800-) [2012]. Born circa 1800. Labour of St Oswald's when he married Mary BILLINGS, Widow, 3 Nov 1827. St. Oswald's, Chester. Witnesses Mary Ann Maguire and Edward Edwards.*
Sp. *Mary BILLINGS (-) [2013].*

The following reference has been included as they lived in Foregate Street and worked in the 'animal' industry.

St John's, Chester

1. *Charles DUTTON (1786-) [1105]. Currier of Foregate Street – (Currier is someone who colours and prepares leather after tanning). Of Foregate Street, Chester in 1817 and 1819. Charles Marr Mary Ann ROWE, 10 Jun 1807, St Oswald's, Chester. Charles was of St. John's, Chester. Charles signed his name.*
   Sp. *Mary Ann ROWE (1785-) [1106]. Of St Oswald's, Chester.*
     2. *Elizabeth DUTTON (1817-) [1107]. Baptised 16 Dec 1817, St John's Chester. Father noted as Charles of Foregate Street, Chester.*
     2. *Charles DUTTON (1819-) [1108]. Baptised 28 Oct 1819, St John's Chester. Father noted as Charles of Foregate Street, Chester. 1841 English Census, Charles, Wine Merchant of Foregate Street, St Oswald's, Chester.*
     2. *Sarah DUTTON (1808-) [1147]. Born 16 Mar 1808, baptised 30 Sept 1808, St John's, Chester. Sarah Marr Timothy Parry WHITBY, 22 Feb 1843, St John's Chester.*
     Sp. *Timothy Parry WHITBY (-) [1707].*
     2. *Ann DUTTON (1809-) [1148]. Born 8 Jul 1809, baptised 27 Jul 1809, St John's, Chester. Ann Marr Thomas BREWER, 26 Aug 1851, St Oswald's Chester.*
     Sp. *Thomas BREWER (-) [1710].*
     2. *Mary DUTTON (1810-) [1149]. Born 29 Sep 1810, baptised 1 May 1812, St John's, Chester.*
     2. *Catherine DUTTON (1815-) [1150]. Baptised 15 Aug 1815, St John's, Chester.*
     2. *Robert DUTTON (1813-) [1246]. Baptised 25 Feb 1813, St John's, Chester.*
     2. *John Rowe DUTTON (1816-) [1247]. Baptised 5 Oct 1816, St John's, Chester.*
     2. *Richard DUTTON (1821-) [1248]. Baptised 10 Feb 1821, St John's, Chester.*
     2. *Margaret DUTTON (1822-) [1648]. Baptised 14 Jul 1822, St John's Chester. Margaret, Widow. Marr Robert Kanzow BOWLEY, 8 Feb 1853, St Oswald's Chester.*
     Sp. *Robert Kanzow BOWLEY (-) [1708], son of Thomas Bowley.*

James Marr Elizabeth WILLIAMS, 1 Aug 1814, St John's Chester.

Marriage details
James Dutton married Elizabeth WILLIAMS, 1 Aug 1814, St John's Chester. James was noted as a Basket Maker. Witnesses Matthew McGivren and Benjamin Linney. (Benjamin was the son of Benjamin Linney, Parish Clerk of St John's. It is not clear if it was Benjamin or his father who was the witness). T Casson was the Vicar performing the marriage.

James has been recorded as having a number of occupations as follows
1814, Basket Maker
1818, Labourer of Boughton, Chester
1822, Pedlar of Boughton
1824, Pedlar of Foregate Street, Chester
1826, Labourer of Boughton
1828, Pedlar of Foregate Street, Chester
1841, Agricultural Labourer
1851, possibly a Ballad Singer,

1841 English Census, Great Boughton, Chester: St John the Baptist
James DUTTON, age 49, Agricultural Labourer, born 1792, Cheshire, Elizabeth DUTTON, wife, age 54, born 1786, Cheshire, Hannah DUTTON, dau, age 15, born Cheshire, William DUTTON, son, age 13, born Cheshire, Elizabeth DICKSON, dau, age 20, born Cheshire, James DICKSON, grandson, age 1, born Cheshire, Charles DICKSON, grandson, age 3, born Cheshire.

It is likely although not confirmed the following English Census refers to James and Elizabeth.
1851 English Census, Chester House of Industry
Ann DUTTON, pauper, widow, 71, born Ireland, Elizabeth DUTTON, pauper, married, 65, house servant, born 1786, Wrexham, Denbighshire, James DUTTON, pauper, married, 61, ballad singer, born 1790, Chester, (the above mentioned Ann Dutton may or may not be a relative).

Interestingly Elizabeth appears to be recorded separately and differently
1851 English Census, Chester House of Industry
Elizabeth DUTTON, Pauper, married, age 54, born 1797, Wrexham, Denbighshire, House Servant.

1861 English Census, Chester, Holy Trinity Institution, Great Boughton
James DUTTON, age 71, born 1789, Elizabeth DUTTON, age 76, born 1784.

Sp. Elizabeth WILLIAMS (1786-) [643]. Residence noted as St John's, Chester in 1814, when Elizabeth married James.

The following reference has been included for interest as it may refer to Elizabeth's sister

1. *William DUTTON (circa 1780-) [1068]. Born circa 1780. Labourer.*
Sp. Mary (-) [1686].
    2. *Thomas DUTTON (1823-) [1066]. Born 9 Dec 1823, St John's Chester. Father noted as a servant of Brook Street, Chester. Thomas Marr Sarah WILLIAMS, 11 Aug 1845, St John's Chester. Thomas noted as a Labourer of Boughton. Witnesses Margaret Roberts and John Thomas. Thomas age 21 when married.*
    Sp. Sarah WILLIAMS (1825-) [1067], *dau. of Henry WILLIAMS (-) [1069]. Age 20 when married.*
        3. *William DUTTON (1845-) [1144]. Baptised 30 Nov 1845, St John's Chester. Father noted as a Labourer of Boughton.*
        3. *Sarah DUTTON (1847-) [1145]. Baptised 6 May 1847, St John's Chester. Father noted as a Labourer of Steam Mill Street, Chester.*
        3. *Margaret DUTTON (1847-) [1146]. Baptised 6 Jun 1847, St John's Chester. Father noted as a Labourer of Steam Mill Street, Chester.*
        3. *Thomas DUTTON (1849-) [1322]. Baptised 12 Jun 1849, St John's, Chester. Twin.*
        3. *Sarah DUTTON (1856-) [1350]. Born Apr 1856, baptised 1 Jun 1857 St Mary's, Chester. Father noted as a Labourer of Potter's Court, Chester.*

    2. **Elizabeth DUTTON (1822-) [209].** Baptised 20 Jan 1822, St John's, Chester. Father noted as James Dutton, a Pedlar of Boughton, Chester. Dau of James Dutton and Elizabeth Williams.

Elizabeth Marr Philip DIXON, 6 Dec 1838, St Mary's Parish Church in the County of the City of Chester. Both noted as residents of Handbridge, Chester.
    Sp. Philip DIXON (1819-) [42], son of Richard or Pat Dixon.

SEE DIXON FAMILY

    2. **William DUTTON (1828-) [593].** Baptised 4 Apr 1828, St John's, Chester. Father noted as James Dutton, a Pedlar of Foregate Street, Chester. Son of James Dutton and Elizabeth Williams. In the 1841 English Census, Great Boughton, St John the Baptist, Chester, William is living with his parents.

1851 English Census, 11 Boughton, St. John the Baptist, Chester
David HARTON, head, age 23, Agricultural Labourer, born Chester, Edward HARTON, nephew, age 26, Sawyer-Journeyman, born Chester, William DUTTON, visitor, age 22, Butcher's Labourer, Chester, Edward FLANKIN, visitor, age 20, Boiler Maker's Labourer, born Liverpool.

By 1861 William was of Potter's Court and noted as a Butcher. It is not clear whether William was directly related to the Dutton family of Butchers in Chester or whether William took up the trade independently.

1861 English Census, 112 Potters Court, Bunce Street, St. Mary's, Chester
William DUTTON, head, 32, butcher, Widower, born Chester, Robert DIXON, nephew, age 11, born Chester (son of Philip Dixon and Elizabeth Dixon nee Dutton).

1861 English Census, Furlong Passage, Burslem, Staffordshire
Robert DICKSON, age 11, nephew, born Chester, William DUTTON, age 32, born Chester

William is noted as a Widow. The only marriage reference that might be relevant would be

William Marr Mary PARR, of Potter's Court, Chester, age 23, 3 Dec 1860, St. Mary's, Chester. William was noted as a Labourer of Potter's Court, age 31. William's father James a Tallow Chandler (someone who makes and or sells candles or soap made from animal fats). Mary's father was noted as Joseph Parr. Witnesses Hannah Forster and Howard Forster. Hannah Forster may have been a sister to William.

William has not been identified in the 1871, 1881 and 1891 English Census

1901 English Census, Withington Workhouse, Withington, Manchester
William DUTTON, married 5 years, age 73, Butcher, born 1828, Chester, Feebleminded

An alternative reference records
1901 English Census, Chorlton Union Workhouse, West Didsbury, Manchester
William DUTTON, single, age 73, Butcher, born Chester, Feebleminded

The first reference would suggest William had married again in approximately 1897. The name of his second wife has not been identified.

2. **Hannah DUTTON (1826-) [644].** Baptised 30 Jun 1826, St John's, Chester. Father noted as James Dutton, Labourer of Boughton, Chester. Mother noted as Elizabeth (Williams).
2. **Margaret DUTTON (1824-) [645].** Baptised 6 May 1824, St John's, Chester. Father noted as James Dutton, Pedlar of Foregate Street, Chester. Mother noted as Elizabeth (Williams).
2. **Mary DUTTON (1818-) [1190].** Baptised 27 Sep 1818, St John's, Chester. Father noted as James Dutton, Labourer of Boughton. Mother noted as Elizabeth (Williams).

Chapter Nine

THE CLOUGH FAMILY

Clough Family Outline

Joseph CLOUGH (1800-)

1. Joseph CLOUGH (1800-) [1966].
Sp. Ann (1801-) [2286].
      2. John CLOUGH (1829-1829) [538].
      2. Ellen CLOUGH (1833-) [1964].
      Sp. Richard SHAW (1826-) [2395].
      2. Mary Ann CLOUGH (1837-) [586].
      2. Edward CLOUGH (1833-) [587].
      2. Samuel CLOUGH (1826-1883) [122].
      Sp. Margaret Ann MURPHY (1828-) [123], dau. of Michael MURPHY (-) [208].
            3. Male CLOUGH (-) [124].
            3. Margaret Ann CLOUGH (1857-) [125].
            3. Female CLOUGH (-) [126].
            3. Sarah CLOUGH (1847-1901) [525].
            Sp. Charles MORGAN (1842-1881) [541].
                  4. Margaret MORGAN (1858-) [1984].
                  4. John MORGAN (1876-) [1985].
            3. Michael Joseph CLOUGH (1850-1881) [526].
            3. John CLOUGH (1851-) [528].
            3. Edward CLOUGH (1861-1937) [63].
            Sp. Sarah Ellen CORDWELL (1866-1933) [64], dau. of John CORDWELL (1847-1916) [65]
                and Elizabeth Ann HUGHES (1847-1882) [66].

SEE CORDWELL AND HUGHES FAMILY
                4. Margaret Ellen CLOUGH (1886-1986) [17].
                Sp. Gilbert DIXON (1885-1956) [16], son of Robert DIXON (1849-1916) [34] and Betsy
                  DEAN (1852-1911) [33].

SEE DIXON AND DEAN FAMILY
                4. Nelly (Ellen) CLOUGH (1903-) [86].
                Sp. Jimmy MANDERS (-) [87], son of James Henry MANDERS (1853-1933) [303] and
                  Louisa NAIL (1854-1913) [605].
                4. Polly (Margaret) CLOUGH (-) [91].
                4. Elizabeth Anne CLOUGH (1886-) [92].
                Sp. Joseph MARTIN (1882-) [777], son of Joseph MARTIN (1836-) [1976] and Ann
                  (1842-) [1977].
                      5. Elizabeth Ann MARTIN (1915-1967) [791].
                    Sp. Thomas ASHTON (-) [792].
                    5. Agnes MARTIN (1918-2004) [795].
                    Sp. Wilfred ASHBROOK (-) [796].
                    Sp. William TRAVIS (-) [798].
                    5. Lily MARTIN (1921-1944) [799].
                    5. Maggie MARTIN (1921-1993) [800].
                    Sp. James WINSTANLEY (-) [801].
                4. Anne CLOUGH (-) [93].
                4. John Samuel CLOUGH (1898-1987) [94].
                Sp. Nelly (Ellen) CONNELL (-1998?) [95], dau. of John CONNELL (-1928) [534] and
                  Sarah GREATOREX (-1939) [535].
                4. Henry CLOUGH (-) [98].
                4. Edward CLOUGH (1894-) [100].
                Sp. Elizabeth Ann Prisilla SELDON (1894-1975) [529], dau. of John SELDON (-) [670]
                and Sarah Hannah MCGUINNESS (-) [671].
                4. Hannah Marie CLOUGH (1901-) [101].
                Sp. John Henry BUCKLEY (1901-) [504], son of John Henry BUCKLEY (-) [755].

Sp. Arthur JONES (-) [533].
4. Joseph CLOUGH (-) [104].
4. Sarah Ellen CLOUGH (1904-) [107].
4. George CLOUGH (1901-) [109].
4. Mary Ann CLOUGH (1889-) [110].
4. George CLOUGH (1893-1893) [115].
4. Daisy CLOUGH (1904-) [119].
4. Alice CLOUGH (-) [523].
4. William Durham CLOUGH (1895-1960) [759].

Clough Lineage

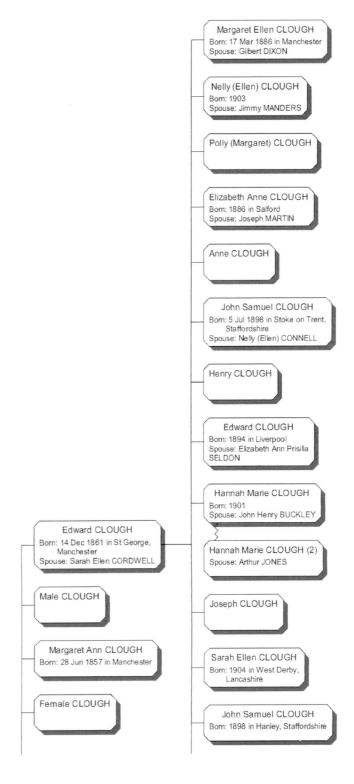

Margaret Ellen CLOUGH
Born: 17 Mar 1886 in Manchester
Spouse: Gilbert DIXON

Nelly (Ellen) CLOUGH
Born: 1903
Spouse: Jimmy MANDERS

Polly (Margaret) CLOUGH

Elizabeth Anne CLOUGH
Born: 1886 in Salford
Spouse: Joseph MARTIN

Anne CLOUGH

John Samuel CLOUGH
Born: 5 Jul 1898 in Stoke on Trent, Staffordshire
Spouse: Nelly (Ellen) CONNELL

Henry CLOUGH

Edward CLOUGH
Born: 1894 in Liverpool
Spouse: Elizabeth Ann Prisilla SELDON

Hannah Marie CLOUGH
Born: 1901
Spouse: John Henry BUCKLEY

Hannah Marie CLOUGH (2)
Spouse: Arthur JONES

Edward CLOUGH
Born: 14 Dec 1861 in St George, Manchester
Spouse: Sarah Ellen CORDWELL

Male CLOUGH

Margaret Ann CLOUGH
Born: 28 Jun 1857 in Manchester

Female CLOUGH

Joseph CLOUGH

Sarah Ellen CLOUGH
Born: 1904 in West Derby, Lancashire

John Samuel CLOUGH
Born: 1898 in Hanley, Staffordshire

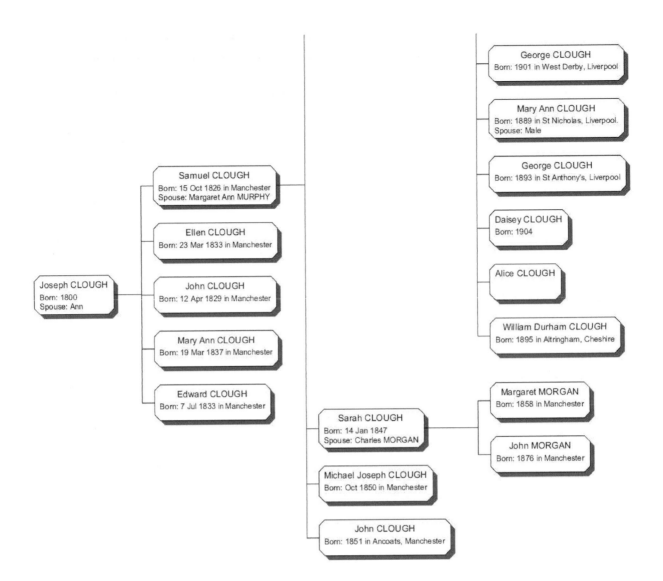

Joseph CLOUGH
Born: 1800
Spouse: Ann

Samuel CLOUGH
Born: 15 Oct 1826 in Manchester
Spouse: Margaret Ann MURPHY

Ellen CLOUGH
Born: 23 Mar 1833 in Manchester

John CLOUGH
Born: 12 Apr 1829 in Manchester

Mary Ann CLOUGH
Born: 19 Mar 1837 in Manchester

Edward CLOUGH
Born: 7 Jul 1833 in Manchester

George CLOUGH
Born: 1901 in West Derby, Liverpool

Mary Ann CLOUGH
Born: 1889 in St Nicholas, Liverpool.
Spouse: Male

George CLOUGH
Born: 1893 in St Anthony's, Liverpool

Daisey CLOUGH
Born: 1904

Alice CLOUGH

William Durham CLOUGH
Born: 1895 in Altringham, Cheshire

Sarah CLOUGH
Born: 14 Jan 1847
Spouse: Charles MORGAN

Margaret MORGAN
Born: 1858 in Manchester

John MORGAN
Born: 1876 in Manchester

Michael Joseph CLOUGH
Born: Oct 1850 in Manchester

John CLOUGH
Born: 1851 in Ancoats, Manchester

Joseph CLOUGH (circa 1800-)

1. Joseph CLOUGH (circa 1800-) [1966]. Born circa 1800

There are two separate families in the Manchester area with both sets of parents called Joseph Clough and Ann and both of similar ages. One reference records Joseph as a foreigner, probably born in Ireland and Ann born in Lancashire. The second reference records a Joseph born in Ashton (Under Lyne), Manchester and Ann born in Ireland. The recorded occupation at all the baptisms for both Josephs was Weaver and Labourer.

Similarly, they both married in Manchester Cathedral
- Joseph Clough married 26 Oct 1829, Ann Stain or Strain, Collegiate, Manchester. (Manchester Cathedral). Witnesses Thomas Perry and Sarah Ewings.
- Joseph Clough married 3 Aug 1819, Ann Fleetwood, Collegiate, Manchester. Witnesses Robert Hilton and William Cook.

Both sets of children were baptised at Manchester Cathedral. The Cathedral was previously known as Collegiate Church until 1847, when it became Manchester Cathedral dedicated to St. Mary, St. Dennis and St. George. In the early 19th Century it was known as Christ Church.

The following English Census has been found for both families

1841 English Census, 19 Bradley Street, Manchester (close to Ancoats)
Joseph CLOUGH, head, age 35, born 1806, Lancashire, Ann CLOUGH, age 35, born 1806, Ireland, Mary CLOUGH, dau, age 3, born 1838, Lancashire, Edward DEGAN, age 25, born 1816, Ireland

1851 English Census, 19 Bradley Street, Manchester (close to Ancoats)
Joseph CLOUGH, head, married, age 50, born 1801, Ashton, Manchester, Weaver, Ann CLOUGH, wife, age 49, born 1802, Ireland, Mary CLOUGH, dau, age 13, born 1838, Manchester, Weaver, Charles MORRIS, lodger, married, age 60, born 1791, Manchester, Marine Dealer, Thomas HUGHES, lodger, unmarried, age 22, born 1829, Ireland, Spinner, James BERESFORD, lodger, widower, age 24, born 1827, Wales, Seaman.

1861 English Census, Regent Road, St. Bartholomew, Salford
Jose CLOUGH, age 60, born 1791, Manchester, Ann CLOUGH, age 47, born 1804

1841 English Census, Little Ancoat's Street, District of London Road, Manchester
Joseph CLOUGH, age 40, Labourer, born 1801 (foreign), Ann CLOUGH, wife, age 40, born 1801, Lancashire, Samuel CLOUGH, son, age 14, born 1826, Lancashire, Ellen CLOUGH, dau, age 10, born 1830, Lancashire, Edward CLOUGH, son, age 7, born 1833, Lancashire, Mary CLOUGH, dau, age 4, born 1837, Lancashire.

The above census for Little Ancoat's Street is likely to be the correct reference for this particular family for a number of reasons
- Joseph and Ann definitely had sons called Samuel and Edward. There is no mention of a Samuel or Edward Clough in the Bradley Street census
- Samuel Clough is noted in the 1851 census for Ancoat's Street, which is the general area where the family lived
- The number and names of the children noted in Ancoat's Street would match the names in the family lines.

Interestingly, nearly all the baptismal records for Joseph and Ann indicated that Joseph was a Labourer with the exception of one which mentions him as a Turner. However, due to the slight uncertainty, other children born to a Joseph and Ann have been noted below as they too may have been born into the same family. They have not been attached to this family tree.

- **William CLOUGH (1822-) [540].** Baptised 13 Oct 1822, Manchester Collegiate Church, parents Joseph Clough and Ann. Joseph noted as a Dyer. Residence Manchester.
- **Sarah CLOUGH (1824-) [539].** Baptised 11 Jan 1824, Manchester Collegiate Church, parents Joseph Clough and Ann. Joseph noted as a Spinner. Residence Manchester.

- **Samuel CLOUGH (1831-) [2287].** Baptised 13 Mar 1831, Manchester Collegiate Church, parents Joseph Clough and Ann. Joseph noted as a Weaver. Residence Manchester.
- **James CLOUGH (1833-) [1961].** Baptised 21 Apr 1833, Manchester Collegiate Church, parents Joseph Clough and Ann. Joseph noted as a Weaver. Residence Manchester.
- **William CLUFF (1836-) [1962].** William Cluff baptised 13 Mar 1836, Manchester Collegiate Church, parents Joseph Cluff and Ann. Born 2 July 1835. Joseph noted as a Weaver. Residence Ancoates
- **Mary CLOUGH (1841-) [1963].** Baptised 13 June 1841, Manchester Collegiate Church, parents Joseph Clough and Ann. Born 4 Sept 1838. Joseph noted as a Weaver. Residence Manchester.

> Joseph's death date is not know and one of the following references might be relevant
> Joseph Clough died 5 May 1891, buried Bardsley, Lancashire
> Joseph Clough died 2 May 1843, Manchester
> Joseph Clough died 29 Aug 1853, buried All Saints, Chorlton upon Medlock
> Joseph Clough died 28 Sept 1874 age 74 Workhouse, Warrington

Given the ages of Joseph and Ann's children it is reasonable to assume that Joseph Clough Marr Ann Stain, or sometimes spelt Strain, 26 Oct 1829, Manchester Collegiate Church. Witnesses Thomas Perry and Sarah Ewings.

Sp. Ann (circa 1801-) [2286]. A birth reference for Ann Stain/Strain has not been found in Manchester. However, there is a record in Liverpool for an Ann which may apply - Ann Strain baptised 24 Oct 1780, St Peter's Priory, Liverpool, born to Patrick and Ann Strain. Sponsors Patrick Carr and Eleanor Abbott. Unfortunately, there is no confirmation this reference refers to Ann.

2. **John CLOUGH (1829-1829) [538].** Baptised 12 Apr 1829, Manchester Collegiate Church, parents Joseph Clough and Ann. Joseph noted as a Labourer. Residence Manchester. John died 8 Nov 1829, 6 months old.
2. **Ellen CLOUGH (1833-) [1964].** Baptised 23 Mar 1833, Manchester Collegiate Church, parents Joseph Clough and Ann. Joseph noted as a Labourer. Residence Manchester. Ellen Marr Richard Shaw, age 29, Widow, Mason, 26 July 1856, Manchester Collegiate, of 18 Rosmond Street, Chorlton upon Medlock, Richard's father Thomas was noted as a Mason. Ellen was age 26, spinster, of Rosmond Street, Chorlton Upon Medlock, father Joseph Clough, noted as a Mechanic. Witnesses Alexander and Sarah Groves.
   Sp. Richard SHAW (1826-) [2395].
2. **Mary Ann CLOUGH (1837-) [586].** Baptised 19 Mar 1837, Manchester Collegiate Church, parents Joseph Clough and Ann. Born 8 March 1837. Joseph noted as a Turner. Residence Manchester.
2. **Edward CLOUGH (1833-) [587].** Baptised 7 Jul 1833 Manchester, Collegiate Church, parents Joseph Clough and Ann. Joseph noted as a Labourer. Residence Manchester.

1851 English Census, Belle Vue Prison, West Gorton Goal
Edward CLOUGH, Prisoner, unmarried, age 17, born 1834, Labourer Factory Manchester, born Lancashire. Admitted 1851. Steeling Lead. Height 4 feet 11 inches, fresh complexion, brown hair and grey eyes. There was a note to say in Salford Goal 6 Sep 1851.

2. **Samuel CLOUGH (1826-1883) [122].** Baptised 15 Oct 1826, Manchester Collegiate Church, parents Joseph Clough and Ann. Joseph noted as a Labourer. Residence Manchester. Samuel Marr Margaret Ann MURPHY 13 Jan 1845, Manchester.

Marriage Certificate
Married Margaret (Ann) Murphy, 13 Jan 1845, Parish of Manchester, age for both was noted as minors, Samuel's residence 20 Garden Street, Manchester, Brass Foundry Worker, his father Joseph Clough a Mechanic. Margaret lived at 3 Well Lane, Manchester, her father Michael Murphy, Labourer. Witnesses to the marriage were James Kemp and Marcy Rourke.

1851 English Census, 39 Tib Street, Township of Manchester, Market Street.
Samuel CLOUGH, head, Brewery Labourer, age 24, born 1826, Manchester, Margaret CLOUGH, wife, age 23, born 1827, Manchester, Sarah CLOUGH, dau, age 4, born 1846, Manchester, Michael CLOUGH, age 5 months, born 1850, Manchester.

1861 English Census, 4 Sutcliffe Court, 4 Silk Street, Ancoat's, Manchester
Saml CLOUGH, head, age 35, born 1826, Manchester, Moulder, Margt CLOUGH,, wife, age 34, born 1827, Manchester, Upholsterer, cotton mill, born Manchester, Margaret (Ann) CLOUGH, dau, age 3, born 1859, Manchester, Jh CLOUGH, son, age 10, born 1851, Manchester, Sarah CLOUGH, dau, age 15, Born 1846, Manchester, Upholsterer cotton mill.

In 1861 when Edward was born Samuel and Margaret were living at 5 Moore Street, St George, Manchester. Samuel was noted as an Foundry Labourer.

Samuel died before the 1871 English Census as Margaret was noted as a Widow. In 1883, when his son Edward married Sarah Ellen Cordwell, Samuel is noted as an Iron Plate Worker and deceased.

Sp. Margaret Ann MURPHY (1828-) [123], dau.of Michael Murphy.

The only birth detail for a Margaret found was that of Margaret born to Michael and Margaret Murphy, 11 March 1827, baptised 18 March 1827, St. Mary's, Liverpool. Godparents Patrick Kinsella and Catherine Flaherty or Rafferty. Unfortunately, there is no confirmation this is the correct reference for Margaret.

Margaret lived at 3 Well Street, Manchester when she married Samuel Clough in 1845. No information on her father Michael Murphy has been found at this address.

Two of Samuel and Margaret's daughters became Nuns and one son became a priest.

After the death of Samuel, Margaret can be found living with his son in law in the following census.

1871 English Census, 9 Gerrards Court, Spittle Street, Manchester
Charles MORGAN, head, age 27 born 1844, Lancashire, Sarah MORGAN, wife, age 23, born 1848, Lancashire, Margaret MORGAN, dau, age 4, born 1867, Lancashire, Margaret Ann CLOFF, mother in law, age 42, Widow, born 1829, Lancashire, Edward CLOFF, brother in law, age 9, born 1862.

1881 English Census, 4 Gerrard's Court, Manchester
Margaret CLUFF, Widow, age 53, born 1828, Manchester, Margare t A CLUFF, unmarried, age 23, born 1858, Manchester, Edward CLUFF, unmarried, age 6, born 1875, Manchester, John W CLUFF, age 2, born 1879, Manchester.

1891 English Census,16, 2 Albert Buildings, Silk Street, Manchester
Sarah MORAN, head, Widow, age 44, born 1847, Manchester, Hawker, Margaret MORAN, dau, single, age 23, born 1858, Manchester, Mill Hand, John MORAN, son, age 15, born 1876, Manchester, Dyer, Margaret CLOUGH, mother, Widow, age 64, born 1827, Manchester.

3. **Male CLOUGH (-) [124].** Became a Priest. Son of Samuel Clough and Margaret Ann Murphy.
3. **Margaret Ann CLOUGH (1857-) [125].** Born 28 Jun 1857, 10 Simpson Street, Manchester. Dau of Samuel Clough and Margaret Ann Murphy. In the 1861 English Census, 4 Sutcliffe Court, 4 Silk Street, Ancote's, Manchester, Margaret Ann was living with her parents. Margaret Ann was a witness to the marriage of Edward and Sarah Ellen Cordwell in 1883. Margaret Ann became a Carmelite Nun and was based at Mount Carmel Church, Salford, where Edward and Sarah Ellen Cordwell married in 1883.
3. **Female CLOUGH (-) [126].** Unfortunately, the name of this female is not known but she also became a Nun based at Mount Carmel Church, Salford. Dau of Samuel Clough and Margaret Ann Murphy.
3. **Sarah CLOUGH (1847-1901) [525].** Born 14 Jan 1847. Dau of Samuel Clough and Margaret Ann Murphy. Sarah Marr Charles MORGAN, 8 Sep 1866, Cathedral, Manchester. In the 1851 English Census, 39 Tib Street, Township of Manchester, Market Street and in the 1861 English Census, 4 Sutcliffe Court, 4 Silk Street, Ancoat's, Manchester, Sarah was living with her parents. Sarah died 1901 at 4 Well Street, Shudehill, Manchester.
Sp. Charles MORGAN (1842-1881) [541].

4. **Margaret MORGAN (1858-) [1984].** Born 1858, Manchester. In the 1871 English Census, 9 Gerrards Court, Spittle Street, Manchester, the 1881 English Census, 4 Gerrard's Court,

Manchester and the 1891 English Census,16, 2 Albert Buildings, Silk Street, Manchester, Margaret living with her parents.
   4. **John MORGAN (1876-) [1985].** Born 1876, Manchester. In the 1881 English Census, 4 Gerrard's Court, Manchester and the 1891 English Census,16, 2 Albert Buildings, Silk Street, Manchester, John living with his parents.

   3. **Michael Joseph CLOUGH (1850-1881) [526].** Born Oct 1850, Manchester. Son of Samuel Clough and Margaret Ann Murphy. In the 1851 English Census, 39 Tib Street, Township of Manchester, Market Street, Michael was living with his parents. Michael died 1881
   3. **John CLOUGH (1851-) [528].** Born 1851, 9 Fielders Yard, Ancoats, Liverpool. Son of Samuel Clough and Margaret Ann Murphy. In the 1861 English Census, 4 Sutcliffe Court, 4 Silk Street, Ancoat's, Manchester, John was living with his parents.
   3. **Edward CLOUGH (1861-1937) [63].** Born 14 Dec 1861, 5 Moore Street, St George, Manchester. Baptised 20 Dec 1861. Son of Samuel Clough and Margaret Ann Murphy. In 1871 English Census, 9 Gerrards Court, Spittle Street, Manchester, Edward living with his mother and sister. Edward died Feb 1937, age 70. Buried All Saints, Golbourne, Wigan, Lancashire.

Edward Marr Sarah Ellen CORDWELL 1883, Mount Carmel Church, Oldfield Road, Salford.

Marriage certificate
Solemnized at Mount Carmel Church, Oldfield Road, Salford in the Sub District of Salford in the County of Lancaster, 28 Nov 1883, Edward Clough, 21 years, bachelor, Dyer of 422 Bigland's Street Salford, father, Samuel Clough (deceased), Iron Plate Worker, married Sarah Ellen Cordwell, age18, spinster, of 44 Wooden Street, Salford, father, John Cordwell, Commercial Traveller. Edward made an x as his mark, Sarah Ellen signed her name. Witnesses William Cordwell (signed his name) and an x was made as the mark for Margaret Ann Clough (later to become a nun at this Convent).

Edward Clough and Sarah Ellen Cordwell had 22 children, 20 were born alive, although not all survived, many were twins.

Unable to find Edward or Sarah Ellen in the 1891 English Census

1901 English Census, Caravans, Trafford Fair Ground, Salford, Lancashire
Edward CLOUGH, head, age 40, born 1860, Manchester, Showman, Sarah E CLOUGH, wife, age 37, born 1863, Manchester, Elizabeth A CLOUGH, dau, age 16, born 1884, Salford, Margaret E CLOUGH, dau, age 14, born 1886, Manchester, George CLOUGH, son, age 1 month, born 1901, Liverpool, Harry MITCHELL, age 27, boarder, born Halifax, Yorkshire, James MADDOX, 17, boarder, born Liverpool, Robert WALKER, 24, boarder, born Rochdale, Lancashire.

1911 English Census, Patricroft, Eccles, Barton upon Irwell, Lancashire.
Edward CLOUGH,, head, age 48, born 1862, Manchester, Showman, Sarah Ellen CLOUGH, wife, age 48, born 1862, Manchester, children born alive 20, 8 alive, 12 dead, married 25 years, Nelly CLOUGH, dau, age 7, born 1903, Daisy CLOUGH, dau, age 6, born 1904, Edward CLOUGH, son, age 21, born 1889, Showman, Willie CLOUGH, son, age 16, born 1894, Showman, Sam CLOUGH, son, age 14, born 1896, Showman,

Edward in a period during his life became a Street Hawker in Liverpool. Sometimes Edward would use his barrow to carry coffins to the grave yard. On one particular occasion he was taking a body to the cemetery . On arrival Edward waited and waited for the family to arrive for the burial. Unfortunately, Edward had been given the wrong instructions and had gone to the wrong cemetery!

Edward died 3 Feb 1937, age 70. Buried All Saints, Golbourne, Wigan, Lancashire.

Death certificate
Registration District of Leigh in the sub district of Lowton in the County of Lancaster, 3rd February 1937, 12 Mill Street, Golbourne, Edward Clough, male, age 75, Fairground Showman, cause of death a) Myocardial Degenerations, b) Senile arteris sclerosis, certified by E W B Shaw RREP, Joseph Twist present at death from 210 Crow Lane, Weat, Earlestown, registered 3rd February 1937, signature of registrar Oliver T Ormrod. (Edward's age at death on the death certificate is incorrect)

Edward was buried at All Saints, Goldbourne, Wigan, Lancashire. Also in this plot is his son William Dunham who died Jan 1960.

"Of your charity pray for the repose of the soul of Edward dearly beloved husband of Sarah Ellen Clough who departed this life 3 February 1937, aged 75 years. RIP Also William Dunham Clough, son of the above, died 15th January 1960, aged 65 years".

Sp. Sarah Ellen CORDWELL (1866-1933) [64], dau. of John Cordwell and Elizabeth Ann Hughes. Born 17 Mar 1866, 12 Back Quay Street, Manchester. Also known as Nellie Clough.

SEE CORDWELL AND HUGHES FAMILY

Sarah Ellen died 26 Oct 1933, Fair Ground, Ellesmere Port. Buried Borough Cemetery, Ruabon Road, Wrexham, North Wales with her father and step mother.

Death Certificate
Registration District Wirral, 1933 in the Sub District of Eastham, Wirral in the County of Chester, 26 Oct 1933, living in a van on Cromwell Road, Ellesmere Port, South Wirral, Cheshire, Sarah Ellen Clough, female, age 67, wife of Edward Clough a Travelling Showman, died of a) Cirrhosis of liver, b) Hypostatic pneumonia, Wolm. Certified by G H Tarras LRD, registered 27 Oct 1933, registrar R.Clough. Present Mrs Daisy Buckley, daughter, living in van on Cromwell Road, Ellesmere Port, South Wirral, Cheshire.

The World's Fair newspaper November 4th 1933
"Death of Mrs E Clough Internment at Wrexham. We regret to have to announce the death, which occurred after a long and painful illness, on Thursday 26 October, in her living van at the Fair Ground, Ellesmere Port, of Mrs E Clough, wife of Edward Clough Snr. She was 68 years of age and was highly respected by all who knew her. She leaves a husband and children to morn a devoted wife and mother. The funeral took place on Monday last at Wrexham. The principal mourners were: Mr Edward Clough Snr (husband), Mrs J Martin and Mrs Gilbert Dixon (daughters), Mr E Clough Jnr, Mr W Clough and Mr S Clough (sons), Mrs James Manders and Mrs J Buckley (daughters), Mr Gilbert Dixon (grandson), Mr Edward Dixon (grandson), Mrs Robert Hines (grand daughter), Mr John Cordwell (brother), Mr James Cordwell (brother), Mrs P Tynan (sister), Mr L Cordwell (brother), Mr & Mrs Guyatt (sister and brother in law), Mrs W Wright and Mrs J Yeats (nieces), Mrs N Clough (grand daughter), Mr J Martin (son in law), Mr Gilbert Dixon snr (son in law), Mrs E Clough jnr (daughter in law), Mrs James Cordwell (sister in law), May Cordwell (sister in law), Mrs James Hall, Mr and Mrs Fred Berry, Liverpool, Mr and Mrs Ryder, Birkenhead, Mrs L Parry, Chester, Mrs Whitley, Liverpool, Mrs G Wallis, Liverpool, Mrs Brennan, Liverpool, Mr A Ryan, Liverpool, Mr and Mrs Tom Bettaney, Liverpool, Mr A Holmes, Manchester, Mr A Hulme, Burslem, Mrs Jack Simons, Mrs John Greatorex, Mrs T Connell, Mrs G Simons, Mr Sam Deeks, Mr Tom Connell and Mr Pat Collins, Blockwich. Funeral Tributes Floral tributes were sent by: Husband, Willie, Sam and Daisy, Mr and Mrs Joe Martin and family, Mr and Mrs Gilbert Dixon, Mr and Mrs E Clough Jnr, Mr and Mrs James Manders, Mr Gilbert Dixon Jnr, Mr Edward Dixon, Mr and Mrs Robert Hines, Mr and Mrs John Cordwell, Mr and Mrs James Cordwell, Mr and Mrs Pat Tynan, Mr and Mrs B Guyatt, Mrs Joe Fletcher, Mr and Mrs W Wright, Mr and Mrs J Yeates, Mr and Mrs Fred Berry, Mr and Mrs Ryder, Mrs Whitley, Mr and Mrs L Harvey and family, Alderman Pat Collins and family, Miss C Mullett, Mr and Mrs George Wallis, Mr and Mrs Tom Cordwell, Little Billy Dixon, Little Nellie Clough, Mr and Mrs Brennan, Mr and Mrs Clayton and family, Mr and Mrs L Braman, Mr and Mrs L Cordwell, Mr and Mrs S Deeks, Mrs R Deeks, Mr and Mrs H Deeks, Mr and Mrs Tom Bettaney, Mr and Mrs James Hall, Mr and Mrs Swann, Joe Smith, Mr and Mrs H Weston snr, Mrs Griffiths, Mr and Mrs Ryan, Whitley Dew, Mr and Mrs Rogers, Miss N Wright, Mr and Mrs E N Ingham, Mrs S Mercer, Mr and Mrs Middlebrook, Mr and Mrs R H Ingham, Tom Taylor, Mr and Mrs H Royle, Mr A Cohen, Anne and Francis Ryder, Little Connie, Mr and Mrs R Jepson and family, Mr and Mrs Sutton and family, Newport. Monmouth, Mr and Mrs Bert Hughes, Mr and Mrs S Salisbury, Mr and Mrs Tom Gates, Mrs G Simons, Mrs T Connell and family, Mrs Jack Simons, Mrs John Greatorex,   Mr Fred Jewell, Mr and Mrs Bates, Mr and Mrs H Pawley and family, Mr and Mrs J N Collins, Mr and Mrs M Jarvis, Mrs Arkinstall and sons, Mr and Mrs C Dixon and family, S alford, Mr and Mrs C Hayes, and family.

4. Margaret Ellen CLOUGH (1886-1986) [17]. Born 17 Mar 1886, Blakely Wakes, Manchester. Baptised 1887, Parish Church, Blakely Wakes, Manchester. Dau of Edward Clough and Sarah Ellen Cordwell.

Margaret Ellen Dixon nee Clough 1886-1986

Margaret Marr Gilbert Dixon, 4 Sep 1907, Trinity Church, Church of England, Salford.

The wedding reception was held at the Black Lion Pub which was on the corner of Blackfriars and Chapel Street, Salford. This is also where the inauguration took place, of what is now known as The Showman's Guild, in the room upstairs.

> **Sp. Gilbert DIXON (1885-1956) [16],** son of Robert DIXON (1849-1916) [34] and Betsy DEAN (1852-1911) [33].

SEE DIXON AND DEAN FAMILY

> **4. Nelly (Ellen) CLOUGH (1903-) [86].** Born 1903. Dau of Edward Clough and Sarah Ellen Cordwell. Nelly (Ellen) Marr Jimmy MANDERS.
> **Sp. Jimmy MANDERS (-) [87],** son of James Henry MANDERS (1853-1933) [303] and Louisa NAIL (1854-1913) [605].

James Henry Manders was the son of James Manders born 1832, died 1907 and Emma Chapman. James Manders was the son of James Manders, born 1800, died 1840, and Jane Whitehead. James Manders was the son of William Manders and Rachael Perry.

> **4. Polly (Margaret) CLOUGH (-) [91].** Dau of Edward Clough and Sarah Ellen Cordwell.

4. **Elizabeth Anne CLOUGH (1886-) [92].** Born 1886, Salford. Dau of Edward Clough and Sarah Ellen Cordwell. Anne Marr Joseph MARTIN, 1904. In the 1891 English Census, 42 Belfort Street, Regent Road, Salford, Elizabeth Ann was living with Richard and Hannah Parr her Uncle and Aunt.

Sp. **Joseph MARTIN (1882-) [777]**, son of Joseph Martin and Ann. In the 1901 English Census, Fairground, Living in a Travelling Caravan, Queen's Road, Manchester, Joseph Martin was living with George Cordwell.

1911 English Census, 12 Mill Street, Golborne, Wigan, Lancashire
Joseph MARTIN, head, married 7 years, age 29, born 1882, Manchester, Carter, Elizabeth Ann MARTIN, wife, age 27, born 1884, Manchester, Annie MARTIN, dau, age 6, born 1905, Manchester, Sarah Ellen MARTIN, dau, age 2, born 1909, Golborne, Wigan.

5. **Sarah MARTIN (1908-) [288].** Born 1908, Golborne, Wigan.
5. **Annie MARTIN (1909-) [289].** Born 1909, Manchester.
5. **Edward MARTIN (1911-1912) [790].** Born 1911. Died 1912.
5. **Elizabeth Ann MARTIN (1915-1967) [791].** Born 1915. Elizabeth Ann Marr Thomas ASHTON. Elizabeth Ann died 1967.
Sp. **Thomas ASHTON (-) [792].**
5. **Agnes MARTIN (1918-2004) [795].** Born 1918. Agnes Marr Wilfred ASHBROOK. Agnes Marr secondly William TRAVIS. Agnes died 2004.
Sp. **Wilfred ASHBROOK (-) [796].**
Sp. **William TRAVIS (-) [798].**
5. **Lily MARTIN (1921-1944) [799].** Born 1921. Died 1944.
5. **Maggie MARTIN (1921-1993) [800].** Born 1921. Maggie Marr James WINSTANLEY. Maggie died 1993.
Sp. **James WINSTANLEY (-) [801].**

4. **Anne CLOUGH (-) [93].** Dau of Edward CLOUGH (1861-1937) [63] and Sarah Ellen CORDWELL (1866-1933) [64].
4. **John Samuel CLOUGH (1898-1987) [94].** Born 5 Jul 1898, Stoke on Trent. Son of Edward Clough and Sarah Ellen Cordwell. John Samuel Marr Nelly (Ellen) CONNELL, 1934, Wrexham. John Samuel died 15 Dec 1987.
Sp. **Nelly (Ellen) CONNELL (-circa 1998) [95]**, dau. of John Connell and Sarah Greatorex.
5. **Anne CLOUGH (-) [96].**
5. **Margaret CLOUGH (-) [97].**

4. **Henry CLOUGH (-) [98].** Son of Edward Clough and Sarah Ellen Cordwell.
4. **Edward CLOUGH (1894-) [100].** Born 1894, Liverpool. Son of Edward Clough and Sarah Ellen Cordwell. Edward Marr Elizabeth Ann Priscilla SELDON 1923, St Thomas, Redbank, Manchester. In the 1901 English Census , 41 Granville Street South, Salford, Edward was living with Richard and Hannah Parr his Aunt and Uncle. Edward is buried at St Helen's, Witton, Northwich, Cheshire.
Sp. **Elizabeth Ann Priscilla SELDON (1894-1975) [529]**, dau. of John Seldon and Sarah Hannah Mc Guinness. Known as Daisy. Elizabeth buried St Helen's, Witton, Northwich, Cheshire.
5. **Sarah CLOUGH (-) [530].** Born Prestwich, Lancashire. Sarah Marr Joseph E SIMPKIN, 1950, Northwich, Cheshire.
Sp. **Joseph E SIMPKIN (-) [531].**

4. **Hannah Marie CLOUGH (1901-) [101].** Born 1901. Dau of Edward Clough and Sarah Ellen Cordwell. Hannah Marie Marr John Henry BUCKLEY, 10 Aug 1925, St John's, Chester. Hannah Marr secondly Arthur JONES.
Sp. **John Henry BUCKLEY (1901-) [504]**, son of John Henry Buckley.
Sp. **Arthur JONES (-) [533].**

4. **Joseph CLOUGH (-) [104].** Son of Edward Clough and Sarah Ellen Cordwell.
4. **Sarah Ellen CLOUGH (1904-) [107].** Born 1904, West Derby, Lancashire. Dau of Edward Clough and Sarah Ellen Cordwell.
4. **George CLOUGH (1901-) [109].** Born 1901, West Derby, Liverpool. Son of Edward Clough and Sarah Ellen Cordwell.

Sp. (unknown).
     5. **Nelly CLOUGH (-) [121].**Affectionately known as little Nelly Clough.

4. **Mary Ann CLOUGH (1889-) [110].** Born 1889, baptised 1890, St Nicholas, Liverpool. Dau of
    Edward Clough and Sarah Ellen Cordwell. In the 1891 English Census, 42 Belfort Street,
    Regent Road, Salford, Mary Ann was living with Richard and Hannah Parr. Aunt and Uncle.
4. **George CLOUGH (1893-1893) [115].** Born 1893, St Anthony's, Liverpool. Son of Edward
    Clough and Sarah Ellen Cordwell. George died 1893, West Derby, Liverpool.
4. **Daisy CLOUGH (1904-) [119].** Born 1904. Dau of Edward Clough and Sarah Ellen Cordwell.
4. **Alice CLOUGH (-) [523].** Died age 21 years. Dau of Edward Clough and Sarah Ellen
    Cordwell.
4. **William Durham CLOUGH (1895-1960) [759].** Born 1895, Dunham, Altringham, Cheshire.
    Registered in Trafford. Son of Edward Clough and Sarah Ellen Cordwell. In 1901 English
    Census, 41 Granville Street South, Salford, William, age 5, living with Richard and Hannah
    Parr, Aunt and Uncle. William died Jan 1960, buried All Saints, Golborne, Wigan, with his
    father Edward Clough.

Betsy Dixon, Nelly Manders, Sammy Clough, Daisy Clouch, Willie Clough circa 1912

Chapter Ten

THE CORDWELL FAMILY

Cordwell Family Outline

John CORDWELL (circa 1789-)

---

1. John CORDWELL (circa 1789-) [512].
Sp. Alicia KELLY (1799-) [542].
   2. James CORDWELL (1828-1829) [545].
   2. Catherine CORDWELL (1817-) [1681].
   2. Emily CORDWELL (1819-) [543].
      3. John CORDWELL (1841-) [1868].
   2. John CORDWELL (1821-) [510].
   Sp. Anne RIGBY (1825-) [511], dau. of James RIGBY (1787-1840) [513] and Ann (1796-) [648].
      3. William CORDWELL (1846-) [405].
      Sp. Sarah Ann (1850-) [589].
         4. John CORDWELL (1868-) [590].
         4. Sarah Ellen CORDWELL (1878-) [930].

At this point there are two John Cordwells - Summarised as

      3. John CORDWELL (1841-) [1868].
      3. John CORDWELL (1847-) [1933].

      Sp. Elizabeth Ann HUGHES (1847-1882) [66]. Dau. of John HUGHES (1819-) [249] and Elizabeth
          TAYLOR (1819-) [558].
SEE HUGHES AND TAYLOR FAMILY
         4. Sarah Ellen CORDWELL (1866-1933) [64].
         Sp. Edward CLOUGH (1861-1937) [63], son of Samuel CLOUGH (1826-1883) [122] and Margaret
           Ann MURPHY (1828-) [123].
SEE THE CLOUGH FAMILY
         4. Johnny Richard CORDWELL (1870-1943) [67].
         Sp. Sarah Ann DORAN (1869-1945) [68], dau. of Thomas DORAN (-) [1716].
            5. Annie CORDWELL (1899-1951) [550].
            Sp. Albert WRIGHT (-) [1903].
               6. Walter WRIGHT (1923-) [1904].
               6. Albert WRIGHT (1931-) [1905].
            5. Thomas CORDWELL (1895-1969) [588].
            Sp. Sarah NEWTON (1893-1983) [551].
               6. John CORDWELL (1919-1919) [552].
               6. Aida CORDWELL (1928-) [553].
               Sp. Albert MULHEARN (1922-1992) [940], son of Joseph MULHEARN (1879-) [1862] and
                 Sarah Ann ROWLEY (1880-) [1863
               6. Thomas E CORDWELL (1921-1992) [910].
               Sp. Nora ROGERS (1902-) [911].
               Sp. Daisy WHYATT (1920-1983) [913].
               Sp. Linda HUBBLE (1945-) [914].
            5. Margarita CORDWELL (1897-) [967].
         4. George C CORDWELL (1872-1920) [73].
         Sp. Harriet COLEMAN (-) [74].
         4. William Henry CORDWELL (1874-1919) [71].
         Sp. Elizabeth SUTHERLAND (1872-1910) [400].
            5. William CORDWELL (1897-1916) [395].
            5. Lilly CORDWELL (1900-) [396].
            Sp. Jack YATES (-) [780].
               6. Jack YATES (1922-) [1879].

6. John YATES (1924-) [1880].
Sp. Agnes May HAGGERTY (1902-) [752], dau. of William HAGGERTY (1854-) [785] and Mary
        STEPHENS (1864-1932) [784].
    5. William CORDWELL (1922-1936) [781].
    5. Annie CORDWELL (1920-1990) [782].
    Sp. Sydney PEPPERMAN (1921-1977) [783].
  4. Elizabeth CORDWELL (1860-) [1883].
  Sp. Joseph FLETCHER (-) [1884].
Sp. Rosina STOKES /ROBINSON (1862-1926) [79].
  4. Leonard CORDWELL (1892-1945) [80].
  Sp. Phyllis MELIA (1889-1956) [565], dau. of Thomas MELIA (-) [1870] and Phyliss
        BUTTERWORTH (1864-1915) [1871].
    5. Marie CORDWELL (1920-) [566].
    5. James CORDWELL (1922-1982) [567].
    Sp. Violet BRATBY (1922-1982) [957], dau. of Richard BATBY (1890-) [1872] and Caroline
        FOSSETT (1890-) [1873].
  4. Rosie CORDWELL (1902-1984) [81].
  Sp. Herbert GUYATT (1900-1968) [554].
    5. Herbert GUYATT (1926-1996) [555].
    5. Leonard GUYATT (1928-) [556].
    5. Lucy GUYATT (1930-) [557].
    5. Frederick J GUYATT (1935-) [994].
  4. Aida CORDWELL (1893-1946) [82]..
  Sp. Joseph FLETCHER (1893-) [1885].
    5. Joseph FLETCHER (1921-1922) [1886].
    5. Nellie FLETCHER (1922-1994) [1887].
    5. Rosina FLETCHER (1923-2005) [1888].
    5. Fanny FLETCHER (1924-) [1889].
    5. Lydia FLETCHER (1927-1975) [1890].
    5. Joseph FLETCHER (1928-) [1891].
    5. James FLETCHER (1930-1995) [1892].
    5. Lily FLETCHER (1932-) [1893].
  4. James CORDWELL (1889-1971) [406].
  Sp. Aida INGAM (-) [407].
    5. Leonard CORDWELL (1922-1982) [942].
    5. Peter CORDWELL (-) [943].
  4. Daisy CORDWELL (1899-) [408].
  4. Martha CORDWELL (1890-1891) [410].
  4. Hannah CORDWELL (-) [411].
  4. Lawrence CORDWELL (-) [904].
  4. Marie CORDWELL (1896-1977) [75].
  Sp. Pat TYNAN (1889-1970) [76].
    5. John TYNAN (1920-) [563].
    5. Nellie TYNAN (1927-) [564].
    5. Nora TYNAN (1924-2005) [995].
    5. Clara TYNAN (1924-) [996].
  4. Elizabeth Ann CORDWELL (1887-) [1720].

Cordwell Lineage

Margaret Ellen CLOUGH
Born: 17 Mar 1886 in Manchester
Spouse: Gilbert DIXON

Nelly (Ellen) CLOUGH
Born: 1903
Spouse: Jimmy MANDERS

Polly (Margaret) CLOUGH

Elizabeth Anne CLOUGH
Born: 1886 in Salford
Spouse: Joseph MARTIN

Anne CLOUGH

Samuel CLOUGH
Born: 1896
Spouse: Nelly (Ellen) CONNELL

Henry CLOUGH

John CORDWELL
Born: 1868 in Salford, Lancashire

Edward CLOUGH
Born: 1894 in Liverpool
Spouse: Elizabeth Ann Prisilla SELDON

Sarah Ellen CORDWELL
Born: 1878 in Salford

Hannah Marie CLOUGH
Born: 1901
Spouse: John Henry BUCKLEY

William CORDWELL
Born: 1846 in Macclesfield
Spouse: Sarah Ann

Hannah Marie CLOUGH (2)
Spouse: Arthur JONES

John CORDWELL
Born: 1847 in Macclesfied, Cheshire

Sarah Ellen CORDWELL
Born: 17 Mar 1866 in Manchester
Spouse: Edward CLOUGH

Joseph CLOUGH

Sarah Ellen CLOUGH
Born: 1904 in West Derby, Lancashire

John Samuel CLOUGH
Born: 1898 in Hanley, Staffordshire

George CLOUGH
Born: 1901 in West Derby, Liverpool

John CORDWELL
Born: 14 Oct 1821 in St Peter's, Chester
Spouse: Anne RIGBY

Mary Ann CLOUGH
Born: 1889 in St Nicholas, Liverpool.
Spouse: Male

George CLOUGH
Born: 1893 in St Anthony's, Liverpool

Daisey CLOUGH
Born: 1904

Alice CLOUGH

William Durham CLOUGH
Born: 1895 in Altringham, Cheshire

John CORDWELL
Born: 1847 in Macclesfield, Cheshire
Spouse: Elizabeth Ann HUGHES

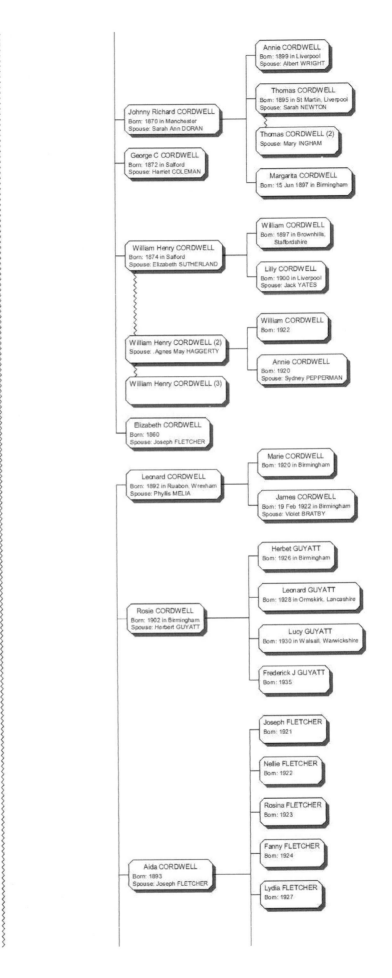

John CORDWELL
Born: 1789 (app)
Spouse: Alicia KELLY

Johnny Richard CORDWELL
Born: 1870 in Manchester
Spouse: Sarah Ann DORAN

George C CORDWELL
Born: 1872 in Salford
Spouse: Harriet COLEMAN

Annie CORDWELL
Born: 1899 in Liverpool
Spouse: Albert WRIGHT

Thomas CORDWELL
Born: 1895 in St Martin, Liverpool
Spouse: Sarah NEWTON

Thomas CORDWELL (2)
Spouse: Mary INGHAM

Margarita CORDWELL
Born: 15 Jun 1897 in Birmingham

William Henry CORDWELL
Born: 1874 in Salford
Spouse: Elizabeth SUTHERLAND

William CORDWELL
Born: 1897 in Brownhills, Staffordshire

Lilly CORDWELL
Born: 1900 in Liverpool
Spouse: Jack YATES

William Henry CORDWELL (2)
Spouse: .Agnes May HAGGERTY

William CORDWELL
Born: 1922

Annie CORDWELL
Born: 1920
Spouse: Sydney PEPPERMAN

William Henry CORDWELL (3)

Elizabeth CORDWELL
Born: 1860
Spouse: Joseph FLETCHER

Leonard CORDWELL
Born: 1892 in Ruabon, Wrexham
Spouse: Phyllis MELIA

Marie CORDWELL
Born: 1920 in Birmingham

James CORDWELL
Born: 19 Feb 1922 in Birmingham
Spouse: Violet BRATBY

Rosie CORDWELL
Born: 1902 in Birmingham
Spouse: Herbert GUYATT

Herbet GUYATT
Born: 1926 in Birmingham

Leonard GUYATT
Born: 1928 in Ormskirk, Lancashire

Lucy GUYATT
Born: 1930 in Walsall, Warwickshire

Frederick J GUYATT
Born: 1935

Aida CORDWELL
Born: 1893
Spouse: Joseph FLETCHER

Joseph FLETCHER
Born: 1921

Nellie FLETCHER
Born: 1922

Rosina FLETCHER
Born: 1923

Fanny FLETCHER
Born: 1924

Lydia FLETCHER
Born: 1927

John CORDWELL (2)
Spouse: Rosina ROBINSON

John CORDWELL (3)

Emily CORDWELL
Born: 22 Aug 1819 in St. John The
Baptist, Chester
Spouse: Thomas BULLOCK

John CORDWELL
Born: 5 Nov 1841 in Macclesfied,
Cheshire

James CORDWELL
Born: 30 Jan 1828 in St Werburgh's,
Chester

Catherine CORDWELL
Born: 7 Feb 1817 in St. Mary's,
Chester

William CORDWELL
Born: 17 Jul 1827

Joseph FLETCHER
Born: 1928

James FLETCHER
Born: 1930

Lily FLETCHER
Born: 1932

James CORDWELL
Born: 28 Oct 1889
Spouse: Aida INGAM

Leonard CORDWELL
Born: 1922 in Bromsgrove

Peter CORDWELL

Daisey CORDWELL
Born: 1899
Spouse: John HART

Martha CORDWELL
Born: 1890

Hannah CORDWELL

Lawrence CORDWELL

Marie CORDWELL
Born: 1896 in Fazley, Staffordshire
Spouse: Pat TYNAN

John TYNAN
Born: 1920 in Wrexham

Nellie TYNAN
Born: 1927 in West Bromwich

Nora TYNAN
Born: 1924

Clara TYNAN
Born: 1924

Lydia CORDWELL
Born: 1865
Spouse: Horatio MANDERS

Lydia CORDWELL (2)
Spouse: Male TETLOW

Elizabeth Ann CORDWELL
Born: 1887

129

John CORDWELL (circa 1789-)

1. John CORDWELL (circa 1789-) [512]. Born circa 1789, Chester, Cheshire.

Unfortunately, John's birth or marriage details have not been identified. However, they are recorded as being in Macclesfield and Manchester in the following census.

1841 English Census, Water Street, Macclesfield West, Prestbury.
John CORDWELL, head, age 52, born 1789, Cheshire, Shoemaker, Alicia CORDWELL, wife, age 42, born 1798, Ireland, Emily CORDWELL, dau, age 20, born 1820, Macclesfield, John CORDWELL, son, age 19, Shoemaker, born 1821, Cheshire.

1851 English Census, 21 Brierley Street, Manchester
John CORDEWELL, Lodger, married, age 60, born 1791, Shropshire, Shoemaker, Ann CORDEWELL, wife, age 56, born 1795, Dublin, Ireland, John CORDEWELL, son age 9, born 1841, Macclesfield. (John born in 1841, is actually their grandson).

No references have been found for John or Alicia in the 1861 Census.
Sp. Alicia KELLY (1799-) [542]. Born 1799, Dublin, Ireland.

> **2. James CORDWELL (1828-1829) [545].** Born 30 Jan 1828, baptised 3 Feb 1828 St. Werburgh's, Chester. Son of John Cordwell and Alicia, Eastgate Street, Chester. Godparents Margaret and John Pearl. There are two death references for a James Cordwell. It is likely the reference for St. Werburgh's applies - James Cordwell died 1884, St. Werburgh's, Chester and James Cordwell died 17 April 1829, Holy Trinity, Chester, Cheshire.
>
> **2. Catherine CORDWELL (1817-) [1681].** Baptised 7 Feb 1817, St. Mary's, Chester. Parents John Cordwell and Elicia. John was noted as a Silk Throster of Duke Street, Chester.
>
> **2. Emily CORDWELL (1819-) [543].** Baptised 22 Aug 1819, St. John the Baptist, Chester. Dau of John Cordwell and Alice. John recorded as a Shoemaker of Eastgate Street, Chester. In the 1841 English Census, Water Street, Macclesfield West, Prestbury, Emily was living with her parents and age 20.
>
>> Emily had a son called John Cordwell born 5 Nov 1841, Water Street, Macclesfield. John's father was named as Thomas Bullock, Farmer. Emily and Thomas were not married and John's surname remained as Cordwell. There is no trace of Emily after 1841, and as her son was living with her parents in 1851, it is assumed Emily died in childbirth.
>>
>>> **3. John CORDWELL (1841-) [1868].** Born 5 Nov 1841, Water Street, Macclesfied. Son of Emily Cordwell and Thomas Bullock. In the 1851 English Census, 21 Brierley Street, Manchester, John was living with his grandparents.
>
> **2. John CORDWELL (1821-) [510].** Baptised 14 Oct 1821, St Peter's, Chester. Father, John Cordwell, Cordwainer, mother Alice. Principal residence St Oswald's, Chester. A second record states baptised 14 Oct 1821, St. Peter's, abode St. Peter's Churchyard. Parents John Cordwell, Cordwinder and Alice. In the 1841 English Census, Water Street, Macclesfield West, Prestbury, John was living with his parents.

It has been assumed that St. Peter's Churchyard in 1821, was a place where tradesmen resided and worked and not a churchyard for burials.

John Marr Anne RIGBY, 21 Apr 1845, St. Michael's, Macclesfield, Cheshire.

Marriage Certificate
Parish of Prestbury, Macclesfield, Parochial Chapel, John Cordwell married Anne Rigby 21 Apr 1845, St. Michael's, Macclesfield, both of full age. Residence, Macclesfield. John, Shoe/Clog Maker, John's father, John Cordwell, Cordwainer. Ann's father, James Rigby, Silk Weaver. John and Ann both made an X as their marks. Witnesses Joseph Gee and Elizabeth Gee.
> **Sp. Anne RIGBY (1825-) [511],** dau. of James RIGBY (1787-1840) [513] and Ann (1796-) [648].

The following English Census refer to Anne Rigby's family

1841 English Census, Exchange Street, Macclesfield
Ann RIGBY, age 45, born 1796, Ireland, Ellen RIGBY, age 20, born 1821, Macclesfield, Esther RIGBY, age 15, born 1826, Macclesfield, Jane RIGBY, age 13, born 1828, Macclesfield, James RIGBY, age 10, born 1831, Macclesfield.

1851 English Census, Cotton Street, Macclesfield, Cheshire.
Ann RIGBY, age 59, born 1792, Dublin, Ireland, Silk Winder, Ellen RIGBY, age 32, born 1819, Macclesfield, Catherine RIGBY, age 29, born 1822, Macclesfield, James RIGBY, age 23, born 1828, Macclesfield.

1861 English Census, 26 Cotton Street, Macclesfield
Ann RIGBY, age 72, born 1789, formally Silk Piecer.

John and Anne moved from Macclesfield to Manchester sometime after 1847, when their son John was born as in the following Census details

1851 English Census, 22 Bedford Street, Chorlton Hulme, Manchester
John CORDWELL, head, age 29, Shoemaker, born 1821, Chester, Anne CORDWELL, wife, age 25, born 1825, Macclesfield, Cheshire, William CORDWELL son, age 5, born 1846, Macclesfield, Cheshire, John CORDWELL, son, age 3, born 1847, Macclesfield.

No records were found for John Cordwell and Anne Cordwell in the 1861, 1871, or 1881 Census.

> **3. William CORDWELL (1846-) [405].** Born 1846, Macclesfield. Son of John Cordwell and Anne Rigby. In the 1851 English Census, 22 Bedford Street, Chorlton Hulme, Manchester, William is living with his parents. William Marr Sarah Ann.
> **Sp. Sarah Ann (1850-) [589].**

William and Sarah Ann have not been identified in the 1861 Census, however, they do appear in the following census

1871 English Census, Back of Quay Street, Cellar under Deansgate no 12, Manchester
William CORDWELL, head, age 35, born 1836, Macclesfield, Hawker, Sarah Ann CORDWELL, wife, age 21, born 1850, Lancashire, John CORDWELL, age 3, born 1868 Lancashire.

1881 English Census, 67 New Bury Street, Salford, Lancashire
William CORDWELL, head, married, age 34, born 1847, Lamp Oil Dealer (Oil Mills), born Macclesfield, Sarah Ann CORDWELL, wife, age 31, born 1850, born Manchester, John CORDWELL, son, age 14, born 1867, Macclesfield, Sarah Ellen CORDWELL, dau, age 3, born 1878, Salford.

> > **4. John CORDWELL (1868-) [590].** Born 1868, Salford, Lancashire. Son of William Cordwell and Sarah Ann.
> > **4. Sarah Ellen CORDWELL (1878-) [930].** Born 1878, Salford. Dau of William Cordwell and Sarah Ann.

> **3. John CORDWELL (1847-1916) [1933].** Born 1847, Macclesfield, son of John Cordwell and Anne Rigby. In the 1851 English Census, 22 Bedford Street, Chorlton Hulme, Manchester, John was living with his parents.

*Also born in Macclesfield was a **John CARDWELL (1847-) [1930]**, son of Frances SWANWICK. Later to become John Cardwell Swanwick. John Cardwell Swanwick died 1857, Macclesfield. His brother was also to become known as Henry Cardwell Swanwick.*

John Swanwick married Frances Sutcliffe, 1842, Manchester Cathedral. Father, Thomas Swanwick, Draper.

1851 English Census, Westside, Market Place, Macclesfield
John SWANWICK, head, age 35, born 1816, Macclesfield, Draper, Frances SWANWICK, wife, age 32, born 1819, Manchester, Draper's wife, John CARDWELL, step son, age 3, born 1848, Macclesfield, Henry CARDWELL, step son, age 1, born 1850, Macclesfield.

1861 English Census, 9 Market Place, Macclesfield
John SWANWICK, head, age 44, born 1817, Macclesfield, Woollen Draper, Frances SWANWICK, wife, age 42, born 1819, Manchester, Woollen Draper's wife, Louise CARDWELL SWANWICK, age 5, dau, born 1856, Macclesfield, Eliza RIGBY, unmarr, Cook, age 41, born 1820, Warford, Cheshire

This Swanwick family cannot be found in the 1871 English Census.

At this point there are two
John Cordwell's appearing in two separate 1851 Census records, all born in Macclesfield .

Summarised as

> 3. **John CORDWELL (1841-) [1868].** Born 5 Nov 1841, Water Street, Macclesfield, Son of Emily Cordwell and Thomas Bullock.

1851 English Census, 21 Brierley Street, Manchester
John CORDEWELL, Lodger, married, age 60, born 1791, Shropshire, Shoemaker, Ann CORDEWELL, wife, age 56, born 1795, Dublin, Ireland, **John CORDEWELL, son age 9, born 1841, Macclesfield.**

> 3. **John CORDWELL (1847-) [1933].** Born 1847, Macclesfield. Son of John Cordwell and Anne Rigby.

1851 English Census, 22 Bedford Street, Chorlton Hulme, Manchester
John CORDWELL, head, age 29, Shoemaker, born 1821, Chester, Anne CORDWELL, wife, age 25, born 1825, Macclesfield, Cheshire, William CORDWELL son, age 5, born 1846, Macclesfield, Cheshire, **John CORDWELL, son, age 3, born 1847, Macclesfield, Cheshire**.

The John Cordwell who married Elizabeth Ann Hughes, noted his father as John Cordwell, Shoemaker. Although, there is some uncertainty of his direct lineage, as stated above, the following details will now reference John as **John CORDWELL (1841-1847-1916) [65].** Born Macclesfield.

> 3. **John CORDWELL (1841-1847-1916) [65].** Born Macclesfield.

John Cordwell circa 1880.

John Marr firstly Elizabeth Ann HUGHES, 2 Aug 1864, The Cathedral Parish Church Manchester.

Marriage certificate
Marriage solemnized at the Catholic Parish Church in the Parish of Manchester in the County of Lancaster, 2 Aug 1864, John Cordwell, age 20, bachelor, Shoemaker of 23 Medlock Street, father's name John Cordwell, Shoemaker, married Elizabeth Ann Hughes, age 18, spinster of 23 Medlock Street, father's name John Hughes, Labourer. Witnesses George Taylor and Hannah C Parr, made an X as their marks. John Cordwell and Elizabeth Ann Hughes also made an X as their marks. H N Westmore Chaplain.

1871 English Census, 43 Hope Street, Christchurch, Salford
John CAULDWELL, age 26, b1844, Licensed Hawker, born Macclesfield, Eliz (abeth) Ann CAULDWELL, wife, age 25, born Manchester, Sarah Ellen CAULDWELL, dau, age 5, born Manchester, John (ny R) CAULDWELL, son, age 1, born Manchester.

1881 English Census, 59 Bigland Street, Salford, Lancashire
John CORDWELL, head, Hawker, married, age 39, born 1841, Macclesfield, Elizabeth Ann CORDWELL, wife, married, age 34, born Manchester, Sarah Ellen CORDWELL, dau, age 15, born Manchester, John (ny) R CORDWELL, son, scholar, age 11, born Manchester, George C CORDWELL, son, scholar, age 9, born 1871 Salford, Lancashire.

John Cordwell and family circa 1910

During John's career he has been recorded as a Clog Maker, Commercial Traveller, Horse Dealer in South Wales and a Travelling Showman. John had a travelling cinema and one of his first films was of Queen Victoria's funeral.

> **Sp. Elizabeth Ann HUGHES (1847-1882) [66].** Born 1847, Preston, Lancashire. Baptised 24 Dec 1847, St. Matthews, Preston. This church amalgamated with St John's and later with St Anne's. Dau of John HUGHES (1819-) [249] and Elizabeth TAYLOR (1819-) [558]. Elizabeth died Dec 1882, age 37, Salford. Death registered at Chorlton Medlock, Lancashire.

SEE HUGHES AND TAYLOR FAMILY

> **4. Sarah Ellen CORDWELL (1866-1933) [64].** Born 17 Mar 1866, 12 Back Quay Street, Manchester. Dau of John Cordwell and Elizabeth Ann Hughes.

Sarah Ellen Cordwell 1866-1933

Birth certificate
Registration District Manchester, born 1866 in the Sub District of Deansgate, Manchester in the County of Lancaster, 17 March 1866 at 12 Back Quay Street, Sarah Ellen, girl, father, John Caldwell, mother, Elizabeth Caldwell formerly Hughes, father Clog Maker, signature, description and residence of informant, X the mark of Elizabeth Caldwell, mother, 12 Back Quay Street, Manchester, registered 20 April 1866. John Leigh was the Registrar.

In the 1871 English Census, 43 Hope Street, Christchurch, Salford and in the 1881 English Census, 59 Bigland Street, Salford, Sarah Ellen was living with her parents.

Sarah Ellen Cordwell Marr Edward CLOUGH, 1883, Mount Carmel Church, Oldfield Road, Salford.

Marriage certificate

Solemnized at Mount Carmel Church, Oldfield Road, Salford in the Sub District of Salford in the County of Lancaster, 28 Nov 1883, Edward Clough, 21 years, bachelor, Dyer of 422 Bigland Street Salford, father, Samuel Clough (deceased), Iron Plate Worker, married Sarah Ellen Cordwell, age18, spinster, of 44 Wooden Street, Salford, father, John Cordwell, Commercial Traveller. According to the Rites and Ceremonies of the Catholic Church by certificate by me, John Lane C Priest, G Yorstone registrar. Edward Clough made an X as his mark and Sarah Ellen Cordwell signed her name. Witnesses William Cordwell (signed his name) and Margaret Ann Clough made an X as her mark. It is thought that Margaret Ann Clough, along with one of her sisters, became Carmelite Nuns in this Parish.

Edward Clough and Sarah Ellen Cordwell had 22 children, although not all survived, many were twins. By 1911, 12 children had died.

> **Sp. Edward CLOUGH (1861-1937) [63],** son of Samuel CLOUGH (1826-1883) [122] and Margaret Ann MURPHY (1828-) [123].

SEE THE CLOUGH FAMILY

> **4. Johnny Richard CORDWELL (1870-1943) [67].** Born 1870, Manchester. Son of John Cordwell and Elizabeth Ann Hughes. Johnny Richard was a Swing Boat proprietor. Johnny Richard died in 1943, buried St Helen's, Witton, Northwich. In the 1871 English Census, 43 Hope Street, Christchurch, Salford and in the 1881 English Census, 59 Bigland Street, Salford, Johnny Richard was living with his parents.

1891 English Census, 35 Caravan, Beast Market, Wrexham Regis, Wrexham
John CORDWELL, single, age 21, born 1870, Manchester, Travelling Bagaar Hawk, William CORDWELL, brother, single, age 16, born 1875, Manchester, Travelling Bagaar Hawk, George CORDWELL, brother, single, age 18, born 1873, Manchester, Travelling Bagaar Hawk, Samuel MERCER, Boarder, single, age 22, born 1869, Manchester, Travelling Bagaar Hawk (Their occupation should probably read Travelling Bazzar Hawker)

Johnny Marr Sarah Ann DORAN ,Mar 1894, Chorlton Medlock, Manchester.

> **Sp. Sarah Ann DORAN (1869-1945) [68],** dau. of Thomas DORAN (-) [1716].

>> **5. Annie CORDWELL (1899-1951) [550].** Born 1899, Liverpool. Dau of Johnny Cordwell and Sarah Ann Doran. Annie Marr Albert WRIGHT. Annie died 1951.
>> **Sp. Albert WRIGHT (-) [1903].**
>>> **6. Walter WRIGHT (1923-) [1904].** Born 1923.
>>> **6. Albert WRIGHT (1931-) [1905].** Born 1931.

>> **5. Thomas CORDWELL (1895-1969) [588].** Born 1895, St. Martin, Liverpool, son of Johnny Cordwell and Sarah Ann Doran. Thomas Marr Sarah NEWTON, Mar 1919, St Mathew, Liverpool. Thomas died 1969, Hyde. There is a possibility that this is the Thomas who also married Mary INGHAM.
>> **Sp. Sarah NEWTON (1893-1983) [551].**
>>> **6. John CORDWELL (1919-1919) [552].** Born 1919. Died 1919, Birkenhead, Wirral.
>>> **6. Aida CORDWELL (1928-) [553].** Born 1928, Birmingham, Warwickshire. Aida Marr Albert MULLHEARN.
>>> **Sp. Albert MULHEARN (1922-1992) [940],** son of Joseph Mulhearn and Sarah Ann Rowley. The following English Census records Albert's family.

1911 English Census, West Derby Road, Liverpool. Joseph MULHEARN, age 31, Rotherham, Yorkshire, Showman, Sarah Ann ROWLEY, wife, age 30, born Hanley, Staffs, married 4 years (1907), Patrick James MULHEARN, born 1911, Albert MULHEARN, born 1922..

>>> **6. Thomas E CORDWELL (1921-1992) [910].** Born 1821, Liverpool. Thomas died in 1992. Thomas Marr Nora ROGERS, 1951, Stoke on Trent, Staffordshire, Thomas Marr secondly Daisy WHYATT 1968, Blackpool, Lancashire, Thomas Marr thirdly Linda HUBBLE,1979, Tameside. Linda's maiden name may have been Mercer.

Sp. Nora ROGERS (1902-) [911].
Sp. Daisy WHYATT (1920-1983) [913].
Sp. Linda HUBBLE (1945-) [914]. Her maiden name was possibly Mercer

5. **Margarita CORDWELL (1897-) [967].** Born 15 Jun 1897, Birmingham, Warwickshire. Dau of Johnny Cordwell and Sarah Ann Doran.

4. **George C CORDWELL (1872-1920) [73].** Born 1872, Salford. Son of John Cordwell and Elizabeth Ann HUGHES. George may have been a twin. George died 7 Jul 1920, age 43, Wolverhampton. In the 1881 English Census, George was living with his parents at 59 Bigland Street, Salford, Lancashire and in the 1891 English Census, 35 Caravan, Beast Market, Wrexham Regis, Wrexham, George was living with his brothers.

1901 English Census Harpurey Ward, Living in Travelling Caravans, Queens Road Fairground, Manchester. George CORDWELL, age 28, single, Travelling Showman, born Salford, Davies STOCKTON, servant, single, age 22, Showmen's Assistant, born Failsworth, Joseph MARTIN, servant, single, age 19, Showmen's Assistant, born Manchester.

George Marr Harriet COLEMAN, 1903, Liverpool.

Sp. **Harriet COLEMAN (-) [74].**

1911 English Census, Queen Street, Warrington, Cheshire (Caravan on Fairground)
George CORDWELL, age 39, born 1872, Salford, Fair Stall Owner, Harriett CORDWELL, age 30, born 1881, Manchester, married 8 years.

4. **William Henry CORDWELL (1874-1919) [71].** Born 1874, Salford, son of John Cordwell and Elizabeth Ann HUGHES. William was a twin. William died 13 Oct 1919. William was a witness at the wedding of his sister Sarah Ellen to Edward Clough in 1883. William Marr Elizabeth SUTHERLAND, Sacred Trinity Church, Salford. William Marr secondly Agnes May HAGGERTY, 1918.

In the 1881 English Census, 47 West Craven Street, Regent Road, Salford, William Henry was living with Richard and Hannah Parr, Uncle and Aunt.

1891 English Census, 35 Caravan, Beast Market, Wrexham Regis, Wrexham
John CORDWELL, single, age 21, born 1870, Manchester, Travelling Bagaar Hawk, William CORDWELL, brother, single, age 16, born 1875, Manchester, Travelling Bagaar Hawk, George CORDWELL, brother, single, age 18, born 1873, Manchester, Travelling Bagaar Hawk, Samuel MERCER, Boarder, single, age 22, born 1869, Manchester, Travelling Bagaar Hawk. (Their occupation should probably read Travelling Bazzar Hawker)

Sp. **Elizabeth SUTHERLAND (1872-1910) [400].**

1901 English Census (Harpurey Ward) (Living in Travelling Caravans) Queens Road Fairground.
William CORDWELL, age 27, Travelling Showman, born Salford, Elizabeth CORDWELL, wife, age 28, born Brigg, Lincolnshire, William CORDWELL, son, age 4, born Brownhills, Staffordshire, Lily CORDWELL, dau, age 1, born Liverpool, Lily PRICE, visitor, single, age 19, born Liverpool.

5. **William CORDWELL (1897-1916) [395].** Born 1897, Brownhills, Staffordshire. Son of William Cordwell and Elizabeth Sutherland. William died 1916, in WWI.
5. **Lilly CORDWELL (1900-) [396].** Born 1900, Liverpool. Dau of William Cordwell and Elizabeth Sutherland. Lilly Marr Jack YATES.
Sp. **Jack YATES (-) [780].**
6. **Jack YATES (1922-) [1879].** Born 1922.
6. **John YATES (1924-) [1880].** Born 1924.

Sp. **Agnes May HAGGERTY (1902-) [752],** dau. of William HAGGERTY (1854-) [785] and Mary STEPHENS (1864-1932) [784].
5. **William CORDWELL (1922-1936) [781].** Born 1922. Son of William Cordwell and Agnes May Haggerty. William died 1936, age14 while on a paper round.

5. Annie CORDWELL (1920-1990) [782]. Born 1920. Dau of William Cordwell and Agnes May Haggerty. Annie Marr Sydney PEPPERMAN. Annie died 1990

Sp. Sydney PEPPERMAN (1921-1977) [783].

4. Elizabeth CORDWELL (1860-) [1883]. Born 1860, dau of John Cordwell and Elizabeth Ann Hughes. Elizabeth Marr Joseph FLETCHER.

Sp. Joseph FLETCHER (-) [1884].

After the death of Elizabeth Ann Hughes in 1882, **John CORDWELL (1841-1847-1916) [65]** John Cordwell, spelt Cardwell, Marr Rosina ROBINSON in 1886, Ashton Under Lyne. Witnesses John Aurthur and Elizabeth Rowe.

However, Rosina Robinson was actually born Rosina Stokes. It is not known why all Rosina's family appear to have changed their names to Robinson.

Sp. Rosina STOKES (1862-1926) [79]. Born 8 Feb 1862, 1 Well Street, Stepney, Parish of St. George, in the East, London. Baptised 8 Apr 1862, Cannon St. Road. Dau of James STOKES (1828-) [927] and Ann (1833-) [928].

1861 English Census, 1 Well Street, Wapping, London, Middlesex
James STOKES, head, married, age 36, born 1828, (place not stated), Photographer Technician, Ann STOKES, wife, age 26, born 1825, England, Maria STOKES, dau, age 6, born 1855, Pickwell, Middlesex, James STOKES, son, age 5, born 1856, Gainsborough, Sussex, Eliza STOKES, dau, age 3, born 1858, Mile End, Middlesex, Mary BIDELL, sister, unmarried, age 16, born 1845, Mile End, Middlesex

The following are two different interpretations of the 1891 English Census

1891 English Census, Caravan at Beast Market, Wrexham, North Wales.
John CORDWELL, Senior, head, married, age 45, born 1845, Macclesfield, Showman, Rosina CORDWELL, Senior, wife, age 29, born Middlesex, London, Assistant to the place, (Mary) Marie CORDWELL, Senior, dau, single, age 4, born, Fazley, Staffordshire.

1891 English Census 35 Caravan, Beast Market, Wrexham Regis, Wrexham
John CORDWELL, married, age 45, born 1845, Macclesfield, Travelling Showman, Rosamond CORDWELL, wife, age 29, born 1862, London, Middlesex, James CORDWELL, son, age 2, born 1889, Edgefoot, Staffordshire, Martha H CORDWELL, dau, age 10 months, born 1891, Lichfield, Staffordshire.

1901 English Census, Beast Market, Wrexham
John CORDWELL, Senior, married, age 59, born 1841, Macclesfield, Travelling Showman, Rosina CORDWELL, Senior, wife, married, age 39, born London, Assistant to the place. James CORDWELL, son, age 12, Eliza LAWTON, age 18, Servant, Arthur HOLLOWAY, age 24, Servant, Edwin MILES, age 22, Servant

1911 English Census, Beast Market, Wrexham
John CORDWELL, Senior, married, age 69, born 1841, Macclesfield, Showman, Rosina CORDWELL, Senior, wife, married 25 years, (married 1885) age 49, born London, Assistant to the place. Aida CORDWELL, Senior, dau, single, age 18, born Morsley, Staffordshire, Assistant, (Mary) Marie CORDWELL, Senior, dau, single, age 15, born Fazley, Staffordshire, Assistant.

Family folklore records that Rosina was managing The Hall Inn, Charles Street, Wrexham.

4. Leonard CORDWELL (1892-1945) [80]. Born 1892, Ruabon, Wrexham. Son of John Cordwell and Rosina Robinson, although when Leonard died in 1945, the newspapers reported Leonard was the grandson of the late Mr and Mrs Stokes. Leonard Marr Phyllis MELIA, Sep 1919, Wolverhampton

Sp. Phyllis MELIA (1889-1956) [565], dau. of Thomas Melia and Phylis Butterworth who married in 1886, Oldham, Lancashire.

5. Marie CORDWELL (1920-) [566]. Born 1920, Birmingham. Dau of Leonard Cordwell and Phyllis Melia. Marie may have married and moved to Canada.

5. **James CORDWELL (1922-1982) [567].** Born 19 Feb 1922, Birmingham. Son of Leonard Cordwell and Phillis Melia. James Marr Violet BRATBY, 1948, Bromsgrove. James died 1982, Walsall.

Sp. **Violet BRATBY (1922-1982) [957]**, dau. of Richard Batby and Caroline Fsssett born 1890. Violet was known as Sandow from the Sandow Circus. Violet remarried to Marius Freeman, 1966, Spilsby, Lincolnshire. Marius was born 11 Mar 1920, Stockport, to Henry Freeman Biddall, born 1894 and died 1961 and Rose. Violet died 1982, Bromsgrove.

4. **Rosie CORDWELL (1902-1984) [81].** Born 1902, Birmingham. Dau of John Cordwell and Rosina Robinson. Rosie Marr Herbert GUYATT. Rosie died 1984, Birmingham.

Sp. **Herbert GUYATT (1900-1968) [554].**
5. **Herbert GUYATT (1926-1996) [555].** Born 1926, Birmingham. Herbert died 1996.
5. **Leonard GUYATT (1928-) [556].** Born 1928, Ormskirk, Lancashire.
5. **Lucy GUYATT (1930-) [557].** Born 1930, Walsall.
5. **Frederick J GUYATT (1935-) [994].** Born 1935.

4. **Aida CORDWELL (1893-1946) [82].** Born 1893, Twin. Dau of John Cordwell and Rosina Robinson. Aida Marr Joseph FLETCHER. Aida died 1946. Buried Birmingham.

Sp. **Joseph FLETCHER (1893-) [1885].** Family of Shoemakers in Manchester.
5. **Joseph FLETCHER (1921-1922) [1886].** Born 1921. Joseph died 1922.
5. **Nellie FLETCHER (1922-1994) [1887].** Born 1922. Nellie died 1994.
5. **Rosina FLETCHER (1923-2005) [1888].** Born 1923. Rosina died 2005.
5. **Fanny FLETCHER (1924-) [1889].** Born 1924.
5. **Lydia FLETCHER (1927-1975) [1890].** Born 1927. Lydia died 1975.
5. **Joseph FLETCHER (1928-) [1891].** Born 1928.
5. **James FLETCHER (1930-1995) [1892].** Born 1930. James died 1995.
5. **Lily FLETCHER (1932-) [1893].** Born 1932.

4. **James CORDWELL (1889-1971) [406].** Born 28 Oct 1889. Son of John Cordwell and Rosina Robinson. James Marr Aida INGAM. James died 1971, Bromsgrove.

Sp. **Aida INGAM (-) [407].**
5. **Leonard CORDWELL (1922-1982) [942].** Born 1922, Bromsgrove. Leonard died 1982.
5. **Peter CORDWELL (-) [943].**

4. **Daisy CORDWELL (1899-) [408].** Born 1899. Dau of John Cordwell and Rosina Robinson.
4. **Martha CORDWELL (1890-1891) [410].** Born 1890. Dau of John Cordwell and Rosina Robinson. Martha died 1891.
4. **Hannah CORDWELL (-) [411].** Dau of John Cordwell and Rosina Robinson.
4. **Lawrence CORDWELL (-) [904].** Son of John Cordwell and Rosina Robinson.
4. **Marie CORDWELL (1896-1977) [75].** Born 1896, Fazley, Staffordshire. Twin. Dau of John Cordwell and Rosina Robinson. Marie Marr Pat TYNAN 1919, Woolstanton, Stafford. Marie died 1977. Buried Birmingham.

Sp. **Pat TYNAN (1889-1970) [76].**
5. **John TYNAN (1920-) [563].** Born 1920, Wrexham.
5. **Nellie TYNAN (1927-) [564].** Born 1927, West Bromwich., Stafford.
5. **Nora TYNAN (1924-2005) [995].** Born 1924. Nora died 2005.
5. **Clara TYNAN (1924-) [996].** Born 1924.

4. **Elizabeth Ann CORDWELL (1887-) [1720].** Born 1887. Dau of John Cordwell and Rosina Robinson.

In his later years John Cordwell was confined to a wheel chair.

John Cordwell died 18 Feb 1916, age 73 , The Hat Inn, Charles St, Wrexham. Buried 22 Feb 1916, Borough Cemetery, Ruabon Rd, Wrexham.

Death certificate,
Registration District of Wrexham, sub district of Wrexham in the County of Denbigh, 18th February 1916, Caravan, Beast Market, Wrexham, U.D. John Cordwell, male, age 73, Travelling Showman, died of a)

Cardiac Disease, b) Senile Decay, certified by K V Palin M.B. Wife Rose Cordwell, widow of the deceased, present at the death in the caravan, Beast Market, Wrexham, registered 18th February 1916, registrar John E Savage.

The World's Fair newspaper, Saturday February 26th 1916

"Death of John Cordwell. We regret to record the death at Wrexham, Friday, February 18th, of Mr John Cordwell, at the age of 73 years. The internment took place on February 22 at Borough Cemetery, Ruabon Road, Wrexham. The funeral was attended by a large number of relatives and friends. There were eleven coaches and a special carriage laden with floral tributes. The principal mourners present were:- Mrs John Cordwell, Miss Rosie Cordwell (dau), Leonard Cordwell (son), Marie Cordwell (dau), James Cordwell (son), A da Cordwell (dau), James and Nellie Cordwell (son and dau), George and Willie Cordwell (sons), Tom Cordwell (grandson), Daisey Cordwell (grand daughter), Mr W Clough (grandson), Edward Clough (grandson), Mrs George Cordwell (dau in law), Mrs John Cordwell (dau in law), Mr and Mrs Mercer (nephew and niece), Mr Clough (son in law), Mrs Tetlow (sister in law), Mrs Gilbert Dixon (grand daughter). The following ladies and gentlemen also attended:- Mr and Mrs P Collins, Mrs Bettaney, Mrs Thomas, Mrs Deeks, Mr and Mrs Alf Birch, Mr James Foley, Miss Foley, Mrs Gilliand, Miss N Felton, Mr Herbert Felton, Miss Nora Wright, Mrs Rogers, Mr and Mrs G Simons, Mrs Gurney, Mr and Mrs Ingham, Mr and Mrs Wallser, Mr and Mrs Lewis, Mr and Mrs J Simons, Mr and Mrs T Manders, Mr and Mrs Harrison, Mr and Mrs Jake Fletcher, Mrs Maud Dixon, Mrs Parry, Mrs Corbett, Mrs Black, Mr and Mrs S Plinton, Mr and Mrs F Plinston, Miss N Foley, Mr Edgar Humphreys, Mr Alf Birch, Mr Patrick Tynan, Mr J D Humphreys, Mrs Harris, Mr J Fletcher, Mr Sheldon, Mr Robert Lloyd, Mr Fitzpatrick, Mr Capper, Mr Herbert Felton, Mrs Winters, Mr F Picitt, Mr Joe Chadwick. Wreaths and other floral tributes were sent by:- loving wife and family, Edward and Nellie (son in law), George and Harriet (son and dau in law), William (son), Maggie and Gilbert Dixon, Teddy and Willie Clough, Mr and Mrs S Mercer, Mrs Tetlow, Mr and Mrs P Collins, Mr John Collins and family, Mr and Mrs Gillihand and Herbert and Nellie, T P Tyas, Messrs. Wright and family, Willie and Phillis Battaney, Mr and Mrs John Ingham, Mrs Weir and family, Mrs Deeks and family, Miss Clare Mullet, Mr J Chaddick, Mr L and, Mrs Lewis and family, Mr and Mrs G Simons, Mr and Mrs T Manders, Mr and Mrs G Corbett, Miss Hannah Farrell, Mr and Mrs John/James Friesner, Mr William Young, Mr and Mrs Harrison, Mrs Holmes and family, Mr and Mrs Fred Parkin, Mr and Mrs A Parkin, Mr and Mrs Edgar Humphreys, Mr and Mrs Jarvis, Mr and Mrs F Rawlins and T Fitzpatrick, Mr and Mrs Plinston, Mr and Mrs S Plinston, Mrs A Hayes and family, Mr and Mrs Gurney, Mr and Mrs Leach, Mr and Mrs Mascall, Mr and Mrs Alf Birch, Mrs Sewell and family, Mrs Simons, Mr and Mrs Horton, Mr and Mrs J Hall, Mr R Peverelle, Mr and Mrs Winters, Mr John Whyatt, Mrs Maud Dixon, Mr Alf Birch and family, Mr and Mrs James Hearon, Mr F Picitt, Mr and Mrs Wallser, Mr and Mrs Jake Fletcher, Employees of Mr P Collin's No. 1 Scenic Railway, Mr and Mrs Luke Parry, John and Mary Greatorex, John and Alice Simons, Mr and Mrs J Chadwick, Mr W Hobbs and family, Mr and Mrs J D Humphreys, Mr and Mrs Black, Mr and Mrs Copper, Mr and Mrs P Collins jnr, Mr and Mrs Clayton, Mrs Brennan, Messrs C and E Gill, Walter Hobbs and family. Mrs Cordwell and family wish to thank their many friends for the kind sympathy shown to them in their sad bereavement".

Chapter Eleven

THE HUGHES FAMILY

Hughes Family Outline

William HUGHES (1791-)

---

1. William HUGHES (1791-) [1715].
Sp. Mary JONES (1780-) [1786].
    2. John HUGHES (1812-) [2385].
    2. Edward HUGHES (1815-) [1787].
    2. John Cartwright HUGHES (1818-) [2383].
    2. Henry HUGHES (1818-) [2384].
    2. William Benjamin HUGHES (1820-) [1906].
    2. Matilda Harriett HUGHES (1824-) [1907].
    2. Thomas HUGHES (1828-) [1908].
    2. John HUGHES (circa 1819-) [249].
    Sp. Elizabeth TAYLOR (1819-) [558], dau. of Matthew TAYLOR (1784-) [1714] and Mary BENNETT
        (1788-) [1724].
SEE TAYLOR FAMILY
        3. Martha HUGHES (1846-) [2386].
        3. Martha HUGHES (1855-) [561].
        3. Sarah Ellen HUGHES (1864-) [562].
        3. William HUGHES (1846-) [787].
        3. Samuel HUGHES (-) [788].
        3. John Matthew HUGHES (1851-) [958].
        3. Elizabeth Ann HUGHES (1847-1882) [66].
        Sp. John CORDWELL (1847-1916) [65], son of John CORDWELL (1821-) [510] and Anne
            RIGBY (1825-) [511].
SEE CORDWELL FAMILY
        3. Hannah HUGHES (1840-1904) [559].
        Sp. Richard PARR (1840-1905) [579], son of John PARR (-) [580] and Ann BURROWS (1800-
) [581].
           4. John Samuel PARR (1864-) [1916].
        3. Mary HUGHES (1842-1924) [560].
        Sp. Robert Naylor MERCER (1842-1913) [789], son of Samuel MERCER (1811-) [1917] and
           Ann YATES (1811-) [1918].
           4. Mary Emma MERCER (1866-) [1909].
           4. Samuel MERCER (1868-) [1910].
           4. John MERCER (1871-) [1911].
           4. Martha MERCER (1872-) [1912].
           4. Elizabeth Ann MERCER (1875-) [1913].
           4. Sarah Ellen MERCER (1880-) [1914].
           4. Edith MERCER (1884-) [1915].

Hughes Lineage

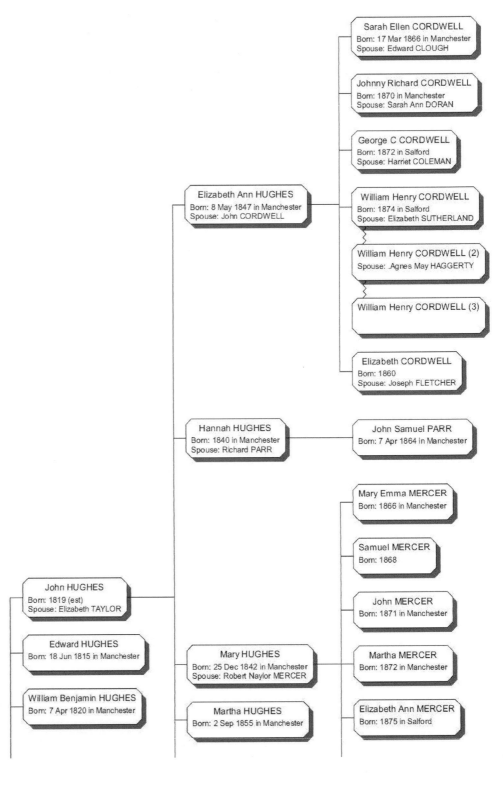

Sarah Ellen CORDWELL
Born: 17 Mar 1866 in Manchester
Spouse: Edward CLOUGH

Johnny Richard CORDWELL
Born: 1870 in Manchester
Spouse: Sarah Ann DORAN

George C CORDWELL
Born: 1872 in Salford
Spouse: Harriet COLEMAN

William Henry CORDWELL
Born: 1874 in Salford
Spouse: Elizabeth SUTHERLAND

William Henry CORDWELL (2)
Spouse: .Agnes May HAGGERTY

William Henry CORDWELL (3)

Elizabeth CORDWELL
Born: 1860
Spouse: Joseph FLETCHER

Elizabeth Ann HUGHES
Born: 8 May 1847 in Manchester
Spouse: John CORDWELL

Hannah HUGHES
Born: 1840 in Manchester
Spouse: Richard PARR

John Samuel PARR
Born: 7 Apr 1864 in Manchester

Mary Emma MERCER
Born: 1866 in Manchester

Samuel MERCER
Born: 1868

John MERCER
Born: 1871 in Manchester

Martha MERCER
Born: 1872 in Manchester

Elizabeth Ann MERCER
Born: 1875 in Salford

John HUGHES
Born: 1819 (est)
Spouse: Elizabeth TAYLOR

Edward HUGHES
Born: 18 Jun 1815 in Manchester

William Benjamin HUGHES
Born: 7 Apr 1820 in Manchester

Mary HUGHES
Born: 25 Dec 1842 in Manchester
Spouse: Robert Naylor MERCER

Martha HUGHES
Born: 2 Sep 1855 in Manchester

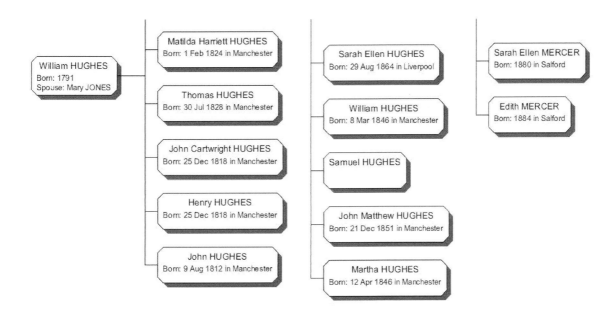

William HUGHES
Born: 1791
Spouse: Mary JONES

Matilda Harriett HUGHES
Born: 1 Feb 1824 in Manchester

Thomas HUGHES
Born: 30 Jul 1828 in Manchester

John Cartwright HUGHES
Born: 25 Dec 1818 in Manchester

Henry HUGHES
Born: 25 Dec 1818 in Manchester

John HUGHES
Born: 9 Aug 1812 in Manchester

Sarah Ellen HUGHES
Born: 29 Aug 1864 in Liverpool

William HUGHES
Born: 8 Mar 1846 in Manchester

Samuel HUGHES

John Matthew HUGHES
Born: 21 Dec 1851 in Manchester

Martha HUGHES
Born: 12 Apr 1846 in Manchester

Sarah Ellen MERCER
Born: 1880 in Salford

Edith MERCER
Born: 1884 in Salford

1. William HUGHES (1791-) [1715]. Born 1791 according to the 1841 census. Unfortunately, due to the number of records for this name it has not been possible to identify William's birth details or where he was born. The following marriage details are likely to refer to William.

William Marr Mary JONES, 7 Jun 1816, St. John's, Preston, Lancashire. Witnesses James Atkinson and George Riley.

The following 1841 English Census has been noted as it is likely to refer to William and Mary as also living in Riga Street was Matthew Taylor, father of Elizabeth who married John Hughes, son of William and Mary Hughes.

1841 English Census, 19 Riga Street, Hulme, Manchester
William HUGHES, age 50, born 1791 (no place of birth given), Warehouseman, Mary HUGHES, wife, age 50, born 1791, Lancashire, William HUGHES, son, age 21, born 1820, Lancashire, Tailor, Matilda HUGHES, dau, age 17, born 1824, Lancashire, Thomas HUGHES, age 10, born 1831, Lancashire, Rebecca WILLIAMSON, age 20, born 1821, Lancashire.

The following census has been added as it may refer to this family

1861 English Census, London Road, St. James, Manchester
Elizabeth HUGHES, born circa 1810, sister, born Manchester, John HUGHES, brother, age 54, born 1807, Manchester, Bricklayer, employing 4 men, William HUGHES, brother, age 65, born 1795, Manchester, Book Keeper.

Sp. Mary JONES (1780-) [1786]. Likely to have been born in Caernarvonshire, Wales.

It has been assumed that Mary was the mother of John Hughes as a Mary was noted on the 1851 English Census, 53 Strand Court, Deansgate, Manchester. In addition it has been confirmed that the following census does refer to this family line.

1851 English Census, 53 Strand Court, Deansgate, Manchester
John HUGHES, head, age 36, Hawker, born 1814, Preston, Lancashire, Elizabeth HUGHES, wife, age 30, Weaver, born 1821, Flixton, Lancashire, Hannah HUGHES, dau, age 11, born 1839, Manchester, Mary HUGHES, dau, age 8, born 1842, Manchester, Elizabeth Ann HUGHES, dau, age 4, born 1847, Preston, Lancashire, John HUGHES, son, age 4 months, born 1851, Manchester, **Mary HUGHES, Lodger, age 70, housekeeper, born 1780, Caernarvonshire.**

Although in 1837 William was noted as a Plasterer, the only other references which note a William and a Mary in the Manchester area also record a Warehouse Man as William's occupation. As there is a mix of William being recorded as a Plasterer and a Warehouse Man it has been assumed the following are all the children of this William and Mary.

> 2. **John HUGHES (1812-) [2385].** Born 22 July, baptised 9 Aug 1812, Manchester Collegate, born to Mary and William Hughes, Warehouse Man. Denomination was Wesleyan.
> 2. **Edward HUGHES (1815-) [1787].** Baptised 18 Jun 1815, Manchester Collegiate, Manchester. Father, William, noted as a Plasterer, mother, Mary.
> 2. **John Cartwright HUGHES (1818-) [2383].** Baptised 25 Dec 1818, Manchester Collegiate, born to William Hughes and Mary. William was noted as a Warehouse Man.
> 2. **Henry HUGHES (1818-) [2384].** Baptised 25 Dec 1818, Manchester Colllegiate, born to William Hughes and Mary. William was noted as a Warehouse Man.
> 2. **William Benjamin HUGHES (1820-) [1906].** Born 7 Apr 1820, Manchester Collegiate. Son of William Hughes and Mary. William noted as a Warehouse Man
> 2. **Matilda Harriet HUGHES (1824-) [1907].** Baptised 1 Feb 1824, Manchester Collegiate. Dau of William Hughes and Mary. William noted as a Warehouse Man.
> 2. **Thomas HUGHES (1828-) [1908].** Baptised 30 Jul 1828, Manchester Collegiate. Son of William Hughes and Mary. William noted as a Warehouse Man
> 2. **John HUGHES (circa 1819-) [249].** Born circa 1819, 'proud' Preston, Lancashire. Son of William Hughes.

In respect to John Hughes, there is some slight confusion as there appear to have been three children named John. It is possible that John Cartwright, born 1818, is ths same person as John born 1819, in Preston, Lancashire.

All the census returns for John show different birth years. However, when John married in 1837, to Elizabeth Taylor, John was younger than Elizabeth and noted a a minor so clearly younger than 21 years old. This would indicate that John would have been born between 1816 and 1821.

John Marr Elizabeth TAYLOR, 25 Dec 1837, Manchester Collegiate Church.

Marriage Certificate
Registration District of Manchester, the Collegiate and Parish Church of Manchester in the County of Lancashire, 25th Dec 1837, John Hughes, minor, bachelor, Brick Maker of 9 Watson Street, Manchester, Father, William Hughes, Plasterer, married Elizabeth Taylor, of full age, Spinster, of 14 Newbury Street, Manchester, Father, Matthew Taylor, Warper. John and Elizabeth made an X as their mark, as did their witnesses Sarah Price and William Kershaw. (Sarah was a sister of Elizabeth)
> Sp. Elizabeth TAYLOR (1819-) [558], dau. of Matthew TAYLOR (1784-) [1714] and Mary BENNETT (1788-) [1724]. Born 15 Jan 1819, Flixton, Manchester. Baptised 12 May 1819, Flixton.

SEE TAYLOR FAMILY

1841 English Census, Fleet Street, Deansgate, Manchester
John HUGHES, head, age 20, born 1820, Preston, Lancashire, Brick Maker, Elizabeth HUGHES, wife, age 20, born 1820, Flixton, Lancashire, Hannah HUGHES, dau, age 5, born 1835, Manchester, Mary HUGHES, dau, age 5, born 1835, Manchester.

1851 English Census, 53 Strand Court, Deansgate, Manchester
John HUGHES, age 36, Hawker, born 1814, Preston, Lancashire, Elizabeth HUGHES, wife, age 30, born 1820, Flixton, Weaver, Hannah HUGHES, dau, age 11, born 1839, Manchester, Mary HUGHES, dau, age 8, born 1842, Manchester, Elizabeth Ann HUGHES, dau, age 4, born 1846, Preston, Lancashire, John HUGHES, son, age 4 months, born 1851, Mary HUGHES, Lodger, age 70, housekeeper, born 1780, Caernarvonshire.

1861 English Census, 131 Deansgate, Manchester, Lancashire, Parish of St. John, 16 Back Quay Street
John HUGHES, head, age 42, Railway Labourer, born 1818, Proud Preston, Lancashire, Railway Labourer, Elizabeth HUGHES, wife, age 40, born 1820, Flixton, Lancashire, Hannah HUGHES, dau, age 18, born 1842, Manchester, Factory Jack Tenter, Mary HUGHES, dau, age 16, born 1844, Manchester, Factory Weaver, Lizth (Elizabeth) Ann HUGHES, dau, age 14, born 1846, Manchester, Factory Card Tenter, Martha HUGHES, dau, age 8, born 1851, Manchester, daily attending school, Sarah Ellen HUGHES, dau, age 16 months, born 1859, Manchester.

A further reference records
1861 English Census, Deansgate, St John's Parish, Manchester
John HUGHES, married, head, age 42, born 1819 Croud, Cretter, Lancashire, Railway Labourer, Elizth HUGHES, wife, age 49, born 1811, Mary HUGHES, dau, age 16, born 1844, Manchester, Eliza Ann HUGHES, age 14, born 1846, Manchester, Hannah HUGHES, dau, age 10, Martha HUGHES, day, age 8, born 1851, Manchester, Sarah Ellen HUGHES, dau age 1 month

1871 English Census, Back of Quay Street Cellar under Deansgate, Manchester
John HUGHES, head, age 55, born 1815, Preston, Lancashire, Brick Maker, Elizabeth HUGHES, wife, age 53, born 1817, Flixton, Lancashire, Martha HUGHES, dau, age 17, born 1853, Manchester, Sarah Ellen HUGHES, dau, age 12, born 1857, Manchester.

There appears to be no references for John and Elizabeth Hughes after the 1871 English Census.

> 3. **Martha HUGHES (1846-) [2386].** Baptised 12 Apr 1846, Manchester Collegiate. Dau of John Hughes and Elizabeth Taylor. John noted as a Brick Maker.
> 3. **Martha HUGHES (1855-) [561].** Born 17 Jun 1854. Baptised 2 Sept 1855, Manchester Collegiate. Dau of John Hughes and Elizabeth Taylor. John noted as a Brick Maker.

3. **Sarah Ellen HUGHES (1864-) [562].** Born 13 Aug 1864, baptised 29 Aug 1864, St. Peter, Liverpool1860, Manchester. Dau of John Hughes and Elizabeth Taylor. John noted as a Labourer.

3. **William HUGHES (1846-) [787].** Born 17 Aug 1845, baptised 8 Mar 1846, Manchester Collegiate. Son of John Hughes and Elizabeth Taylor. John noted as a Brick Maker.

3. **Samuel HUGHES (-) [788].** Son of John Hughes and Elizabeth Taylor. Unable to located baptismal details.

3. **John Matthew HUGHES (1851-) [958].** Baptised 21 Dec 1851, Manchester Collegiate. Son of John Hughes and Elizabeth Taylor. John noted as a Brick Maker.

3. **Elizabeth Ann HUGHES (1847-1882) [66].** Born 8 May 1847, Preston, Lancashire. Baptised 24 Dec 1847, St Matthews, Manchester. This church amalgamated with St John's and later with St Anne's. Dau of John Hughes and Elizabeth Taylor. John noted as a Brick Maker. Residence Manor Street, Manchester.

Elizabeth was living with her parents in the 1851 English Census, 53 Strand Court, Deansgate, Manchester and in the 1861 English Census, 131 Deansgate, Lancashire, Civil Parish of Manchester, Ecclesiastical Parish of St. John, 16 Back Quay Street.

Elizabeth Marr John CORDWELL, 2 Aug 1864, The Cathedral Parish Church Manchester.

Marriage certificate
Marriage solemnized at the Catholic Parish Church in the Parish of Manchester in the County of Lancaster, 2nd August 1864, John Cordwell, 20, bachelor, Shoemaker of 23 Medlock Street, father's name and surname, John Cordwell, Shoemaker, married Elizabeth Ann Hughes,18, spinster of 23 Medlock Street, father's name and surname John Hughes, Labourer. X the mark of John Cordwell, X the mark of Elizabeth Ann Hughes, in the presence of us X mark of George Taylor and X mark of Hannah C Parr. H N Westmore Chaplain.

Elizabeth died Dec 1882, age 37, Salford. Death registered at Chorlton Medlock, Lancashire.

    Sp. John CORDWELL (circa 1841-1847 -1916) [00]

SEE CORDWELL FAMILY

3. **Hannah HUGHES (1840-1904) [559].** Born 1840, Manchester. Dau of John Hughes and Elizabeth Taylor. Hannah was living with her parents in the 1841 English Census, Fleet Street, Deansgate, Manchester, in the 1851 English Census, 53 Strand Court, Deansgate, Manchester and in the 1861 English Census, 131 Deansgate, Manchester, Lancashire, Parish of St. John, 16 Back Quay Street.

Hannah Marr Richard PARR, 14 Apr 1861, Manchester Cathedral formally Manchester Colligate Church. Witnesses John Cordwell and Elizabeth Ann Hughes. Hannah died 1904, age 64, Salford.
    Sp. Richard PARR (1840-1905) [579], son of John Parr and Ann Burrows.

1871 English Census, West Union Street, Regent Road, Salford, Lancashire.
Richard PARR, age 30, born Manchester, Quarryman, Hannah PARR, wife, age 30, born Manchester.

1881 English Census, 47 West Craven Street, Regent Road, Salford, Lancashire.
Richard PARR, age 40, born Manchester, Carter, Hannah PARR, wife, age 40, born Manchester, Shopkeeper, Mary Ann PARR, mother, age 81, born London, Middlesex, formerly Silk Minder, William Henry, nephew, age 7, born Salford.

1891 English Census, 42 Belfort Street, Regent Road, Salford , Lancashire.
Richard PARR, age 50, born Manchester, Lurrfman, Hannah PARR, wife, age 50, born Manchester, Elizabeth Anne CLOUGH, niece, age 5, born Salford, Lancashire, Mary Ann CLOUGH, niece, age 2, born Salford, Lancashire.

1901 English Census, 41 Granville Street South, Salford, Lancashire.
Richard PARR, age 61, born Manchester, Railway Carter formally, Hannah PARR, wife, age 61, born Manchester, Edward CLOUGH, nephew, age 10, born Liverpool, John S CLOUGH, nephew, born Hanley, Staffordshire, William Durham CLOUGH, nephew, age 5, born Dunham, Cheshire.

4. John Samuel PARR (1864-) [1916]. Born 7 Apr 1864, Manchester Cathedral formally Manchester Colligate Church . Godparents John Cordwell and Elizabeth Ann Hughes.

3. Mary HUGHES (1842-1924) [560]. Baptised 25 Dec 1842, St. Matthew, Manchester. Dau of John Hughes and Elizabeth Taylor. John noted as a Carter. Mary was living with her parents in the 1841 English Census, Fleet Street, Deansgate, Manchester, the 1851 English Census, 53 Strand Court, Deansgate, Manchester and the 1861 English Census, 131 Deansgate, Manchester, Lancashire, Parish of St. John, 16 Back Quay Street. Mary died 1924, age 81, Salford

Mary Marr Robert Naylor MERCER, 15 May 1864, Manchester Cathedral. Witnesses John Cordwell and Elizabeth Ann Hughes.

Sp. Robert Naylor MERCER (1842-1913) [789], son of Samuel Mercer and Ann Yates.

1871 English Census, Medlock Street, St, Matthew, Manchester
Robert NAYLOR MERCER, age 27, born 1844, Manchester, Mary MERCER, wife, age 27, born 1844, Manchester, Mary Emma MERCER, dau, age 5, born 1866, Manchester, Samuel MERCER, son, age 3, born 1868, Manchester, John MERCER, son age 0, born 1871, Manchester, S amuel MERCER, Boarder, age 57, born 1814, Manchester, William MERCER, Boarder, age 33, born 1838, Manchester.

1881 English Census, 61 New Bury Street, Salford
Robert MERCER, age 38, born 1843, Manchester, Carter, Mary MERCER, wife, age 38, born 1834, Manchester, Mary Emma MERCER, dau, age 15, born 1866, Manchester, Samuel MERCER, son, age 13, born 1868, Hulme, Manchester, Martha H, dau, age 9, born 1872, Manchester, Elizabeth Ann MERCER, dau, age 6, born 1875, Salford, Sarah Ellen MERCER, age 1, born 1880, Salford, Martha AYRES, Lodger, Widow, age 73, born 1808, Flixton, Chairwoman.

1891 English Census, 31 Granville Street, Salford
Robert MERCER, age 49, born 1842, Manchester, Moulder Labourer, Mary MERCER, wife, age 49, born 1842, Manchester, Martha A MERCER, dau, age 18, Born 1873, Manchester, Cotton Weaver, Elizabeth A MERCER, dau, age 16, born 1875, Manchester, Cotton Weaver, Nelly MERCER, dau, age 11, born 1880, Manchester, Edith MERCER, dau, age 7, born 1884, Manchester, Isabella AXON, Boarder, age 18, born 1873, Manchester, Shop Assistant.

1901 English Census, 31 Granville Street, Saltford
Robert N MERCER, age 59, born 1842, Manchester, General Labourer, Mary MERCER, wife, age 59, born 1842, Manchester, Elizabeth A, dau, single, age 25, born 1876, Salford, Cotton Weaver, Ellen MERCER, dau, single, age 21, born 1880, Salford, Cotton Weaver, Edith MERCER, dau, single, age 18, born 1883, Salford, Cotton Weaver, Anne CLOUGH, Nurse Child, age 1, born 1900, Manchester.

1911 English Census, 31 Granville Street, Salford
Robert Naylor MERCER, age 68, born 1843, Manchester, Labourer Iron Foundry now out of work, Mary MERCER, wife, married 47 years, age 68, born 1843, Manchester, Edith MERCER, dau, single, age 27, born 1884, Salford, Cotton Winder, Annie CLOUGH, grandchild, age 11, born 1900, Manchester, Betha BURTAIN, Boarder, single, age 28, Born 1883, Salford, Cotton Minders.

   4. Mary Emma MERCER (1866-) [1909]. Born 1866, Manchester.
   4. Samuel MERCER (1868-) [1910]. Born 1868.
   4. John MERCER (1871-) [1911]. Born 1871, Manchester.
   4. Martha MERCER (1872-) [1912]. Born 1872, Manchester.
   4. Elizabeth Ann MERCER (1875-) [1913]. Born 1875, Salford.
   4. Sarah Ellen MERCER (1880-) [1914]. Born 1880, Salford.
   4. Edith MERCER (1884-) [1915]. Born 1884, Salford.

Chapter Twelve

THE TAYLOR FAMILY

Taylor Family Outline

John TAYLOR (-)

---

1. John TAYLOR (-) [1851].
Sp. Ann (-) [1855].
      2. James TAYLOR (1787-) [1852].
      2. John TAYLOR (1794-) [1853].
      2. Thomas TAYLOR (1779-) [1854].
      2. Betty TAYLOR (1771-) [2387].
      2. James TAYLOR (1773-) [2388].
      2. Ellin TAYLOR (1791-) [2389].
      2. William TAYLOR (1789-) [2390].
      2. Peggy TAYLOR (1789-) [2391].
      2. Betty TAYLOR (1787-) [2392].
      2. Ann TAYLOR (1779-) [2393].
      2. Edmund TAYLOR (1776-) [2394].
      2. Matthew TAYLOR (1784-1849) [1714].
      Sp. Mary BENNETT (1788-) [1724].
            3. George TAYLOR (1824-) [1725].
            3. Hannah TAYLOR (1827-) [1726].
            3. Sarah TAYLOR (1821-) [1727
                  4. Mary TAYLOR (1814-) [1728].
            3. Mary TAYLOR (1816-) [1729].
            3. Edward TAYLOR (1827-1828) [1730].
            3. Elizabeth TAYLOR (1819-) [558].
            Sp. John HUGHES (1819?-) [249], son of William HUGHES (1791-) [1715] and Mary JONES
                (1780-) [1786].
SEE HUGHES FAMILY

Taylor Lineage

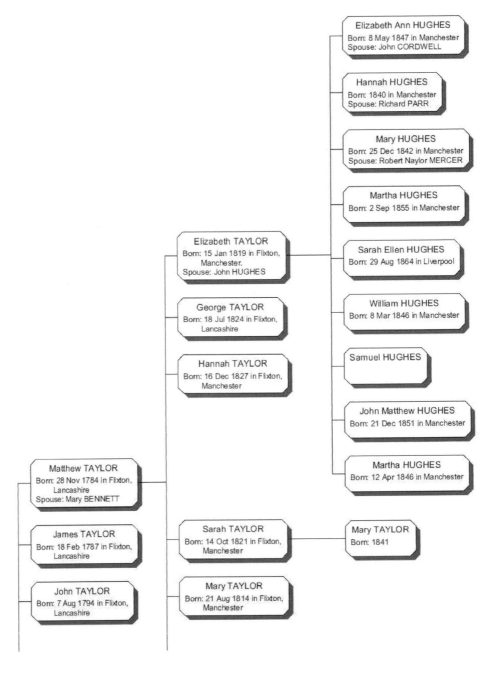

Elizabeth Ann HUGHES
Born: 8 May 1847 in Manchester
Spouse: John CORDWELL

Hannah HUGHES
Born: 1840 in Manchester
Spouse: Richard PARR

Mary HUGHES
Born: 25 Dec 1842 in Manchester
Spouse: Robert Naylor MERCER

Martha HUGHES
Born: 2 Sep 1855 in Manchester

Sarah Ellen HUGHES
Born: 29 Aug 1864 in Liverpool

William HUGHES
Born: 8 Mar 1846 in Manchester

Samuel HUGHES

John Matthew HUGHES
Born: 21 Dec 1851 in Manchester

Martha HUGHES
Born: 12 Apr 1846 in Manchester

Elizabeth TAYLOR
Born: 15 Jan 1819 in Flixton,
Manchester.
Spouse: John HUGHES

George TAYLOR
Born: 18 Jul 1824 in Flixton,
Lancashire

Hannah TAYLOR
Born: 16 Dec 1827 in Flixton,
Manchester

Matthew TAYLOR
Born: 28 Nov 1784 in Flixton,
Lancashire
Spouse: Mary BENNETT

James TAYLOR
Born: 18 Feb 1787 in Flixton,
Lancashire

John TAYLOR
Born: 7 Aug 1794 in Flixton,
Lancashire

Sarah TAYLOR
Born: 14 Oct 1821 in Flixton,
Manchester

Mary TAYLOR
Born: 1841

Mary TAYLOR
Born: 21 Aug 1814 in Flixton,
Manchester

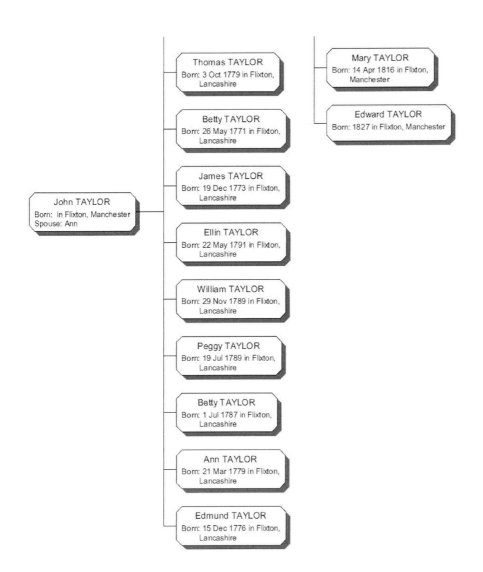

John TAYLOR
Born: in Flixton, Manchester
Spouse: Ann

Thomas TAYLOR
Born: 3 Oct 1779 in Flixton, Lancashire

Mary TAYLOR
Born: 14 Apr 1816 in Flixton, Manchester

Edward TAYLOR
Born: 1827 in Flixton, Manchester

Betty TAYLOR
Born: 26 May 1771 in Flixton, Lancashire

James TAYLOR
Born: 19 Dec 1773 in Flixton, Lancashire

Ellin TAYLOR
Born: 22 May 1791 in Flixton, Lancashire

William TAYLOR
Born: 29 Nov 1789 in Flixton, Lancashire

Peggy TAYLOR
Born: 19 Jul 1789 in Flixton, Lancashire

Betty TAYLOR
Born: 1 Jul 1787 in Flixton, Lancashire

Ann TAYLOR
Born: 21 Mar 1779 in Flixton, Lancashire

Edmund TAYLOR
Born: 15 Dec 1776 in Flixton, Lancashire

John TAYLOR (-)

1. John TAYLOR (-) [1851]. Born Flixton, Lancashire between 1734 and 1767.

References for births of a John Taylor in Flixton are numerous therefore it has not been possible to confirm exactly which refers to John on this direct line. However, the following are possible births for John.

- John Taylor born 11 Aug 1735, baptised 17 Aug 1735, St Michael, Flixton, parent John Taylor
- John born 29 Oct 1743, baptised 20 Nov 1743, St. Michael, Flixton, parent, Jonathan Taylor
- Jonathan born 30 Aug 1746, baptised 25 Sept 1746, St. Michael, Flixton, parent William Taylor
- John born 29 May 1754, baptised 23 June 1754, St. Michael, Flixton, parents Edmund Taylor and Lydia living at Davyhulme
- John born 5 Oct 1757, baptised 23 Oct 1757, St. Michael, Flixton, parents John Taylor and Alice living at Carrington
- John born 27 July 1762, baptised 29 Aug 1762, St. Michael, Flixton, parents John Taylor and Ann
- John born 14 Apr 1762, baptised 9 May 1762, St. Michael, Flixton, parents John Taylor and Ann

Likewise there are a number of marriage references for John who married an Ann in Flixton.

- Ann Irlam, St. Michael, Flixton, Lancashire, 15 Apr 1759
- Ann Hesketh, St. Michael, Flixton, Lancashire, 1 March 1778. John was noted as a Widower
- Ann Allen, St. Michael, Flixton, Lancashire, 17 Aug 1784. John was a Weaver. Witnesses were Thomas Taylor and John Erlam
- Ann Derbyshire, St. Michael, Flixton, Lancashire, 21 Dec 1786. Witnesses were Margaret Derbyshire and Thomas Rogers

Given the number of marriage references it is possible that the following children of John and Ann, may in fact belong to three separate families in Flixton. In any event they are all related.

Sp. Ann (-) [1855].

- **2. James TAYLOR (1787-) [1852].** Born 18 Feb 1787, baptised 18 Feb 1787, St. Michael, Flixton, Lancashire. Son of John Taylor and Ann.
- **2. John TAYLOR (1794-) [1853].** Born 7 Aug 1794, baptised 7 Aug 1794, St. Michael, Flixton, Lancashire. Son of John Taylor and Ann of Tan House, Flixton.
- **2. Thomas TAYLOR (1779-) [1854].** Born 3 Oct 1779, baptised 3 Oct 1779, St. Michael. Flixton, Lancashire. Son of John Taylor and Ann.
- **2. Betty TAYLOR (1771-) [2387].** Born 8 May 1771, baptised 26 May 1771, St Michael, Flixton, Lancashire. Dau of John Taylor and Ann.
- **2. James TAYLOR (1773-) [2388].** Born 23 Nov 1773, baptised 19 Dec 1773, St. Michael, Flixton, Lancashire. Son of John Taylor and Ann.
- **2. Ellin TAYLOR (1791-) [2389].** Baptised 22 May 1791, St Michael, Flixton, Lancashire. Dau of John Taylor and Ann.
- **2. William TAYLOR (1789-) [2390].** Baptised 29 Nov 1789, St. Michael, Flixton, Lancashire. Son of John Taylor and Ann, residing in Davyhulme.
- **2. Peggy TAYLOR (1789-) [2391].** Baptised 19 Jul 1789, St. Michael, Flixton, Lancashire. Dau of John Taylor and Ann.
- **2. Betty TAYLOR (1787-) [2392].** Baptised 1 Jul 1787, St. Michael, Flixton, Lancashire. Dau of John Taylor and Ann.
- **2. Ann TAYLOR (1779-) [2393].** Baptised 21 Mar 1779, St. Michael, Flixton, Lancashire. Dau of John Taylor and Ann.
- **2. Edmund TAYLOR (1776-) [2394].** Baptised 15 Dec 1776, St. Michael, Flixton, Lancashire. Son of John Taylor and Ann.
- **2. Matthew TAYLOR (1784-1849) [1714].** Baptised 28 Nov 1784, St Michael, Flixton, Lancashire. Son of John Taylor and Ann.

Matthew Marr Mary BENNETT, 2 Nov 1809, St. Mary the Virgin, Eccles, Manchester.

Marriage Details
28 Nov 1809, St Mary the Virgin, Eccles, Lancashire, Matthew Taylor age 25, married Mary Bennett, age 20. Witness: Joseph Isherwood; James Carrington and James Taylor.

1841 English Census, Riga Street, Hulme, Manchester
Thomas PRYCE, age 35, born 1806, (no birth place given), Ann PRYCE, age 30, born 1811, (no birth place given), Sarah PRYCE, age 10, born 1831, Lancashire, Mary PRYCE, age 8, born 1833, Lancashire, Thomas PRYCE, age 3, born 1838, Lancashire, Susana THOMPSON, age 35, born 1806, (no birth place given), **Matthew TAYLOR, age 56, born 1785, (no birth place given), Cotton Beamer**, George TAYLOR, age 16, born 1825.

Matthew was residing at 15 Bridgewater Street, Hulme, St. George, a Cotton Beamer in the cotton mill, when he died June 1849, age 62, buried 17 June 1849.
>   **Sp. Mary BENNETT (1788 -) [1724].** Mary had died before the 1841 English Census as Matthew and her son George were living at Riga Street, Hulme.

>> 3. **George TAYLOR (1824-) [1725].** Baptised 18 Jul 1824, St. Michael, Flixton, Manchester. Son of Matthew Taylor and Mary Bennett. Residence Flixton. Matthew noted as a Weaver. In the 1841 English Census, Riga Street, Hulme, Manchester, George living with his father.

>> 3. **Hannah TAYLOR (1827-) [1726].** Baptised 16 Dec 1827, St. Michael, Flixton, Manchester. Dau of Matthew Taylor and Mary Bennett. Residence Flixton. Matthew noted as a Weaver.

>> 3. **Sarah TAYLOR (1821-) [1727].** Baptised 14 Oct 1821, St. Michael, Flixton, Manchester. Dau of Matthew Taylor and Mary Bennett. Residence Flixton. Matthew noted as a Weaver.
>>> 4. **Mary TAYLOR (1841-) [1788].** Born 1841. Dau of Sarah Taylor.

1841 English Census, Peter Street, Little, Manchester
Sarah Taylor, age 20, born 1821, Lancashire, Mary Taylor, age 2 months, born 1841, Lancashire.

>> 3. **Mary TAYLOR (1814-) [1728].** Baptised 21 Aug 1814, St. Michael, Flixton, Manchester. Dau of Matthew Taylor and Mary Bennett. Residence Flixton. Matthew noted as a Weaver.
>> 3. **Mary TAYLOR (1816-) [1729].** Baptised 14 Apr 1816, St. Michael, Flixton, Manchester. Dau of Matthew Taylor and Mary Bennett. Residence Flixton. Matthew noted as a Weaver.
>> 3. **Edward TAYLOR (1827-1828) [1730].** Died Mar 1828, buried 10 March 1828. 10 to 12 months old. Son of Matthew Taylor and Mary Bennett.
>> 3. **Elizabeth TAYLOR (1819-) [558].** Born 15 Jan 1819, Flixton, Manchester. Baptised 12 May 1819, Wesleyan, Flixton. Dau of John Taylor and Mary Bennett. Also noted in the Wesleyan Chapel was Elizabeth Taylor, parents Matthew Taylor and Mary Taylor, baptised 12 May 1819, Davy Hulme, Wesleyan, Flixton, Lancashire, birth date 15 Jan 1819.

Elizabeth Marr John HUGHES 25 Dec 1837, Manchester Cathedral

Marriage Certificate
Registration District of Manchester
In the Collegiate and Parish Church of Manchester in the County of Lancashire, 25th Dec 1837, John Hughes, minor, bachelor, Brick Maker of 9 Watson Street, Manchester, Father, William Hughes, Plasterer, married Elizabeth Taylor, of full age, Spinster, of 14 Newbury Street, Manchester, Father, Matthew Taylor, Warper .(a Cotton mill operator who sets the warp thread (yarns) on the looms before weaving) John and Elizabeth made an X as their mark, as did their witnesses Sarah Price and William Kershaw.
>   **Sp. John HUGHES (1819-) [249],** son of William HUGHES (1791 -) [1715] and Mary JONES (1780-) [1786].

SEE HUGHES FAMILY

Chapter Thirteen

THE HINES FAMILY

Hines Family Outline

Robert HINES (-)

---

1. Robert HINDS (-) [1758].
Sp. (unknown).
    2. William (Gulielmi) HINDS (1847-1875) [238].
   Sp. Margaret FINN (1849-) [908], dau. of Patrick FINN (-) [1757].
      3. Robert W HINES (1875-1956) [224].
     Sp. Mary Elizabeth STOCKDALE (1880-1952) [225], dau. of William STOCKDALE (circa 1830-) [239]
        and Isabella SCOTT (1842-) [240].
SEE SCOTT AND STOCKDALE FAMILY
        4. Robert HINES (1901-1951) [8].
       Sp. Betsy DIXON (1908-1983) [9], dau. of Gilbert DIXON (1885-1956) [16] and Margaret Ellen
          CLOUGH (1886-1986) [17].
SEE DIXON AND CLOUGH FAMILY
        4. Edward HINES (1910-1976) [228].
        4. Mary Elizabeth HINES (1908-) [229].
        4. Josephine HINES (1914 -) [230].
        4. Joseph HINES (-) [231].
        4. James HINES (1921 -) [232].
        4. John HINES (1906-) [233].
        4. Katie HINES (1920 -) [234].
        4. Ann HINES (1912 -) [235].
        4. Lucy HINES (1916 -) [236].
        4. Frances HINES (1902-) [237].
      3. Frances HINES (1872-) [226].
     Sp. John MILLER Squire(-) [227].

Hines Lineage

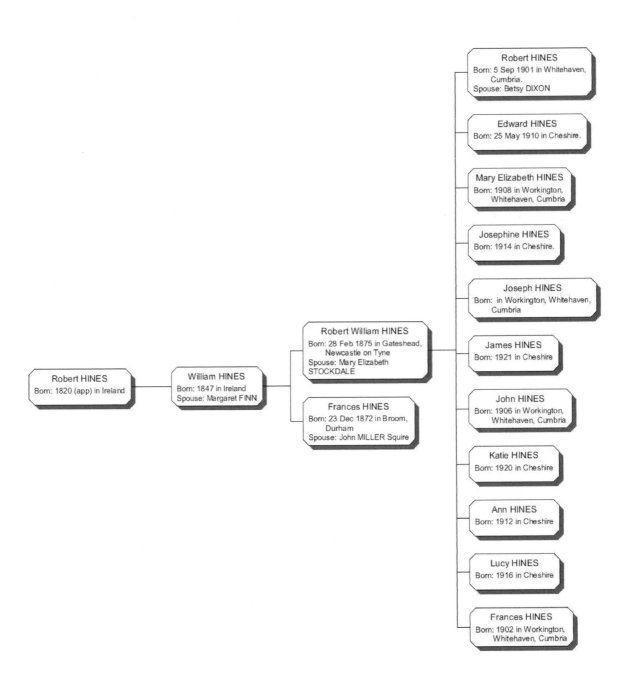

Robert HINES (-)

1. Robert HINES (-) [1758]. When Robert's son William married in 1870, Robert's surname was spelt as Hinde and Robert was noted as a House Joiner.

This surname has many spellings, such as Hind, Hiner, Hines, Hynes etc. As the present day family spell the surname as Hines all names reflect this spelling.

The details of the earlier part of this family have been difficult to determine as there are numerous references to Hines families in the English Census, particularly in the areas of Durham and Cumberland.

Robert had a child called William, also recorded as Gulielmi. The reference confirming this was a marriage record between William and Margaret Finn in 1870. William's father Robert was noted as a House Joiner. So far this has been the only identified child of Robert.

Several searches have been undertaken for a Robert Hines but unfortunately the correct reference has not been identified.

However, there was one record from the 1851 English Census for High Street, Crosscanonby, Maryport, Cumberland which noted a Robert HINDE, age 41, born 1810, Dearham, Cumberland, Master Joiner and Cabinet Maker employing 4 Men, 5 Apprentices. Although the occupation would be the same references and folklore would suggest Robert was born in Ireland. The lack of references for Robert might confirm that whilst some of his family moved to England Robert remained in Ireland.

There is another possibility in that, if like his son, Robert had a second name of William there are possible references which might confirm that Robert did move to England and the family may well be connected to the Irish Hind family who appear in Cumberland in the 1851 English Census. By the 1861 English Census this family had moved to Durham. Interestingly, the Christian names are very similar in both families which would reflect the Irish naming system and both families first appeared in Cumberland and both families moved to Durham.

A lineage and detail of this particular family can be seen at the end of this section – reference William Hines Lineage.

2. William (Gulielmi) HINDS (1847-1875) [238]. Born 1847, Ireland. Father Robert Hinds.

William Marr Margaret FINN, 23 May 1870, Whitehaven, Cumberland.

Marriage Certificate
Marriage solomnized in St. Begas Catholic Chapel Cleaton, in the District of Whitehaven, Cumberland. On the 23 May 1870, William Hinds, age 22 years, Bachelor, Iron Ore Miner, residence Frizington, Anleadon, father Robert Hinds, House Joiner, married Margaret Finn, age 21 years, Spinster, Domestic Servant, residence Frizington, Anleadon, father Patrick Finn, deceased, Iron Ore Miner. William signed his name and Margaret made an X as her mark. Witnesses John Kerion and Ellen Toole. (St, Begas generally known as St. Bees).

William and Margaret moved from Frizington, Anleadon, Whitehaven to Ayreshire as they appear in the following 1871 Scottish Census.

1871 Scottish Census, 11 Gass Brae, Dalmellington, Ayrshire
William HINES, age 22, b1849, Ireland, Coalminer, Margaret HINES, wife, age 22, b1849, Ireland.

Family folklore confirmed by following extracts from Durham Mining Museum illustrate that William died in a coal pit accident.

"1875 Mines Inspectors Report (C 1499)
Hiner, William, 09 Apr 1875, aged 25, b1850, Shifter, South Durham mine, returned to a shot before it exploded".

The occupation of a 'Shifter' has been recorded as a number of interpretations as follows
* The shift boss assigned to certain areas to undertake certain tasks within the mine

- Men who repair and maintain horse ways and or other passages of the mine, both under and over ground
- Men who are paid by the shift rather than by the amount of coal they extract from the coal face

William died in Durham about 4 weeks after the birth of his son Robert, leaving his wife Margaret with two young children.

Sp. Margaret FINN (1849-) [908], born Ireland, dau. of Patrick Finn. Margaret has also been recorded as Mariae Flynn and Margaritae Flynn.

As with William it is not clear if Margaret moved to England on her own or whether she came with her family. The 1841, 1851, 1861 Census have been searched for Patrick Finn and Patrick Flynn. Although there are a few references which may be relevant it is not possible to confirm they are the correct references for this family. However, as Patrick was noted as an Iron Ore Miner on Margaret's marriage certificate, it would suggest Patrick was living in England, although deceased at the time of her marriage.

After the death of William in 1875, Margaret re married to a John Mallard and by 1881, Margaret, John and her children Frances and Robert William Hines had returned to Maryport, Cumberland.

1881 English Census, Furness Cottage, 3 Court, Cross Canonby with Maryport, Cockermouth, Cumberland
John MALAARD, head, age 31, b1850, Stone Mason, Margaret MALAARD, wife, age 30, b1851 Ireland, Frances HINES, step dau, age 7, born 1874, Gateshead, Durham, Robert W HINES, step son, age 5, born 1876, Gateshead, Durham.

1891 English Census, Waterloo Street, Cockermouth, Cumberland
John MALLARD, age 37, born 1854, Ireland, Hawker, Margaret MALLARD, wife, age 37, born 1854, Ireland, Frances HUIE, step dau, single, age 17, born 1874, Co. Durham, Domestic Servant, Robert HUIE, step son, single, age 15, born 1876, Co. Durham, General Labourer, Josephina MALLARD, dau, age 7, born 1884, Maryport, Cumberland, Mary Elizth, dau, age 6, born 1885, Ullock, Cumberland.

1901 English Census, 2 Irving Court, Udale Street, Workington, Cumberland
John MALLARD, head, age 36, born 1865, Ireland, Pedlar, Margaret MALLARD, wife, age 44, born 1857, Ireland, Josephinna MALLARD, dau, age 18, born 1883, Maryport, Cumberland, Pedlar, Mary Elizabeth MALLARD, dau, age 17, born 1884, Ullock, Cumberland, Pedlar.

3. **Robert William HINES (1875-1956) [224].** Robertus Hind, baptised 28 Feb 1875, St Joseph's, Gateshead, Newcastle on Tyne, Co Durham, father Gulielmi Hind, mother Mariae Flynn. In the 1881 English Census, Furness Cottage, 3 Court, Cross Canonby with Maryport, Cockermouth, Cumberland and the 1891 English Census, Waterloo Street, Cockermouth, Cumberland, Robert William was living with his mother and step father.

Robert Marr Mary Elizabeth STOCKDALE, 29 Jan 1898, St Michael and St Mary's RC, Workington, Cumbria. Robert's residence was Church Street, Workington, Cumberland.

Marriage certificate
Church of Our Lady and St. Michael, in the District of Cockermouth in the County of Cumberland, 29 Jan 1898, Robert Hines, age 21, bachelor, Steelworks Labourer, residence Church Street, Workington, father William Hines, Iron Ore Miner, married Mary Elizabeth Stockdale, age 19, spinster, residence Udale Street, Workington, father, William Stockdale, deceased, French Polisher, Witnesses Thomas Graham and Hannah Redhead.

Sp. Mary Elizabeth STOCKDALE (1880-1952) [225], dau. of William STOCKDALE (circa 1830-) [239] and Isabella SCOTT (1842-) [240]. Baptised 27 Sep 1880, Cockermouth, St Michaels & St Mary's, Workington, Cumbria.

SEE SCOTT AND STOCKDALE FAMILY

1901 English Census, 1 Irving Court, Udale Street, Workington, Cumberland
Robert HINES, head, age 23, born 1878, Northumberland, Steel Worker, Mary Elizabeth HINES, wife, age 20, born 1881, Workington, Cumberland, Robert HINES, son, age 6 months, born 1901, Workington, Cumberland, Annie Elizabeth STOCKDALE, sister-in-law, single age 16, born 1885, Workington, Cumberland, Servant (Domestic), Isabella STOCKDALE, mother-in-law, widow, age 60, born 1841,

Workington, Cumberland, John MORLEY, visitor, single, age 40, born 1861, Carlisle, Cumberland, French Polisher.

1911 English Census 19 Oldfield Road, Ellesmere Port, Cheshire
Robert HINES, age 32, born Newcastle on Tyne, Labourer in corrugated sheet factory. Mary HINES, age 31, born Workington, Cumberland, married 13 years, 8 children, 3 died, Robert HINES, son, age 11, born Workington, Cumberland, Fanny HINES, dau, age 10, born Workington, Cumberland, John HINES, son, age 5, born Workington, Cumberland, Mary HINES, dau, age 3, born Workington, Cumberland, Edward HINES, son, age 1, born Workington, Cumberland.

Robert worked for a time in a pencil factory in Cumbria before leaving for Ellesmere Port.

Robert was in WW1 stationed at Lord Derby's Park, Liverpool, he was in the 4th Liverpool Pals. The 20th Battalion Kings, Liverpool Regiment were part of the 89th Brigade, 30th Division, fighting on the Western front in Russia, serving at the garrison in Russia and in India. After the war Robert belonged to one of the garrisons who stayed in Russia for approximately four years to ensure the peace was kept (occupation force). After the war Robert worked in the Iron Foundry at Ellesmere Port, Cheshire.

Robert died 28 Feb 1956, age 81. Death registered in Bebington, Wirral, Cheshire. Robert is buried at the Cemetery Gates, Ellesmere Port, Cheshire, along with his wife Mary Elizabeth and daughter Lucy.

4. **Robert HINES (1901-1951) [8].** Born 5 Sept 1901, Youdle Street, Workington, Whitehaven, Cumbria, son of Robert Hines and Mary Elizabeth Stockdale. In the 1901 English Census, 1 Irving Court, Udale Street, Workington, Cumberland and the 1911 English Census 19 Oldfield Road, Ellesmere Port, Cheshire, Robert was living with his parents.

Robert Marr Betsy DIXON, Feb 1928, St. Werburgh's Church, Grange Road, Birkenhead, Wirral, Cheshire.
Sp. Betsy DIXON (1908-1983) [9], dau. of Gilbert DIXON (1885-1956) [16] and Margaret Ellen CLOUGH (1886-1986) [17]. Birth, Sub District Mottram, Cheshire, 12 Aug 1908.

SEE DIXON AND CLOUGH FAMILY

Robert Hines, Betsy Dixon, at Nelly Manders Wedding

Robert died 6 Jun 1951, age 50, buried Cemetery Gates, Ellesmere Port, Cheshire.

Extract from The Ellesmere Port Pioneer newspaper. Newspaper Obituary

Mr R Hines "We regret to record the death at the age of 50 of Mr Robert Hines of 15 Wellesley Avenue (Ellesmere Port, Wirral). Mr Hines passed away at Clatterbridge Hospital on Wednesday after a long illness. A Cumberland man he had resided in this district for about 40 years and was an old employee of the Cement Works. Since they were closed down he had worked for Burnell & Co. He leaves a widow, one daughter and one son. The funeral took place on Saturday. Requiem Mass was celebrated at Our Lady's Star of the Sea Church by Rev Father Campbell and O'Donnell and the internment followed at the Cemetery. Mourners were Mrs B Hines (widow), Miss Mary Hines (daughter) Mr Robert Hines (son) Mr R Hines (father), Miss L Hines (sister), Mr J Hines (brother) Mr and Mrs G Dixon (father in law and mother in law) Mr and Mrs E Hines (brother and sister in law) Mr and Mrs J Barber (sister & brother in law), Misses M and B Barber, Mrs J Hall (nieces) Mr and Mrs J Howell, Mr and Mrs B Barrett, Messrs E and G Dixon (brothers in law and sisters in law), Mrs J Donoghue, Mrs W Tully, Nurse Ankers, Mr Mitchelmore (representing Messrs Burnell), Messrs T Hughes, T Short, Royle and Durling were the bearers. Floral tributes were received from: Wife, Mary and Bobbie, Mother, Father, Lucy and Jim, Edward, Katie and family, Fanny, Jim and family, Mr and Mrs Barrett, Mr and Mrs J Howell and family, Mr and Mrs G Dixon, Mr and Mrs W Dixon, Mr Patrick Green Jnr, Caswell's and family, Workmates, Black Iron, Burnell's, The Nursing Association, Colleagues from the Ambulance Room, Mr and Mrs J Philips, Mr and Mrs Hanson, Friends and Neighbours (font & flowers), Donald Philips, Mr and Mrs Makeham and Joyce, Margaret Makeham, Elsie, George, Joan and Joe, Mr and Mrs Howitt, Miss L Parkes, Burnell's Nursing Fund. Mass cards: Father, Mother, Lucy and Jimmy, Edward, Katie and children, sister Frances and Jim, Betty and Mary, Arthur Gallagher, Mrs Tully, Mrs Witton and Rose Tully, Mrs Donoghue, Mr Patrick Green Jnr, Peggy, Albert and Children, Mr and Mrs Green, Danny and Hazel Green, Martin and Bridie Green, Mr and Mrs P J Hodges, The Women's Guild (two) Mrs Roberts and Mary, Katie Grant, Arthur and Mary Anstis, Mrs Kane, Mrs Monoghan, Mr and Mrs L Hill, Mrs Farrell, Mrs Hill, Park Road, Evelyn Fitzgerald. R F Walton and Sons were the undertakers".

> 4. **Edward HINES (1910-1976) [228].** Baptised 26 May 1910, Cheshire. Son of Robert Hines and Mary Elizabeth Stockdale. Edward died 1976, Cheshire.
> 4. **Mary Elizabeth HINES (1908-) [229].** Born 1908, Cockermouth, Cumberland. Dau of Robert Hines and Mary Elizabeth Stockdale.
> 4. **Josephine HINES (1914 -) [230].** Born 1914, Cheshire. Dau of Robert Hines and Mary Elizabeth Stockdale.
> 4. **Joseph HINES (-) [231].** Son of Robert Hines and Mary Elizabeth Stockdale.
> 4. **James HINES (1921 -) [232].** Born 1921, Cheshire. Son of Robert Hines and Mary Elizabeth Stockdale.
> 4. **John HINES (1906-) [233].** Born 1906, Workington, Whitehaven, Cumbria. Son of Robert Hines and Mary Elizabeth Stockdale.
> 4. **Katie HINES (1820 -) [234]. Born 1920, Cheshire.** Dau of Robert Hines and Mary Elizabeth Stockdale.
> 4. **Ann HINES (1912-) [235].** Born 1912, Cheshire. Dau of Robert Hines and Mary Elizabeth Stockdale.
> 4. **Lucy HINES (1916-) [236].** Born 1916, Cheshire. Dau of Robert Hines and Mary Elizabeth Stockdale.
> 4. **Frances HINES (1902-) [237].** Born 1902, Workington, Whitehaven, Cumbria. Son of Robert Hines and Mary Elizabeth Stockdale.

> 3. **Frances HINES (1872-) [226].** Born 23 Dec 1872, Bear Park Colliery, Durham. Baptised 29 Dec 1872, St. Joseph's, Gateshead, Durham. Father Gulielmi Hind, mother Mariae Flynn.

Birth Certificate
Registration District of Durham, Sub district St Oswald, County of Durham, 23 Dec 1872, at Bear Park Colliery, Broom, Frances, girl, father William Hines, Coal Miner Bear Park Colliery, Broom, mother Margaret Hines formerly Finn (the mark of). Registered 10 Jan 1873.

In the 1881 English Census, Furness Cottage, 3 Court, Cross Canonby with Maryport, Cockermouth, Cumberland and the 1891 English Census, Waterloo Street, Cockermouth, Cumberland, Frances was living with his mother and step father.

Frances Marr John Miller, Squire of Bassenthwaite, 1925, Cockermouth, Cumberland. There were two brothers named Miller who farmed in Bassenthwaite, Cumbria in the 1920s.

Sp. John MILLER (-) [227] Squire.

William Hines Lineage

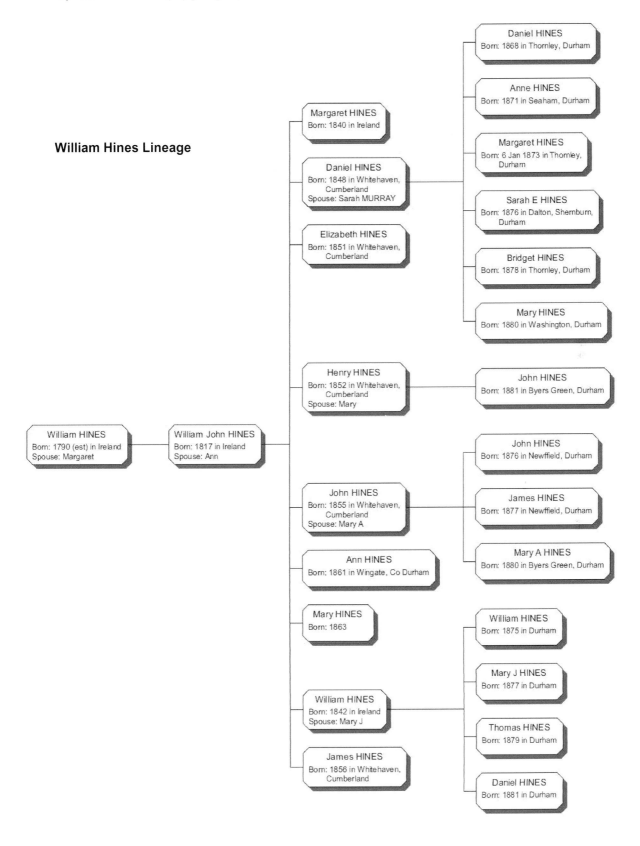

William Hines Lineage

Note - On the 1851 and 1861 English Census, the birth years for William and Ann are incorrect. However, more realistic birth years appear in the 1871 English Census.

1851 English Census, Ginns Street, Whitehaven, Cumberland
William HIND, married age 28, born 1823, Ireland, Coal Miner, Ann HIND, wife, age 26, born 1825, Ireland, Margaret HIND, dau, age 11, born 1840, Ireland, William HIND, son age 8, born 1843, Ireland, Daniel HIND, son, age 3, born 1848, Whitehaven, Cumberland, Elizabeth HIND, dau, age 3 months, born 1851, Whitehaven, Cumberland.

1861 English Census, Wellington Street, Easington, Co Durham, Civil Parish of Thornley
William HINES, age 33, born 1827, Ireland, Coal Miner, Ann HINES, wife, age 30, born 1830, Ireland, Margaret HINES, dau, age 21, born 1840, Ireland, William HINES, son, age 19, born 1842, Ireland, Coal Miner, Daniel HINES, son, age 13, born 1848, Whitehaven, Cumberland, Coal Miner, Elizabeth HINES, dau, age 9, born 1851, Whitehaven, Cumberland, Henry HINES, son, age 8 born 1852, Whitehaven, Cumberland, John HINES, son, age 5, born 1855, Whitehaven, Cumberland, James HINES, son, age 4 born 1856, Whitehaven, Cumberland, Ann HINES, dau, age 9 months, born 1861, Wingate, Co Durham.

1871 English Census, German or Doctor's Row, Seaham, Easington, Durham
William HINDE, age 54, born 1817, Ireland, Anne HINDE, wife, age 50, born 1821, Ireland, Henry HINDE, son, age 18, born 1853, England, John HINDE, son, age 16, born 1855, England, James, HINDE, son, age 14, born 1857, England, Anne HINDE, dau, age 11, born 1860, England, Mary HINDE, age 8, born 1863 England, Philip CASHEDY, boarder, age 28, born 1843, Ireland.

William born in 1842, does not appear in the above census and has not been identified elsewhere apart from the 1871 Scottish Census. It is possible that William found in the 1871 Scottish Census, married to Margaret Finn in 1870, is the same William which would confirm the two families in this chapter are related. Unfortunately, there is no evidence to confirm this.

Chapter Fourteen

THE SCOTT AND STOCKDALE FAMILY

Scott and Stockdale Family Outline

James SCOTT (-)

---

1. James SCOTT (-) [981].
Sp. Mary (-) [987].
  2. James SCOTT (1806-1808) [988].
  2. Isabella SCOTT (1805-) [1761].
  2. Mary SCOTT (1811-) [1762].
  2. Lancaster SCOTT (1816-) [1763].
  2. Ann SCOTT (1809-) [2373].
  2. Thomas SCOTT (1811-1811) [2374].
  2. William SCOTT (1813-) [646].
  2. Sarah SCOTT (1814-) [1759].
  2. James SCOTT (1808-) [982].
  Sp. Elizabeth (1811-) [983].
    3. James Dorthwaite SCOTT (1845-) [985].
    3. Georgina SCOTT (1850-) [986].
    3. Ann SCOTT (1840-) [1764].
    3. Isabella SCOTT (1842-) [240].
    Sp. William HARDING (-) [546].
      4. Margaret HARDING (1868-) [547].
      4. Isaac HARDING (1870-) [548].
    Sp. William STOCKDALE (circa 1830-) [239], son of Thomas STOCKDALE (-) [241].
      4. Annie Isabella STOCKDALE (1885-) [549].
      4. Mary Elizabeth STOCKDALE (1880-1952) [225].
      Sp. Robert W HINES (1875-1956) [224], son of William (Gulielmi) HINDS (1847- circa
        1881) [238] and Margaret (Marie) FINN or FLYNN (1849-) [908].

SEE HINES FAMILY

Scott and Stockdale Lineage

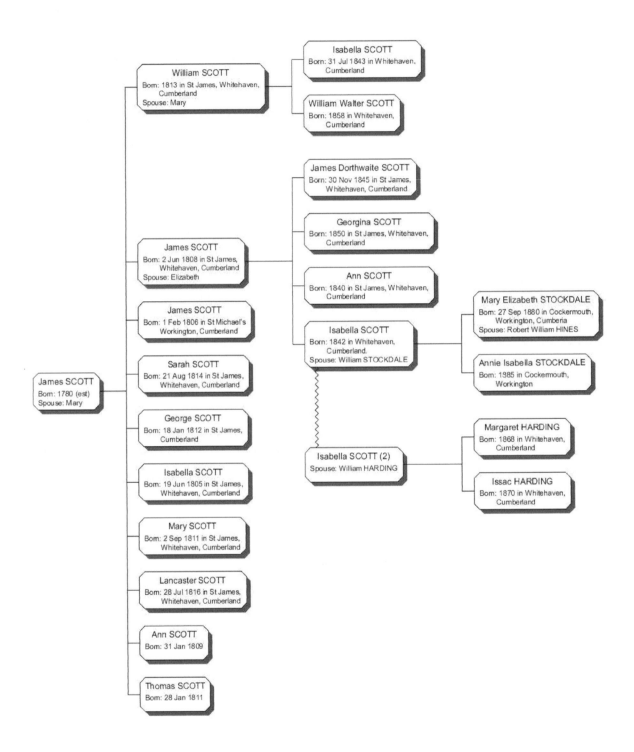

James SCOTT (-)

1. James SCOTT (-) [981]. Born between 1756 and 1788. Unfortunately, it has not been confirmed where James was born or the name of his parents.

There are a number of referemces for Scottish Presbyteran baptisms in St. James, Whitehaven, as are there a number of possible references which might suggest the family were from Scotland or Ireland.

The baptismal records for their children confirm that James married a Mary. It has not been possible to identify their marriage details.
Sp. Mary (-) [987].

2. James SCOTT (1806-1808) [988]. Baptised 1 Feb 1806, St. Michael's Workington, Cumberland. Son of James Scott and Mary. James died 24 May 1808.

2. Isabella SCOTT (1805-) [1761]. Born 9 Jun 1805, Baptised 7 Jun 1805, St. James, Whitehaven, Cumberland. Dau of James Scott and Mary.

2. Mary SCOTT (1811-) [1762]. Born 2 Sep 1811, Baptised 15 Sept 1811, St. James, Whitehaven, Cumberland. Dau of James Scott and Mary.

2. Lancaster SCOTT (1816-) [1763]. Born 28 Jul 1816, St. James, Whitehaven, Cumberland. Son of James Scott and Mary.

2. Ann SCOTT (1809-) [2373]. Dau of James Scott and Mary. One reference states Ann was 6 years old when she died the 31 Jan 1809 and was born 1 Feb 1809. Clearly this is slightly incorrect.

2. Thomas SCOTT (1811-1811) [2374]. Born 28 Jan 1811. Thomas died 29 Jan 1811. Son of James Scott and Mary.

2. William SCOTT (1813-) [646]. Baptised 1813, St. James, Whitehaven, Cumberland. Son of James Scott and Mary.

2. Sarah SCOTT (1814-) [1759]. Born 21 Aug 1814, Baptised St. James, Cumberland. Dau of James Scott and Mary.

2. George SCOTT (1812-) [1760]. Born 18 Jan 1812, Baptised 2 Feb 1812, St. James, Cumberland. Son of James Scott and Mary.

2. James SCOTT (1808-) [982]. Born 2 Jun 1808. Baptised 25 June 1808, St. James, Whitehaven, Cumberland. Son of James Scott and Mary. When James was born in 1808 his father, James was noted as a Mason. James was a Shipwright Journeyman (Ship Carpenter).

James Marr Elizabeth. Unfortunately her surname has not been identified. Likewise James and Elizabeth could not be identified in the 1841 Census but do appear in the following 1851 and 1861 English Census.
Sp. Elizabeth (1811-) [983]. Born 1811, Cumberland.

1851 English Census, 1 Queen Street, Selaney's Passage, Cumberland
James SCOTT, age 42, born 1808, Whitehaven, Cumberland, Shipwright, Elizth SCOTT, wife, age 40, born 1811, Keswick, Cumberland, Anne SCOTT, dau, age 11, born 1840, Whitehaven, Cumberland, Isabella SCOTT, dau, age 8, born 1843, Whitehaven, Cumberland, James SCOTT, son, age 5, born 1846, Whitehaven, Cumberland, Georgeina SCOTT, dau, age 1, born 1850, Whitehaven, Cumberland.

1861 English Census, 1 Spittal's Court, Church Street, St Bees, Whitehaven, Cumberland, St Nicholas
James SCOTT, age 53, Shipwright Journeyman, born 1808, Whitehaven, Cumberland, Elizth SCOTT, wife, age 49, Shipwrights wife, born 1812, Keswick, Cumberland, Isabella SCOTT, dau, unmarried, age 18, born 1843, Whitehaven, Cumberland, Shipwright's dau, James SCOTT, son, age 15, Shipwrights son, born 1846, Whitehaven, Cumberland, Georgiana SCOTT, dau, age 11, Shipwright's dau, born 1850, Whitehaven, Cumberland.

James died between the 1861 and 1871 Census.

1871 English Census, Roper Street, Rod's Court, Whitehaven
Elizabeth SCOTT, age 60, born 1811, Cumberland, James SCOTT, son, age 25, born 1864, Cumberland, Printer's Compo.

3. James Dorthwaite SCOTT (1845-) [985]. Baptised 30 Nov 1845, St. James, Whitehaven. Son of James Scott and Elizabeth. In the 1871 English Census, Roper Street, Rod's Court, Whitehaven, James was living with his mother.

1881 English Census, 24 Senhouse, Street, Whitehaven, Cumberland
James SCOTT, Lodger, married, age 38, born 1843, Whitehaven, Cumberland, Printer's Compo.

   3. **Georgina SCOTT (1850-) [986].** Baptised 1850, St. James, Whitehaven, Cumberland. Dau of
      James Scott and Elizabeth.
   3. **Ann SCOTT (1840-) [1764].** Baptised 1840, St. James, Whitehaven, Cumberland. Dau of James
      Scott and Elizabeth.
   3. **Isabella SCOTT (1842-) [240].** Baptised June 1842, St. James, Whitehaven, Cumberland.
      Dau of James Scott and Elizabeth. Isabella firstly Marr William HARDING, Sep 1866,
      Whitehaven, Cumberland.
   Sp. William HARDING (-) [546].

1871 English Census, 107 Town of Whitehaven, Cumberland, Parish of Holy Trinity
Isabella HARDING age 28, born 1843, Whitehaven, Margaret HARDING, dau, age 3, Isaac HARDING,
son age 1.

   4. **Margaret HARDING (1868-) [547].** Born 1868, Whitehaven, Cumberland. Dau of Isabella
      Scott and William Harding.
   4. **Isaac HARDING (1870-) [548].** Born 1870, Whitehaven, Cumberland. Dau of Isabella Scott
      and William Harding.

It is assumed that William Harding died after 1870 and before the 1871 English Census.

After the death of William Harding, Isabella Marr William STOCKDALE, Widower, 2 Nov 1876,
Cockermouth, Workington, Cumberland.

Marriage Certificate
At the Registrar's Office, Cockermouth, Cumberland, on the 2nd Nov 1876, William Stockdale, age 46,
Widower, French Polisher, Udale Street, Workington, Cumberland, Father, Thomas Stockdale, Office Clerk,
Deceased, married Elizabeth Harding, age 35, Widow, Udale Street, Workington, Cumberland, Father,
James Scott, Ship Carpenter, Deceased. William signed his name and Elizabeth made an X as her mark.
Witnesses C Shilton and Mary Mc Laughlin. Shilton signed his name and Mary made an X as her mark.
   Sp. William STOCKDALE (circa 1830-) [239]. Born circa 1830, Tyrone, Ireland. Son of Thomas
      Stockdale.

STOCKDALE FAMILY

The English Census have been searched for Thomas Stockdale, without success. It is likely Thomas
remained in Ireland and the following information is likely to apply to this Stockdale family.

Tithe Applotment Books 1824-1837, Ireland. Courtesy of The National Archives of Ireland
  - Thomas Stockdale, Anahagh, Monaghan Township, City of Monaghan, 1826
  - Thol Stockdale, Township, City of Monaghan

Richard Griffiths' Primary Valuation of Ireland 1848-1864. Civil Parish of Co Tyrone, Ireland, 1851
  - Thomas Stockdale, Townland of Glasdrummond, Parish of Aghaloo, County Tyrone.

Although not confirmed it is likely William Stockdale was of Glasdrummond Aghaloo Tyrone, Northern
Ireland.

William first appears in the 1851 Scottish Census as follows

1851 Scottish Census, 288 Back Land, Buchanan Street, Barony, District Milton, Lanarkshire
William STOCKDALE, Lodger, unmarried, age 23, born 1828, Tyrone, Ireland. French Polisher
(Journeyman), Thomas HARRISON, Lodger, unmarried, age 22, born 1829, Belfast, Ireland. French
Polisher (Journeyman).

William became a soldier as the following census confirms

1861 Scottish Census, St. Gile's, Edinburgh, Canongate, Co Midlothian, Edinburgh Castle.
William STOCKDALE, Soldier, single, age 28, born 1833, Tyrone, Ireland.

At the time of the Scottish Census the regiment stationed at Edinburgh Castle was the 78th Highland
Regiment (Ross-shire Buffs). The regiment was actually based at Edinburgh Castle between 21 Feb 1860
and 8 May 1861. Previous to this the Regiment had been in India until 1859. The Regiment had also been
dispatched to many other places such as Ireland, Gibraltar and Canada.

It is not clear when William left the regiment and where he went from 1861 to 1876, when he is recorded as
marrying Elizabeth Harding nee Scott, 2 Nov 1876, Cockermouth. William was noted as a Widower. To date
no details have been found on his previous marriage.

1881 English Census, 5 Udale Street, Cockermouth, Workington, Cumberland
William STOCKDALE, born 1832, Tyrone, Ireland, age 48, French Polisher, Isabella STOCKDALE, wife,
born Whitehaven, age 36, French Polisher, Margaret HARDING, step dau, age 14, Isaac HARDING, step
son, age 12, Mary Elizabeth STOCKDALE, dau, age 6 months.

1891 English Census, Institution in Cockermouth, (Workhouse), Sullart Street, Cockermouth, Cumbria
William STOCKDALE, age 53, born 1837, Ireland, noted as being Infirm.

William died after 1885 when his daughter Annie Isabella was born and before 1898, when his daughter,
Mary, married Robert Hines.

1891 English Census, Parish of St John, Cumberland
Isabella STOCKDALE, age 46, born Whitehaven, Cumberland, French Polisher (Em'ee), Isaac HARDING,
son, age 22, Steelworker (Em'ee), born Whitehaven, Cumberland, Mary Elizabeth STOCKDALE, dau, age
10, Workington, Cumberland, Annie Isabella STOCKDALE, dau, age 6, born Workington, Cumberland,
William WILSON, Lodger, age 52, Joiner, born Workington, Cumberland.

1901 English Census, 1 Irving Court, Udale Street, Workington, Cockermouth, Cumberland
Robert HINES, age 23, born 1878, Northumberland, Steel Worker, Mary Elizabeth HINES, wife, age 20,
born 1881, Workington, Cumberland, Robert HINES, son, age 6 months, born 1901, Workington,
Cumberland, Annie Elizabeth STOCKDALE, sister-in-law, single age 16, born 1885, Workington,
Cumberland, Servant (Domestic), **Isabella STOCKDALE, Mother-in-law, Widow,** age 60, born 1841,
Workington, Cumberland, John MORLEY, visitor, single, age 40, born 1861, Carlisle, Cumberland, French
Polisher.

> 4. **Annie Isabella STOCKDALE (1885-) [549].** Born 1885, Cockermouth, Workington. Dau of
> William Stockdale and Isabella Harding nee Scott. In the 1891 English Census, Parish of St
> John, Cumberland and the 1901 English Census, 1 Irving Court, Udale Street, Workington,
> Cumberland, Annie Isabella was living with her mother.

> 4. **Mary Elizabeth STOCKDALE (1880-1952) [225].** Born 27 Sep 1880, Cockermouth,
> Workington. Baptised St Michael's and St Mary's, Workington, Cumbria. Dau of William
> Stockdale and Isabella Harding nee Scott. In the 1881 English Census, 5 Udale Street,
> Cockermouth, Workington, Cumberland, Mary Elizabeth was living with her mother and
> father and in the 1891 English Census, Parish of St John, Cumberland, Mary Elizabeth was
> living with her mother.

Birth Certificate
Registration District Cockermouth, Sub District Workington, County of Cumberland, Mary Elizabeth
Stockdale, 27 Sept 1880, 5 Udale Street, Workington, father William Stockdale, mother Isabella Stockdale,
late Harding, formerly Scott, father, French Polisher, registered by William Stockdale, father, 5 Udale Street,
Workington, 30 Sept 1880, John Lister Registrar.

Mary Elizabeth Marr Robert W HINES 1898, St. Michael's and St. Mary's RC, Workington, Cumbria.

Mary died 3 Sep 1952, age 73 years, Moston Hospital, Chester, Cheshire, buried Cemetery Gates,
Ellesmere Port, Cheshire with her daughter Lucy.

Sp. Robert W HINES (1875-1956) [224], son of William (Gulielmi) HINDS (1847-1875) [238] and Margaret (Marie) FLYNN or Finn (1849-) [908].

SEE HINES FAMILY

Chapter Fifteen

THE MERRYWEATHER FAMILY

Merryweather Family Outline

Male MERRYWEATHER (-)

1. Male MERRYWEATHER (-) [150].
   2. William MERRYWEATHER (-) [94].
   Sp. Female KITCHING / Mary WARD (-) [199].
      3. Charlotte MERRYWEATHER (1765-1832) [40].
      Sp. George DUTY (1759-1802) [114], son of Thomas DUTY (circa 1730-) [121] and Nancy
            BIRKETT (circa 1730-) [122].
         4. Birkett DUTY (1800-1879) [43].
         Sp. Ann (-1884) [42].
            5. William DUTY (1829-) [44].
            5. Birkett Merryweather DUTY (1878-) [123].
            5. Ann D DUTY (1847-) [41].
         4. Horatio Merryweather DUTY (1802-) [115].
         4. Thomas DUTY (1795-) [116].
         4. Richard DUTY (1790-) [118].
         4. Matilda DUTY (1793-) [117].
         4. Nancy DUTY (1789-) [119].
         4. George DUTY (1786-) [120].
         4. Ann DUTY (1789-) [182].
         Sp. Jeremiah WHITHAM (1772-1835) [205], son of James WITHAM (1749-1823) [206] and
               Anne MASON (-) [207].
            5. Richard WHITHAM (1824-) [209].
            5. John Merryweather WHITHAM (1822-) [210].
            5. Martha WHITHAM (1812-) [211].
            Sp. Thomas ASHTON (-) [212].
            5. Sarah WHITHAM (1811-) [213].
            Sp. Joseph TAYLOR (-) [214], son of Henry TAYLOR (-) [215].
            5. Mary Ann WHITHAM (1815-) [216].
            Sp. John BAGSHAW (-) [217], son of Jonathan BAGSHAW (-) [218].
            5. Thomas WHITHAM (1817-) [219].
         4. Robert DUTY (1797-) [198].
      3. Richard MANEYWEATHER (1766-1837) [80].
      Sp. Sarah NEWTON (1770-1828) [79].
         4. Horatio MERRYWEATHER (1798-1877) [13].
         Sp. Mary HOYLE (1806-1876) [12].
            5. Sarah Ann MERRYWEATHER (1834-) [18].
            5. Richard J MERRYWEATHER (1835-1907) [4].
            Sp. Emma WOOD (1841-1917) [3], dau. of James WOOD (1820-) [151].
               6. Ann MERRYWEATHER (1862-1907) [6].
               6. Walter MERRYWEATHER (1867-) [9].
               6. Emily MERRYWEATHER (1870-1873) [7].
               6. George MERRYWEATHER (1872-1949) [11].
               Sp. Selina TAYLOR (1875-1950) [77].
                  7. Richard James MERRYWEATHER (1904-1959) [90].
                  Sp. Eleanor GILBERT (-) [156], dau. of Hezekiah GILBERT (-) [157].
                  7. Arthur MERRYWEATHER (1906-1967) [88].
                  7. Alfred MERRYWEATHER (1908-1924) [89].
                  7. Mabel MERRYWEATHER (1908-) [76].
                  7. Harry MERRYWEATHER (1911-1987) [87].
                  7. Evelyn MERRYWEATHER (1912-) [86].
                  7. William MERRYWEATHER (1915-1972) [158].
                  Sp. Joan SYKES (-) [159].

6. Louisa MERRYWEATHER (1877-) [10].
6. Joseph MERRYWEATHER (1882-) [2].
Sp. Jessie MCLEOD (1881-1962) [5], dau. of Hugh MCLEOD (-) [152].
    7. Walter Hugh MERRYWEATHER (1906-1990) [1].
    Sp. Rose GRIFFITHS (1905-) [75], dau. of James GRIFFITHS (1886-) [73] and
        Eizabeth STEADMAN (1883-) [74].
        8. Joseph MERRYWEATHER (1928-) [85].
        8. Mabel BRACKLEY (-) [223].
        8. Robert MERRYWEATHER (1930-2000) [84].
        Sp. Francis Rose PRICE (1934-1983) [146], dau. of Joseph Leonard PRICE
           (1912-1987) [148] and Frances Rose SAYCE (1911-1993) [147].
    Sp. Daphne LM LILLEY (-) [153].
    7. Nelly MERRYWEATHER (-) [154].
    Sp. Benjamin MARKS (-) [155].
6. Horatio MERRYWEATHER (1864-) [160].
6. Thomas MERRYWEATHER (1865-) [200].
Sp. Ada (1880-) [201].
    7. Leonard MERRYWEATHER (1903-) [202].
    7. Doris MERRYWEATHER (1905-) [203].
    7. Walter MERRYWEATHER (1907-) [204].
5. Mary MERRYWEATHER (1837-) [19].
5. Hannah Newton MERRYWEATHER (1840-1858) [15].
5. Horatio MERRYWEATHER (1842-1918) [17].
6. Mary MERRYWEATHER (1866-) [26].
6. Thomas H MERRYWEATHER (1868-) [23].
Sp. Isabella KENYON (1873-) [149].
    7. Ida MERRYWEATHER (1897-) [177].
    7. Thomas MERRYWEATHER (1898-) [178].
    7. Alice MERRYWEATHER (1900-) [179].
    7. Edith MERRYWEATHER (1902-) [180].
    7. Doris MERRYWEATHER (1904-) [181].
6. Jane MERRYWEATHER (1870-) [24].
6. Horatio MERRYWEATHER (1872-1941) [22].
Sp. Rossetta CONNOLLY (1882 -) [169].
    7. Horatio MERRYWEATHER (1904-) [170].
    Sp. Marjorie C STANFORD (-) [171].
    7. Rossetta MERRYWEATHER (1906-) [172].
    Sp. Joseph William FITTON (-) [173].
    7. Andrew MERRYWEATHER (1911-) [174].
6. Alice Ann MERRYWEATHER (1874-) [20].
Sp. Albert SHAW (1878-) [175].
    7. Albert Nelson SHAW (1906-) [176].
6. Ada MERRYWEATHER (1879-) [25].
5. Jane MERRYWEATHER (1843-) [16].
5. Ellen / Helen MERRYWEATHER (1849-) [14].
4. Harriet MERRYWEATHER (1799-) [78].
3. Melissa MERRYWEATHER (1767-) [38].
Sp. George FRANCE (-) [37].
3. Edward MERRYWEATHER (1774-) [31].
Sp. Lucy KAY (-1806) [221].
4. Lucy MERRYWEATHER (1806-1806) [222].
Sp. Catherine MILES (1792-1867) [27].
4. George Edward MERRYWEATHER (1817-) [30].
Sp. Hannah (1823-) [34].
5. John MERRYWEATHER (1848-) [35].
4. Julia MERRYWEATHER (1826-) [28].
5. Eleanor Florence MERRYWEATHER (1856-) [32].
5. Henry MERRYWEATHER (1860-) [33].
3. Mary MANEYWETHERS (1759-) [183].
Sp. Joseph PEACE (1761-) [184].

      4. Mary PEACE (1789-) [185].
      4. Hannah PEACE (1791-) [186].
      4. George PEACE (1793-) [187].
      4. Henry PEACE (1795-) [188].
      4. Melissa PEACE (1796-) [189].
      4. Joseph PEACE (1800-) [190].
    3. George MANEYWEATHER (1770-) [220].
    3. Elizabeth MANEYWETHERS (1755-) [191].
    Sp. George HANLEY (-) [192].
2. John MERRYWEATHER (1742-) [193].
Sp. (unknown).
    3. Charlotte MERRYWEATHER (1763-) [194].
    3. John MERRYWEATHER (1776-) [195].
    Sp. Martha SAVILLE (-) [196].
      4. Alfred John MERRYWEATHER (1815-) [197].

Merryweather Lineage

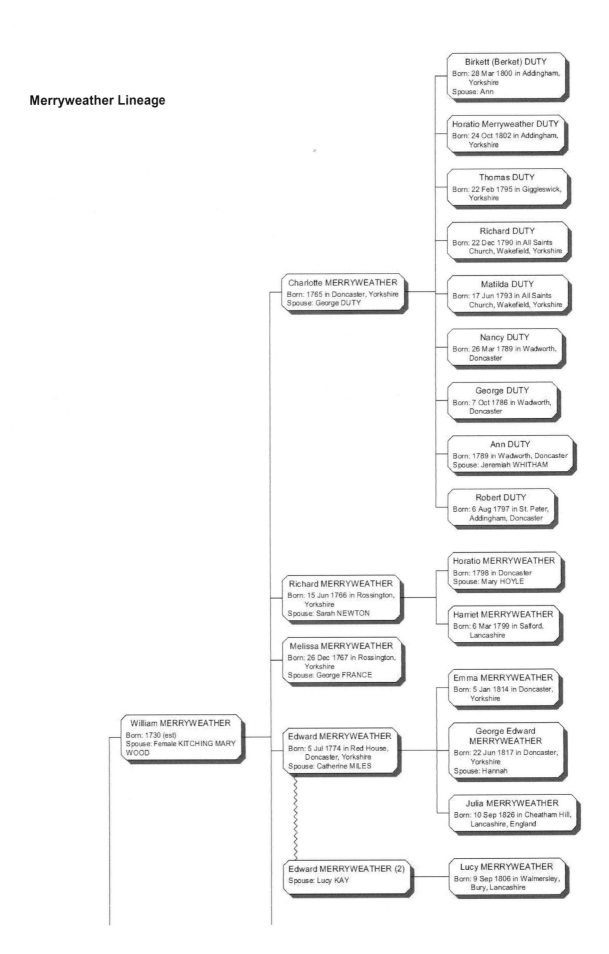

Birkett (Berket) DUTY
Born: 28 Mar 1800 in Addingham, Yorkshire
Spouse: Ann

Horatio Merryweather DUTY
Born: 24 Oct 1802 in Addingham, Yorkshire

Thomas DUTY
Born: 22 Feb 1795 in Giggleswick, Yorkshire

Richard DUTY
Born: 22 Dec 1790 in All Saints Church, Wakefield, Yorkshire

Matilda DUTY
Born: 17 Jun 1793 in All Saints Church, Wakefield, Yorkshire

Nancy DUTY
Born: 26 Mar 1789 in Wadworth, Doncaster

George DUTY
Born: 7 Oct 1786 in Wadworth, Doncaster

Ann DUTY
Born: 1789 in Wadworth, Doncaster
Spouse: Jeremiah WHITHAM

Robert DUTY
Born: 6 Aug 1797 in St. Peter, Addingham, Doncaster

Charlotte MERRYWEATHER
Born: 1765 in Doncaster, Yorkshire
Spouse: George DUTY

Horatio MERRYWEATHER
Born: 1798 in Doncaster
Spouse: Mary HOYLE

Harriet MERRYWEATHER
Born: 6 Mar 1799 in Salford, Lancashire

Richard MERRYWEATHER
Born: 15 Jun 1766 in Rossington, Yorkshire
Spouse: Sarah NEWTON

Melissa MERRYWEATHER
Born: 26 Dec 1767 in Rossington, Yorkshire
Spouse: George FRANCE

Emma MERRYWEATHER
Born: 5 Jan 1814 in Doncaster, Yorkshire

George Edward MERRYWEATHER
Born: 22 Jun 1817 in Doncaster, Yorkshire
Spouse: Hannah

Julia MERRYWEATHER
Born: 10 Sep 1826 in Cheatham Hill, Lancashire, England

William MERRYWEATHER
Born: 1730 (est)
Spouse: Female KITCHING MARY WOOD

Edward MERRYWEATHER
Born: 5 Jul 1774 in Red House, Doncaster, Yorkshire
Spouse: Catherine MILES

Edward MERRYWEATHER (2)
Spouse: Lucy KAY

Lucy MERRYWEATHER
Born: 9 Sep 1806 in Walmersley, Bury, Lancashire

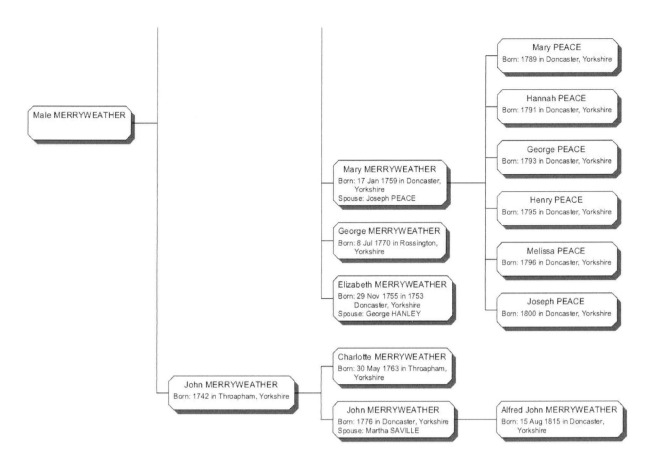

Male MERRYWEATHER

Mary MERRYWEATHER
Born: 17 Jan 1759 in Doncaster, Yorkshire
Spouse: Joseph PEACE

George MERRYWEATHER
Born: 8 Jul 1770 in Rossington, Yorkshire

Elizabeth MERRYWEATHER
Born: 29 Nov 1755 in 1753 Doncaster, Yorkshire
Spouse: George HANLEY

Mary PEACE
Born: 1789 in Doncaster, Yorkshire

Hannah PEACE
Born: 1791 in Doncaster, Yorkshire

George PEACE
Born: 1793 in Doncaster, Yorkshire

Henry PEACE
Born: 1795 in Doncaster, Yorkshire

Melissa PEACE
Born: 1796 in Doncaster, Yorkshire

Joseph PEACE
Born: 1800 in Doncaster, Yorkshire

John MERRYWEATHER
Born: 1742 in Throapham, Yorkshire

Charlotte MERRYWEATHER
Born: 30 May 1763 in Throapham, Yorkshire

John MERRYWEATHER
Born: 1776 in Doncaster, Yorkshire
Spouse: Martha SAVILLE

Alfred John MERRYWEATHER
Born: 15 Aug 1815 in Doncaster, Yorkshire

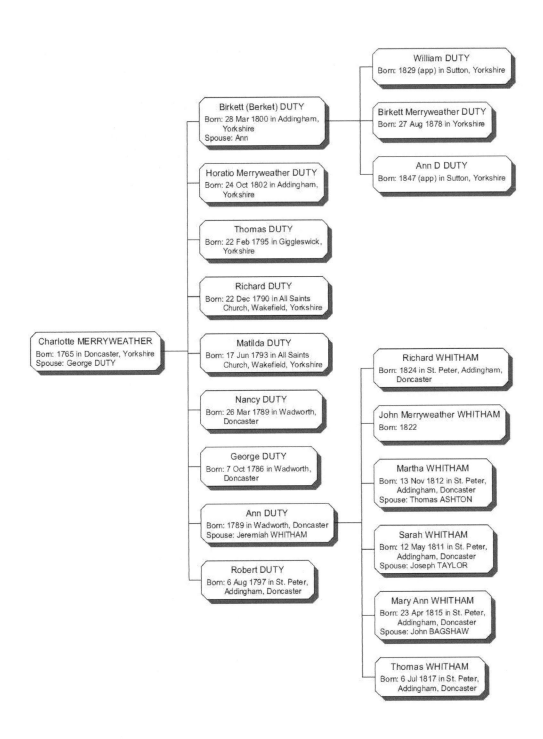

William DUTY
Born: 1829 (app) in Sutton, Yorkshire

Birkett Merryweather DUTY
Born: 27 Aug 1878 in Yorkshire

Ann D DUTY
Born: 1847 (app) in Sutton, Yorkshire

Birkett (Berket) DUTY
Born: 28 Mar 1800 in Addingham,
Yorkshire
Spouse: Ann

Horatio Merryweather DUTY
Born: 24 Oct 1802 in Addingham,
Yorkshire

Thomas DUTY
Born: 22 Feb 1795 in Giggleswick,
Yorkshire

Richard DUTY
Born: 22 Dec 1790 in All Saints
Church, Wakefield, Yorkshire

Charlotte MERRYWEATHER
Born: 1765 in Doncaster, Yorkshire
Spouse: George DUTY

Matilda DUTY
Born: 17 Jun 1793 in All Saints
Church, Wakefield, Yorkshire

Richard WHITHAM
Born: 1824 in St. Peter, Addingham,
Doncaster

John Merryweather WHITHAM
Born: 1822

Nancy DUTY
Born: 26 Mar 1789 in Wadworth,
Doncaster

Martha WHITHAM
Born: 13 Nov 1812 in St. Peter,
Addingham, Doncaster
Spouse: Thomas ASHTON

George DUTY
Born: 7 Oct 1786 in Wadworth,
Doncaster

Sarah WHITHAM
Born: 12 May 1811 in St. Peter,
Addingham, Doncaster
Spouse: Joseph TAYLOR

Ann DUTY
Born: 1789 in Wadworth, Doncaster
Spouse: Jeremiah WHITHAM

Mary Ann WHITHAM
Born: 23 Apr 1815 in St. Peter,
Addingham, Doncaster
Spouse: John BAGSHAW

Robert DUTY
Born: 6 Aug 1797 in St. Peter,
Addingham, Doncaster

Thomas WHITHAM
Born: 6 Jul 1817 in St. Peter,
Addingham, Doncaster

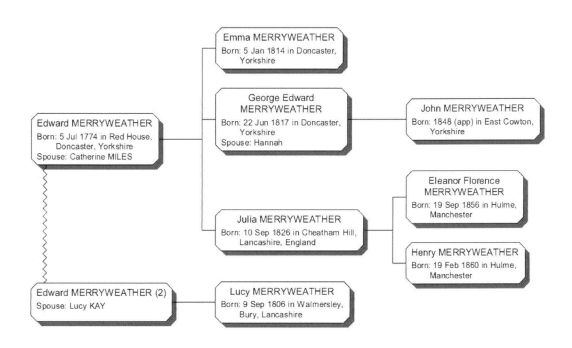

Edward MERRYWEATHER
Born: 5 Jul 1774 in Red House, Doncaster, Yorkshire
Spouse: Catherine MILES

Emma MERRYWEATHER
Born: 5 Jan 1814 in Doncaster, Yorkshire

George Edward MERRYWEATHER
Born: 22 Jun 1817 in Doncaster, Yorkshire
Spouse: Hannah

John MERRYWEATHER
Born: 1848 (app) in East Cowton, Yorkshire

Julia MERRYWEATHER
Born: 10 Sep 1826 in Cheatham Hill, Lancashire, England

Eleanor Florence MERRYWEATHER
Born: 19 Sep 1856 in Hulme, Manchester

Henry MERRYWEATHER
Born: 19 Feb 1860 in Hulme, Manchester

Edward MERRYWEATHER (2)
Spouse: Lucy KAY

Lucy MERRYWEATHER
Born: 9 Sep 1806 in Walmersley, Bury, Lancashire

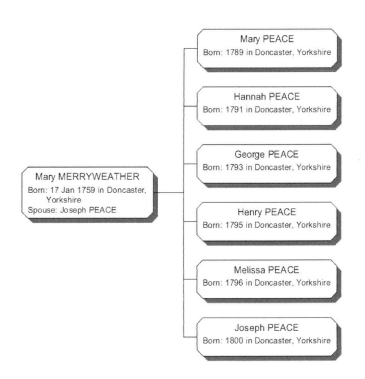

Mary MERRYWEATHER
Born: 17 Jan 1759 in Doncaster, Yorkshire
Spouse: Joseph PEACE

Mary PEACE
Born: 1789 in Doncaster, Yorkshire

Hannah PEACE
Born: 1791 in Doncaster, Yorkshire

George PEACE
Born: 1793 in Doncaster, Yorkshire

Henry PEACE
Born: 1795 in Doncaster, Yorkshire

Melissa PEACE
Born: 1796 in Doncaster, Yorkshire

Joseph PEACE
Born: 1800 in Doncaster, Yorkshire

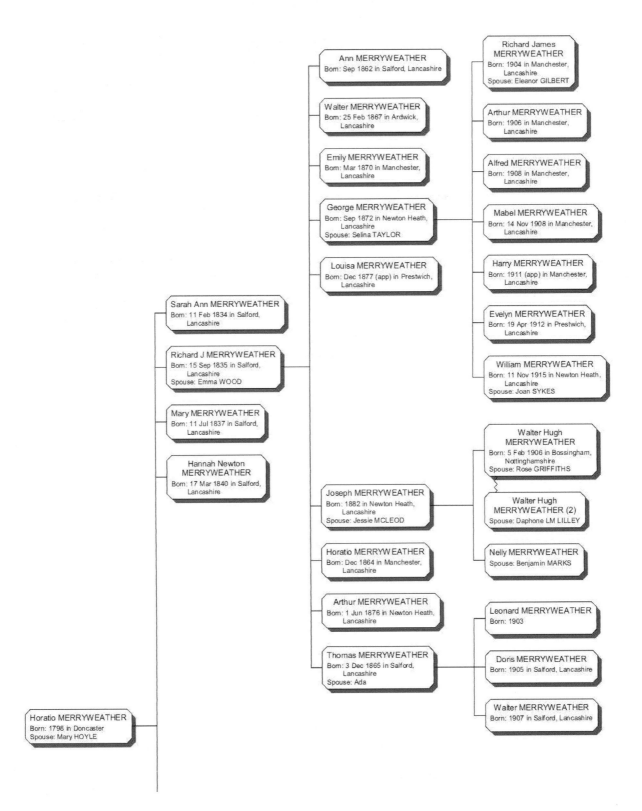

Ann MERRYWEATHER
Born: Sep 1862 in Salford, Lancashire

Walter MERRYWEATHER
Born: 25 Feb 1867 in Ardwick, Lancashire

Emily MERRYWEATHER
Born: Mar 1870 in Manchester, Lancashire

George MERRYWEATHER
Born: Sep 1872 in Newton Heath, Lancashire
Spouse: Selina TAYLOR

Louisa MERRYWEATHER
Born: Dec 1877 (app) in Prestwich, Lancashire

Richard James MERRYWEATHER
Born: 1904 in Manchester, Lancashire
Spouse: Eleanor GILBERT

Arthur MERRYWEATHER
Born: 1906 in Manchester, Lancashire

Alfred MERRYWEATHER
Born: 1908 in Manchester, Lancashire

Mabel MERRYWEATHER
Born: 14 Nov 1908 in Manchester, Lancashire

Harry MERRYWEATHER
Born: 1911 (app) in Manchester, Lancashire

Evelyn MERRYWEATHER
Born: 19 Apr 1912 in Prestwich, Lancashire

William MERRYWEATHER
Born: 11 Nov 1915 in Newton Heath, Lancashire
Spouse: Joan SYKES

Sarah Ann MERRYWEATHER
Born: 11 Feb 1834 in Salford, Lancashire

Richard J MERRYWEATHER
Born: 15 Sep 1835 in Salford, Lancashire
Spouse: Emma WOOD

Mary MERRYWEATHER
Born: 11 Jul 1837 in Salford, Lancashire

Hannah Newton MERRYWEATHER
Born: 17 Mar 1840 in Salford, Lancashire

Joseph MERRYWEATHER
Born: 1882 in Newton Heath, Lancashire
Spouse: Jessie MCLEOD

Horatio MERRYWEATHER
Born: Dec 1864 in Manchester, Lancashire

Arthur MERRYWEATHER
Born: 1 Jun 1876 in Newton Heath, Lancashire

Thomas MERRYWEATHER
Born: 3 Dec 1865 in Salford, Lancashire
Spouse: Ada

Walter Hugh MERRYWEATHER
Born: 5 Feb 1906 in Bossingham, Nottinghamshire
Spouse: Rose GRIFFITHS

Walter Hugh MERRYWEATHER (2)
Spouse: Daphone LM LILLEY

Nelly MERRYWEATHER
Spouse: Benjamin MARKS

Leonard MERRYWEATHER
Born: 1903

Doris MERRYWEATHER
Born: 1905 in Salford, Lancashire

Walter MERRYWEATHER
Born: 1907 in Salford, Lancashire

Horatio MERRYWEATHER
Born: 1798 in Doncaster
Spouse: Mary HOYLE

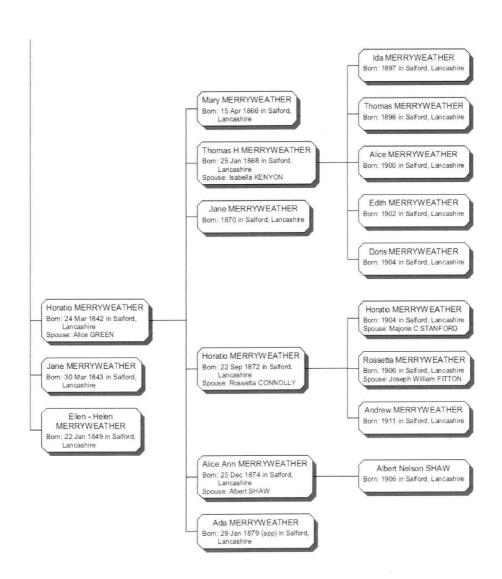

Horatio MERRYWEATHER
Born: 24 Mar 1842 in Salford, Lancashire
Spouse: Alice GREEN

Jane MERRYWEATHER
Born: 30 Mar 1843 in Salford, Lancashire

Ellen - Helen MERRYWEATHER
Born: 22 Jan 1849 in Salford, Lancashire

Mary MERRYWEATHER
Born: 15 Apr 1866 in Salford, Lancashire

Thomas H MERRYWEATHER
Born: 25 Jan 1868 in Salford, Lancashire
Spouse: Isabella KENYON

Jane MERRYWEATHER
Born: 1870 in Salford, Lancashire

Horatio MERRYWEATHER
Born: 22 Sep 1872 in Salford, Lancashire
Spouse: Rossetta CONNOLLY

Alice Ann MERRYWEATHER
Born: 25 Dec 1874 in Salford, Lancashire
Spouse: Albert SHAW

Ada MERRYWEATHER
Born: 29 Jan 1879 (app) in Salford, Lancashire

Ida MERRYWEATHER
Born: 1897 in Salford, Lancashire

Thomas MERRYWEATHER
Born: 1898 in Salford, Lancashire

Alice MERRYWEATHER
Born: 1900 in Salford, Lancashire

Edith MERRYWEATHER
Born: 1902 in Salford, Lancashire

Doris MERRYWEATHER
Born: 1904 in Salford, Lancashire

Horatio MERRYWEATHER
Born: 1904 in Salford, Lancashire
Spouse: Majorie C STANFORD

Rossetta MERRYWEATHER
Born: 1906 in Salford, Lancashire
Spouse: Joseph William FITTON

Andrew MERRYWEATHER
Born: 1911 in Salford, Lancashire

Albert Nelson SHAW
Born: 1906 in Salford, Lancashire

1. Male MERRYWEATHER (-) [150]. The name or where this person came from has not been confirmed as there are numerous possibilities. Identifying relationships have been difficult due to the number of spellings of the surname and the fact that these Merryweathers in the earlier years appear to have moved from place to place.

What is certain is that Richard Merryweather and Sarah Newton are the confirmed direct line. Richard was born in Doncaster and his father was William Merryweather/Maneyweather of Red House, Doncaster.

As much detail as possible has been gathered which is detailed below in an attempt to identify and assume the lineage to the above mentioned William.

2. William MERRYWEATHER (-) [94]. Born between 1730 to 1753.

Folklore suggests this family are
- originally Irish, then Scottish
- linked to the Merryweather family of Lincolnshire - William Merryweather baptised 1 June 1740, Treswell, Nottinghamshire born to John Merriweather and Mary
- closely related to the surname Merrilees
- linked to the Merryweather family of Besdale, Yorkshire – Richard born 1665, father of Dorothy Merryweather baptised 9 Dec 1686, Besdale and Richard Merryweather baptised 1691, Besdale, who married Mary Johnson 10 Nov 1738, Hornby by Besdale.

  Richard Merryweather and Mary Johnson had the following -Thomas Merryweather baptised 30 Sept 1739, Hornby by Besdale and married Ann Cumin, Richard Merryweaher born 1745, Hornby by Besdale, William Merryweather born 1740, Hornby by Besdale, who died Sept 1743 and William Merryweather born 1743, Hornby by Besdale, Yorkshire. This may be William of Rossington, Yorkshire and the following family line.

William Merryweather was the Inn Keeper at Red House, Doncaster in at least 1774, when his son Edward was born, until 1790, as the following Affidavits of Debt and Writs confirms.

An Affidavits of Debt and Writs of Capias document dated 1790 regarding William Merryweather, Innkeeper, being in debt to Lucy and John Howarth. – Courtesy of Doncaster Archives.

The details of this document are difficult to read but they appear to suggest William Merryweather, on 2 May 1773, wrote a promise note to John Howarth to pay a debt. It is not clear what the debt was for but it appears as though it may be damage through trespass.

- 8 Feb 1790, John Howarth took William Merryweather to court for what appears to be non payment on his promise note. John Howarth plaintiff, and amount of forty three pounds, eleven shillings and 6 pence was mentioned
- 8 Feb 1790, Lucy Howarth, claimed the interest on non payment of twenty two pounds, eighteen shillings and four pence, from William Merryweather, Inn Keeper, Red House, Doncaster
- 8 Feb 1790, a receipt is issued by John Howarth for twenty two pounds and eighteen shillings and four pence for the debt and costs from William Merryweather. The witness is Richard Merryweather.

Red House, so called because it was painted red, is situated on Red House Lane which connects Adwick-le-Street, Doncaster with the main road. Red House was a coaching inn which stood on the corner. This coaching house would have had room for about 20 horses. It closed as a coaching house in the mid 19th century. The property still stands and is now a farm house. The old stabling area also still stands. There is now a junction at the location and known as Red House interchange.

The following information has been included for interest

- A book recording Addingham Registers 1797-98, notes William Merryweather was married to a Kitching
- William is also recorded as William Maneyweather

- A William Maneweathers, sometimes spelt Meanyweathers married Mary Ward, widow, 12 Feb 1756, Cantley Parish, Yorkshire (this parish is not far from Rossington) by William Grice, Vicar, witnesses Thomas Chester and Thomas Singleton
- It is possible Mary Ward may have previously been a Kitching
- The following children were born to William

  - Elizabeth MANEYWETHERS (1755-) [191]. Born 29 Nov 1755, Cantley, Yorkshire, dau of William and Mary Maneyweather, of Gate, Farmer. – As Elizabeth was born before William's marriage to Mary Ward was Elizabeth from a previous marriage. Elizabeth married George Hanley, 1 Nov 1774, Adwick-le-Street, Doncaster.
  - Charlotte MERRYWEATHER (1765-1832) [40]. Born 1765, Doncaster, Yorkshire, dau of William Merryweather and Kitching.
  - Mary MANEYWETHERS (1759-) [183]. Born 17 Jan 1759, Cantley, Yorkshire, dau of William and Mary Maneyweather, of Gate, Farmer.
  - Richard MANEYWEATHER (1766-1837) [80]. Born 15 Jun 1766, Rossington, Yorkshire, son of William Maneyweather
  - Melissa MERRYWEATHER (1767-) [38]. Baptised 6 Dec 1767, Rossington, Yorkshire, dau of William Merryweather,
  - George MANEYWEATHER (1770-) [220]. Born 8 Jul 1770, Rossington, Yorkshire, Son of William Maneyweather.
  - Edward MERRYWEATHER (1774-) [31]. Baptised 5 Jul 1774, Adwick-le-Street, born Red House, Doncaster, Yorkshire, son of William Merryweather.

If indeed this is the same William the above records would suggest William Merryweather/Maneyweather was in Cantley, (Borough of Doncaster) Yorkshire until 1759 and by 1766, had moved to Rossington, (Borough of Doncaster), Yorkshire and by 1774 he was the Inn Keeper at Red House, Doncaster.
> Sp. Female KITCHING /Mary WARD (-) [199]. William's wife was noted as a Kitching when Charlotte's (his daughter), grand daughter was born in 1811. Therefore, it is possible a 'female' Kitching married a Ward before marrying William in 1756.

> 3. **Charlotte MERRYWEATHER (1765-1832) [40].** Born 1765, Doncaster, Yorkshire. Dau of William Merryweather, Inn Keeper Red House. A book recording Addingham Registers 1797-98, notes William Merryweather was married to a Kitching.

There were two different Charlottes, one baptised 30 May 1763, Throapham, Doncaster, Yorkshire born to John Merryweather and Charlotte born 1765, Doncaster, Yorkshire to William Merryweather.

Charlotte, daughter of William Merryweather and Kitching, Marr George DUTY, 7 Oct 1786, Adwick-le-Street, Doncaster Yorkshire. A further record states Charlotte of Adwick le Street Marr George Duty, 12 May 1784. It is not clear which is correct. On her marriage details it states she was born in 1763.

Charlotte died Jan 1832, Addingham Yorkshire.

> Sp. **George DUTY (1759-1802) [114]**, son of Thomas Duty and nancy Birkett.

> > 4. **Birkett DUTY (1800-1879) [43].** Born 28 Mar 1800, baptised 27 Apr 1800, St. Peter, Addingham, Yorkshire. Son of Charlotte and George Duty. Birkett died 11 Jul 1879, Sutton, Keighly, Yorkshire.
> > Sp. **Ann (-1884) [42].**
> > > 5. **William DUTY (1829-) [44].** Born 1829, Sutton, Yorkshire.
> > > 5. **Birkett Merryweather DUTY (1878-) [123].** Born 27 Aug 1878, Yorkshire.
> > > 5. **Ann D DUTY (1847-) [41].** Born 1847, Sutton, Yorkshire,
> > 4. **Horatio Merryweather DUTY (1802-) [115].** Born 16 Jan 1802, baptised 24 Oct 1802, St. Peter, Addingham, Yorkshire.
> > 4. **Thomas DUTY (1795-) [116].** Born 22 Feb 1795, Giggleswick, Yorkshire.
> > 4. **Richard DUTY (1790-) [118].** Baptised 22 Dec 1790, All Saints, Wakefield, Yorkshire.
> > 4. **Matilda DUTY (1793-) [117].** Baptised 17 Jun 1793, All Saints, Wakefield, Yorkshire.
> > 4. **Nancy DUTY (1789-) [119].** Baptised 26 Mar 1789, Wadworth, Doncaster, Yorkshire.
> > 4. **George DUTY (1786-) [120].** Born 7 Oct 1786, baptised 7 Oct 1786, Wadworth, Doncaster, Yorkshire.

4. **Ann DUTY (1789-) [182].** Born 1789, Wadworth, Doncaster, Yorkshire. Ann Marr Jeremiah WHITHAM, 3 Dec 1810, St. Peter, Addingham, Yorkshire. Witnesses Joseph Atkinson, John Cockshott and William Booth. Witham surname spelt Whiteham.

Sp. **Jeremiah WHITHAM (1772-1835) [205].** Baptised 6 Jan 1772, St. Peter, Addingham, Yorkshire. Son of James Witham born 1749, died 1823 and Anne Mason.. Jeremiah was noted as a Jobber and Farmer. Jeremiah died Apr 1835, Addingham.

5. **Richard WHITHAM (1824-) [209].** Baptised 1824, St. Peter, Addingham, Yorkshire.
5. **John Merryweather WHITHAM (1822-) [210].** Born 1822, Addingham, Yorkshire.
5. **Martha WHITHAM (1812-) [211].** Baptised 13 Nov 1812, St. Peter, Addingham, Yorkshire. Martha Marr Thomas ASHTON, 18 Jan 1836.
Sp. **Thomas ASHTON (-) [212].**
5. **Sarah WHITHAM (1811-) [213].** Born 20 March 1811, baptised 12 May 1811, St. Peter, Addingham, Yorkshire. Sarah Marr Joseph TAYLOR, 13 Apr 1838, St. Peter, Addingham, Yorkshire.
Sp. **Joseph TAYLOR (-) [214],** son of Henry Taylor.
5. **Mary Ann WHITHAM (1815-) [216].** Baptised 23 Apr 1815, St. Peter, Addingham, Yorkshire. Mary Ann Marr John BAGSHAW, 3 Aug 1844, St. Peter, Addingham, Yorkshire.
Sp. **John BAGSHAW (-) [217],** son of Jonathan Bagshaw.
5. **Thomas WHITHAM (1817-) [219].** Baptised 6 Jul 1817, St. Peter, Addingham, Yorkshire.

4. **Robert DUTY (1797-) [198].** Baptised 6 Aug 1797, St. Peter, Addingham, Yorkshire.

3. **Richard MANEYWEATHER (1766-1837) [80].** Baptised 15 Jun 1766, Rossington, Yorkshire. Surname spelt manyweather. Son of William Maneyweather. Richard Marr Sarah NEWTON, 26 Oct 1791, Manchester Cathedral, Lancashire. Witnesses John Tyass and T Boardman. Richard was noted as an Agent. Richard, died Oct 1837, Widower, buried 11 Oct 1837, St. Luke, Chorlton-upon-Medlock, Lancashire age 71.

Sp. **Sarah NEWTON (1770-1828) [79].** Born 1770. Sarah died 1828, age 63.

4. **Horatio MERRYWEATHER (1798-1877) [13].** Born 1798. One census states born Salford, Lancashire, however, the 1871, Census records born at Doncaster. Given the family details it is likely he was born in Doncaster. Son of Richard Merryweather and Sarah Newton. Horatio Marr Mary HOYLE, 16 Dec 1832, Manchester Cathedral, Lancashire. Horatio died Sep 1877, Salford, Lancashire, age 78.

1841 English Census Mount Pleasant, Salford, Lancashire
Horatio MARYWEATHER, age 43, born 1798, Lancashire, Agent, Mary MARYWEATHER, wife, age 35, born 1806, Lancashire, Richard MARYWEATHER, son, age 6, born 1835, Lancashire, Mary MARYWEATHER, dau, age 4, born 1837, Lancashire, Hannah F MARYWEATHER, dau, age 1, born 1840, Lancashire.

1851 English Census, 3 Paradise Hill, Manchester
Horatio MERRYWEATHER, age 52, born 1799, Manchester, Collector of Poor Rate, Mary MERRYWEATHER, wife, age 44, born 1807, Manchester, Sarah Anne MERRYWEATHER, dau, unmar, age 17, born 1834, Salford, Richard J MERRYWEATHER, son, unmarr, age 15, born 1836, Salford, Mary MERRYWEATHER, dau, age 13, born 1838, Salford, Hannah N MERRYWEATHER, dau, age 10, born 1841, Salford, Horatio MERRYWEATHER, son, age 9, born 1842, Salford, Jane MERRYWEATHER, dau, age 7, born 1844, Salford, Ellen MERRYWEATHER, dau, age 2, born 1849, Salford, Julia MERRYWEATHER, cousin, unmarr, age 24, born 1827, Manchester, Dress Maker.

(Julia mentioned above is the daughter of Edward Merryweather and Catherine Miles)

1861 English Census, 3 Square, Mason Street, Manchester
Horatio MERRYWEATHER, age 62, born 1799, Manchester, Book Keeper, Mary MERRYWEATHER, wife, age 50, born 1808, Manchester, Helen MERRYWEATHER, dau, age 12, born 1849, Manchester, Nurse.

1871 English Census, Copper Street, Manchester
Horatio MERRYWEATHER, age 72, born 1799, Doncaster, Gas Man, Mary MERRYWEATHER, wife, age 65, born 1806, Lancashire.

Sp. Mary HOYLE (1806-1876) [12]. Born 1806. Mary died Jun 1876 Salford, age 69

5. Sarah Ann MERRYWEATHER (1834-) [18]. Born 11 Feb 1833, Salford, St Stephen, Lancashire, baptised 25 Dec 1874, St. Matthew, Lancashire. Dau of Horatio Merryweather and Mary Hoyle.

In the 1841 English Census, Cook Street, Chorlton Upon Medlock, Lancashire. Sarah Ann, age 3, born 1835, was living with Sarah Bullock, age 37, James Bullock, age 14, Jane Ashworth, age 68, Ralph Andrew, age 50 and Samuel Ashworth age 32. It is not known what relation Sarah Ann is to them. In the 1851 English Census, 3 Paradise Hill, Manchester Sarah Ann is living with her parents.

5. Richard J MERRYWEATHER (1835-1907) [4]. Baptised 15 Sep 1835, St. Stephen, Salford, Lancashire. Son of Horatio Merryweather and Mary Hoyle. Richard J, age 24, Marr Emma WOOD, 19 Feb 1860, St. Simons, Salford, Lancashire. Richard J died Mar 1907, Fylde, Lancashire, age 71. In the 1841 English Census, Mount Pleasant, Salford and 1851 English Census, 3 Paradise Hill, Manchester, Richard is living with his parents

1861 English Census 4 High Prospect Street, Salford, Lancashire
Richard Jas MERRYWEATHER, age 26, born 1837, Lancashire, Tin plate worker, Emma MERRYWEATHER, wife, age 20, born 1841, Lancashire, Horatio MERRYWEATHER, Brother, age 19, born 1842, Blacksmith.

1871 English Census, Pickstone Street, Newton Heath, Manchester
Richard Jas MERRYWEATHER, age 34, born 1837, Lancashire, Tin plate worker, Emma MERRYWEATHER, wife, age 30, born 1841, Lancashire, Ann MERRYWEATHER, dau, age 8, born 1863, Lancashire, Thomas MERRYWEATHER, son, age 5, born 1866, Lancashire, Walter MERRYWEATHER, son, age 3, born 1868, Lancashire, Emily MERRYWEATHER, dau, age 1, born 1870, Lancashire.

1881 English Census 104 Oldham Road, Newton, Lancashire
Richard James MERRYWEATHER, age 45, born 1836, Salford, Tin Plate Worker, Emma MERRYWEATHER, wife, age 40, born 1841, Salford, Thomas MERRYWEATHER, son, age 15, born 1866, Salford, Tin Plate Worker, Walter MERRYWEATHER, son, age 14, born 1867, Ardwick, Lancashire, Optician, George MERRYWEATHER, son, age 8 born 1873, Newton, Lancashire, Ann MERRYWEATHER, dau, age 18, born 1863, Salford, Louisa MERRYWEATHER, dau, age 3, born 1878, Newton, Lancashire.

1891 English Census 30 Cresswell Street, Newton, Manchester
Richard J MERRYWEATHER, age 55, born 1836, Salford, Tin Plate Worker, Emma MERRYWEATHER, wife, age 50, born 1841, Salford, Anne MERRYWEATHER, dau, single, age 27, born 1864, Salford, Tailoress, Thomas MERRYWEATHER, son, single, age 25, born 1866, Salford, Tin Plate Worker, George MERRYWEATHER, son, single, age 18, born 1873, Salford, Iron Turner, Louisa MERRYWEATHER, dau, age 13, born 1873, Newton Heath, Lancashire, Joseph MERRYWEATHER, son, age 9, born 1882, Newton Heath, Lancashire.

1901 English Census, 70 Ashley Lane, Failsworth, Harpurhey, North Manchester
Richard J MERRYWEATHER, age 65, born 1836, Salford, Sheet Metal Worker, Emma MERRYWEATHER, wife, age 60, born 1841, Salford, Thomas MERRYWEATHER, son, single, age 35, born 1866, Salford, Sheet Metal Worker, George MERRYWEATHER, son, single, age 23, born 1873, Manchester, Turner Tool Makers, Joseph MERRYWEATHER, son, age 19, born 1882, Salford, Apprentice Sheet Metal Worker, Louisa MERRYWEATHER, dau, single, age 23, born 1873, Manchester, Ann MERRYWEATHER, dau, single, age 38, born 1863, Salford.

Sp. Emma WOOD (1841-1917) [3]. Born 1841, dau. of James Wood born 1820.. Emma died March 1917, Fylde, Lancashire, age 75.

6. **Ann MERRYWEATHER (1862-1907) [6].** Born Sep 1862, Salford, Lancashire. Dau of Richard J Merryweather and Emma Wood. In the 1871 English Census, Pickstone Street, Newton Heath, Lancashire, the 1881 English Census, 104 Oldham Road, Newton, Lancashire, the 1891 English Census, 30 Cresswell Street, Newton, Manchester and the 1901 English Census, 70 Ashley Lane, Failsworth, Harpurhey, North Manchester, Ann was living with her parents. Ann died Dec 1906 Fylde, age 44, shown as Annie Merryweather.

6. **Walter MERRYWEATHER (1867-) [9].** Born Sep 1867, Chorlton, Ardwick, Lancashire, Son of Richard J Merryweather and Emma Wood. Walter noted as an Optician. In the 1871 English Census, Pickstone Street, Newton Heath, Manchester and the 1881 English Census, 104 Oldham Road, Newton, Lancashire, Walter was living with his parents.

6. **Emily MERRYWEATHER (1870-1873) [7].** Born Mar 1870, Salford, Lancashire. Dau of Richard J Merryweather and Emma Wood. Emily died Jun 1873, Salford, Lancashire.

6. **George MERRYWEATHER (1872-1949) [11].** Born Sep 1872, Newton Heath, Lancashire. Son of Richard J Merryweather and Emma Wood. In the 1881 English Census, 104 Oldham Road, Newton, Lancashire, the 1891 English Census, 30 Cresswell Street, Newton, Manchester and 1901 English Census, 70 Ashley Lane, Failsworth, Harpurhey, North Manchester, George was living with his parents. George Marr Selina TAYLOR 1902, Lancashire, Prestwich. George died Dec 1949, Manchester.

1911 English Census, 17 Bute Street, Moston, Manchester
George MERRYWEATHER, age 38, born 1873, Manchester, Assistant Foreman Engineer, Selina MERRYWEATHER, wife, married 8 years, age 36, born 1875, Birmingham, Richard James, son, age 7, born 1904, Manchester, Arthur MERRYWEATHER, son, age 5, born 1906, Manchester, Alfred MERRYWEATHER, son age 3, born 1908, Manchester, Mabel MERRYWEATHER, dau, age 2, born 1909, Manchester, Harry MERRYWEATHER, son, age 5 months, born 1911, Manchester.
Sp. Selina TAYLOR (1875-1950) [77]. Born 1875.

7. **Richard James MERRYWEATHER (1904-1959) [90].** Born 1904, Manchester, Lancashire. Richard James Marr Eleanor GILBERT, 3 Jan 1931, St. Luke, Miles Platting, Lancashire. Richard James died 4 Mar 1959, Blackpool, Lancashire.

Sp. Eleanor GILBERT (-) [156], dau. of Hezekiah Gilbert.

7. **Arthur MERRYWEATHER (1906-1967) [88].** Born 1906, Manchester, Lancashire. Arthur died Jun 1967, Manchester, Lancashire. In the 1911 English Census, 17 Bute Street, Moston, Manchester, Arthur was living with his parents.

7. **Alfred MERRYWEATHER (1908-1924) [89].** Born 1908, Manchester, Lancashire. Alfred died Dec 1924, Prestwich, Lancashire. In the 1911 English Census, 17 Bute Street, Moston, Manchester, Alfred was living with his parents.

7. **Mabel MERRYWEATHER (1908-) [76].** Born 14 Nov 1908, Manchester, Baptised 6 Dec 1908, Collyhurst, St James, Lancashire. In the 1911 English Census, 17 Bute Street, Moston, Manchester, Mabel was living with her parents.

7. **Harry MERRYWEATHER (1911-1987) [87].** Born 1911, Manchester, Lancashire. Harry died Jun 1987, Manchester, Lancashire. In the 1911 English Census, 17 Bute Street, Moston, Manchester, Harry was living with his parents.

7. **Evelyn MERRYWEATHER (1912-) [86].** Born 19 Apr 1912, Prestwich, Lancashire, baptised 8 May 1912, Collyhurst, St James, Lancashire.

7. **William MERRYWEATHER (1915-1972) [158].** Born 11 Nov 1915, Newton Heath, Lancashire. William Marr Joan SYKES, 1949. William died 4 Oct 1972, Newton Heath, Lancashire.

Sp. Joan SYKES (-) [159].

6. **Louisa MERRYWEATHER (1877-) [10].** Born Dec 1877, Lancashire. Dau of Richard J Merryweather and Emma Wood. In the 1881 English Census, 104 Oldham Road, Newton, Lancashire, the 1891 English Census, 30 Cresswell Street, Newton, Manchester and the 1901 English Census, 70 Ashley Lane, Failsworth, Harpurhey, North Manchester, Lousia was living with her parents.

6. **Joseph MERRYWEATHER (1882-) [2].** Born 1882, Newton Heath, Lancashire. Son of Richard J Merryweather and Emma Wood. Joseph Marr Jessie MCLEOD, 21 Oct 1905, Nottingham. Joseph of 17 Shelton Street, Nottingham. In the 1891 English Census, 30 Cresswell Street, Newton, Manchester and the 1901 English Census, 70 Ashley Lane, Failsworth, Harpurhey, North Manchester, Joseph was living with his parents.

1911 Census, 2 Pym Street, Moston, Manchester
Joseph MERRYWEATHER, age 29, born 1882, Manchester, Gas Meter Maker, 5 years married, Jessie MERRYWEATHER, wife, age 30, born 1881, Nottingham, Walter Hugh MERRYWEATHER, son, age 5, born 1906, Nottingham.

Sp. Jessie MCLEOD (1881-1962) [5], dau. of Hugh McLeod. Jessie was a Lace Dresser.

7. **Walter Hugh MERRYWEATHER (1906-1990) [1].** Born 5 Feb 1906, Bossingham, Nottinghamshire. In the 1911 English Census, 2 Pym Street, Moston, Manchester, Walter Hugh was living with his parents. Walter Hugh Marr firstly Rose GRIFFITHS, 1928, Wirral, Cheshire.

Sp. Rose GRIFFITHS (1905-) [75], dau. of James Griffiths born 1886 and Elizabeth Steadman born 1883.

James Griffiths born 1886

8. Joseph MERRYWEATHER (1928-2006) [85]. Born 2 Nov 1928, baptised Dec 1928, Wirral, Cheshire. Son of Walter Hugh Merryweather and Rose Griffiths. Joseph Marr Mabel Brackley. Joseph died Feb 2006.

Joseph Merryweather 1928-2006

Joseph Merryweather and the banjo quintet receiving their cup, circa 1950s.

8. **Mabel BRACKLEY (-) [223].**
8. **Robert MERRYWEATHER (1930-2000) [84].** Born 7 Sep 1930, Wirral, Cheshire. Son of Walter Hugh Merryweather and Rose Griffiths. Robert Marr Francis Rose PRICE. Robert died 20 Dec 2000, Chester, Cheshire.
Sp. Francis Rose PRICE (1934-1983) [146], dau. of Joseph Leonard Price and Frances Rose Sayce.

Walter Hugh Merryweather married secondly Daphne LM LILLEY, 1961. Walter Hugh died Feb 1990, Birkenhead, Cheshire.
Sp. Daphne LM LILLEY (-) [153].

7. **Nelly MERRYWEATHER (-) [154].** Born 1913, Lancashire. Nelly Marr Benjamin MARKS, 1951, Salford, Lancashire.
Sp. Benjamin MARKS (-) [155].

6. **Horatio MERRYWEATHER (1864-) [160].** Born Dec 1864, Manchester, Lancashire. Son of Richard J Merryweather and Emma Wood.
6. **Arthur MERRYWEATHER (1876-) [161].** Baptised 1 Jun 1876, All Saints, Newton Heath, Lancashire. Son of Richard J Merryweather and Emma Wood.
6. **Thomas MERRYWEATHER (1865-) [200].** Born 13 Apri 1865, Salford, Lancashire, baptised 3 Dec 1865. Son of Richard J Merryweather and Emma Wood. In the 1871 English Census, Pickstone Street, Newton Heath, Manchester, the 1881 English Census, 104 Oldham Road, Newton, Lancashire, the 1891 English Census, 30 Cresswell Street, Newton, Manchester and the 1901 English Census, 70 Ashley Lane, Failsworth, Harpurhey, North Manchester, Thomas was living with his parents. Thomas Marr Ada.

1911 English Census, 30 Wembury Street, Harpurhey, Salford, Lancashire
Thomas MERRYWEATHER, age 46, born 1865, Salford, Sheet Metal Worker, Ada MERRYWEATHER, age 31, born 1880, Wolverhampton, Leonard MERRYWEATHER, age 8, born 1903, Doris MERRYWEATHER, age 6, born 1905, Salford, Walter MERRYWEATHER, age 4, born 1907, Salford.
Sp. Ada (1880-) [201]. Born 1880.

7. **Leonard MERRYWEATHER (1903-) [202].** Born 1903, Salford, Lancashire. In the 1911 English Census, 30 Wembury Street, Harpurhey, Salford, Leonard was living with his parents.
7. **Doris MERRYWEATHER (1905-) [203].** Born 1905, Salford, Lancashire. In the 1911 English Census, 30 Wembury Street, Harpurhey, Salford, Doris was living with her parents.
7. **Walter MERRYWEATHER (1907-) [204].** Born 1907, Salford, Lancashire. In the 1911 English Census, 30 Wembury Street, Harpurhey, Salford, Walter was living with his parents.

5. **Mary MERRYWEATHER (1837-) [19].** Born 11 Jul 1837, St. Stephen, Salford, Lancashire. Dau of Horatio Merryweather and Mary Hoyle. In the 1841 English Census, Mount Pleasant, Salford and the 1851 English Census, 3 Paradise Hill, Manchester, Mary was living with her parents.
5. **Hannah Newton MERRYWEATHER (1840-1858) [15].** Born 18 Feb 1840, Baptised 17 Mar 1840, St. Stephen, Salford, Lancashire. Dau of Horatio Merryweather and Mary Hoyle. In the 1841 English Census, Mount Pleasant, Salford and the 1851 English Census, 3 Paradise Hill, Manchester, Hannah was living with her parents. Hannah died Mar 1858, Manchester, Lancashire.
5. **Horatio MERRYWEATHER (1842-1918) [17].** Born 4 May 1841, baptised 24 Mar 1842, St. Stephen, Salford, Lancashire. Son of Horatio Merryweather and Mary Hoyle. In the 1851 English Census, 3 Paradise Hill, Manchester and the 1861 English Census, 4 High Prospect St, Salford, Horatio was living with his parents.

In the 1861 English Census, Horatio age 19 living with his Sister in Law Emma and Brother Richard James.

Horatio Marr Alice GREEN, 4 Dec 1864, Manchester Cathedral
Sp. Alice GREEN (1845-) [21]. Born 1845, Wiston.

1871 English Census, Regent Street, Salford, Lancashire
Horatio MERRYWEATHER, age 28, born 1843, Salford, Blacksmith, Alice MERRYWEATHER, wife, age 24, born Wiston, Mary MERRYWEATHER, dau, age 5, born Salford, born 1866, Thomas H MERRYWEATHER, age 3, born 1868, Salford, Jane MERRYWEATHER, age 1, born 1870, Salford, Elizabeth GIBSON, age 20, Lodger

1881 English Census, 2 Armitage Street, Salford, Lancashire
Horatio MERRYWEATHER, age 39, born 1842, Salford, Whitesmith employing 1 Man, Alice MERRYWEATHER, age 35, born 1846, Wiston, Mary MERRYWEATHER, dau, age 15, born 1866, Salford, Thomas MERRYWEATHER, son, age 13, born 1868, Salford, Jane MERRYWEATHER, dau, age 11. Born 1870, Salford, Horatio MERRYWEATHER, son, age 8, born 1872, Salford, Alice Ann MERRYWEATHER, dau, age 5, born 1876, Salford, Ada MERRYWEATHER, dau, age 2, born 1879, Salford.

1891 English Census, 2 Armitage Street, Salford, Lancashire.
Horatio MERRYWEATHER, age 48, born 1843, Salford, Grocer, Alice MERRYWEATHER, age 46, born 1846, Wiston, Thomas MERRYWEATHER, son, age 23, born 1868, Salford, Whitesmith, Jane MERRYWEATHER, dau, age 20. Born 1870, Salford, Horatio MERRYWEATHER, son, age 18, born 1872, Salford, Silversmith, Alice Ann MERRYWEATHER, dau, age 14, born 1876, Salford, Ada MERRYWEATHER, dau, age 12, born 1879, Salford.

1901 English Census, Regent Street, Salford, Lancashire
Horatio MERRYWEATHER, age 60, born 1841, Salford, Blacksmith (garden Rails), Employer, Alice MERRYWEATHER, age 50, born 1851, Wiston, Horatio MERRYWEATHER, son, age 28, born 1873, Salford, Blacksmith (Garden Rails) worker, Alice Ann MERRYWEATHER, dau, age 24, born 1876, Salford.

1911 English Census, 64 Isaac Street, Salford, Lancashire
Albert SHAW, head, age 33, born 1878, Manchester, Brass Moulder, Alice Ann SHAW, wife, age 34, born 1877, Salford, Albert Nelson SHAW, son, age 5, born 1906, Salford, Horatio MERRYWEATHER, son in law, age 68, widower, Blacksmith, general,

Horatio died Sept 1918, Chorlton, Lancashire, age 77.

> 6. **Mary MERRYWEATHER (1866-) [26].** Born 15 Apr 1866, Salford, Lancashire. Dau of Horatio Merryweather and Alice Green. In 1871 English Census, Regent Street, Salford, Lancashire and the 1881 English Census, 2 Armitage Street, Salford, Mary was living with her parents.
> 6. **Thomas H MERRYWEATHER (1868-) [23].** Born 25 Jan 1868, Salford, Lancashire. Son of Horatio Merryweather and Alice Green. In the 1871 English Census, Regent Street, Salford, Lancashire, the 1881 English Census, 2 Armitage Street, Salford and the 1891 English Census, 2 Armitage Street, Salford, Thomas was living with his parents. Thomas H Marr Isabella KENYON, 1892.

1901 English Census, 94 Bigland Street, Salford, Lancashire
Thomas H MERRYWEATHER, age 32, born 1868, Salford, Blacksmith, Isabella MERRYWEATHER, wife, age 28, born 1873, Salford, Ida MERRYWEATHER, dau, age 14, born 1897, Salford, Thomas H MERRYWEATHER, son, age 13, born 1898, Salford, Alice M MERRYWEATHER, dau, age 1, born 1900, Salford.

1911 English Census, 34 Clement Street, Salford, Lancashire
Thomas H MERRYWEATHER, age 43, born 1868, Salford, Master Blacksmith, employer, Isabella MERRYWEATHER, wife, age 38, born 1873, Salford, Ida MERRYWEATHER, dau, age 4, born 1897, Salford, Thomas H MERRYWEATHER, son, age 3, born 1898, Salford, Alice MERRYWEATHER, dau, age

11, born 1900, Salford, Edith MERRYWEATHER, dau, age 9, born 1902, Salford, Doris MERRYWEATHER, dau, age 7, born 1904, Salford.

Sp. Isabella KENYON (1873-) [149]. Born 1873, Salford, Lancashire.

7. **Ida MERRYWEATHER (1897-) [177].** Born 1897, Salford, Lancashire. In the 1901 English Census, 94 Bigland Street, Salford, Lancashire and the 1911 English Census, 34 Clement Street, Salford, Ida was living with her parents.

7. **Thomas MERRYWEATHER (1898-) [178].** Born 1898, Salford, Lancashire. In the 1901 English Census, 94 Bigland Street, Salford and the 1911 English Census, 34 Clement Street, Salford, Thomas was living with his parents.

7. **Alice MERRYWEATHER (1900-) [179].** Born 1900, Salford, Lancashire. In the 1901 English Census, 94 Bigland Street, Salford and the 1911 English Census, 34 Clement Street, Salford, Alice was living with her parents.

7. **Edith MERRYWEATHER (1902-) [180].** Born 1902, Salford, Lancashire. In the 1911 English Census, 34 Clement Street, Salford, Edith was living with her parents.

7. **Doris MERRYWEATHER (1904-) [181].** Born 1904, Salford, Lancashire. In the 1911 English Census, 34 Clement Street, Salford, Doris was living with her parents.

6. **Jane MERRYWEATHER (1870-) [24].** Born 1870, Salford, Lancashire. Dau of Horatio Merryweather and Alice Green. In the 1871 English Census, Regent Street, Salford, Lancashire, the 1881 English Census, 2 Armitage Street, Salford and the 1891 English Census, 2 Armitage Street, Salford, Jane was living with her parents.

6. **Horatio MERRYWEATHER (1872-1941) [22].** Baptised 22 Sep 1872, St. Bartholomew, Salford, Lancashire. Son of Horatio Merryweather and Alice Green. In the 1871 English Census, Regent Street, Salford, Lancashire, the 1881 English Census, 2 Armitage Street, Salford, the 1891 English Census, 2 Armitage Street, Salford and the 1901 English Census, Regent Street, Salford, Horatio was living with his parents.

Horatio Marr Rossetta CONNOLLY, 1903, St. Bartholomew, Salford, Lancashire. Horatio was age 28, a Blacksmith of Armitage Street, Rossetta, age 20, of 94 Gloucester Street, daughter of Andrew Connolly. Witnesses Thomas Henry Merryweather, Gertrude Baybut and Horatio Merryweather. Horatio died 1941, Bucklow, Cheshire, age 68.

1911 English Census, 37 Clare Moor Grove, Didsbury, Lancashire
Horatio MERRYWEATHER, age 38, born 1873, Salford, Electric Theabre, Rossetta MERRYWEATHER, wife, age 27,born 1884, Salford, Horatio MERRYWEATHER, son, age 7, born 1904, Salford, Rossetta MERRYWEATHER, dau, age 5, born 1899, Salford, Andrew MERRYWEATHER, son, age 9 months, born 1910, Salford, Mary CONNELLY, aunt, age 62, single, born 1849, Salford

Sp. Rossetta CONNOLLY (1882 -) [169]. Born 1882.

7. **Horatio MERRYWEATHER (1904-) [170].** Born 1904, Salford, Lancashire. Son of Horatio Merryweather and Rossetta Connolly. Horatio Marr Marjorie C STANFORD, 1930, Lancashire. In the 1911 English Census, 37 Clare Moor Grove, Didsbury, Lancashire, Horatio was living with his parents.

Sp. Marjorie C STANFORD (-) [171].

7. **Rossetta MERRYWEATHER (1906-) [172].** Born 1906, Salford, Lancashire. Dau of Horatio Merryweather and Rossetta Connolly. Rossetta Marr Joseph William FITTON, 3 Sep 1930, Chorlton -cum-Hardy, Lancashire. In the 1911 English Census, 37 Clare Moor Grove, Didsbury, Lancashire, Roseetta was living with her parents.

Sp. Joseph William FITTON (-) [173].

7. **Andrew MERRYWEATHER (1911-) [174].** Born 1911, Salford, Lancashire. Son of Horatio Merryweather and Rossetta Connolly. In the 1911 English Census, 37 Clare Moor Grove, Didsbury, Lancashire, Andrew was living with his parents.

6. **Alice Ann MERRYWEATHER (1874-) [20].** Baptised 25 Dec 1874, St. Matthews, Salford, Lancashire. Dau of Horatio Merryweather and Alice Green. In the 1871 English Census, Regent Street, Salford, Lancashire, the 1881 English Census, 2 Armitage Street, Salford, the 1891 English Census, 2 Armitage Street, Salford and the 1901 English Census, Regent Street, Salford, Alice Ann was living with her parents. Alice Ann Marr Albert SHAW.
Sp. Albert SHAW (1878-) [175]. Born 1878, Manchester.

1911 English Census, 64 Isaac Street, Salford, Lancashire
Albert SHAW, age 33, born 1878, Manchester, Brass Moulder, Alice Ann SHAW, wife, age 34, born 1877, Salford, Albert Nelson SHAW, son, age 5, born 1906, Salford, Horatio MERRYWEATHER, son in law, age 68, widower, Blacksmith, general.

7. **Albert Nelson SHAW (1906-) [176].** Born 1906, Salford, Lancashire. Born 1906, Salford, Lancashire. In the 1911 English Census, 64 Isaac Street, Salford, Albert was living with his parents.

6. **Ada MERRYWEATHER (1879-) [25].** Baptised 29 Jan 1879 Chapelry of St. Clement, Ordsall-in-Salford, Lancashire. Dau of Horatio and Alice Green. In the 1881 English Census, 2 Armitage Street, Salford and the 1891 English Census, 2 Armitage Street, Salford, Ada was living with her parents.

5. **Jane MERRYWEATHER (1843-) [16].** Baptised 30 Mar 1843, St. Stephen, Salford, Lancashire. Dau of Horatio Merryweather and Mary Hoyle. In 1851 English Census, 3 Paradise Hill, Manchester, living with parents.

5. **Ellen / Helen MERRYWEATHER (1849-) [14].** Born 18 Dec 1848, baptised 22 Jan 1849, St. Stephen, Salford, Lancashire. Dau of Horatio Merryweather and Mary Hoyle. In the 1851 English Census, 3 Paradise Hill, Manchester and the 1861 English Census, 3 Square, Mason Street, Manchester, Ellen / Hellen was living with her parents. Noted as a Nurse.

4. **Harriet MERRYWEATHER (1799-) [78].** Baptised 6 Mar 1799, Manchester Cathedral. Dau of Richard and Sarah Newton.

3. **Melissa MERRYWEATHER (1767-) [38].** Baptised 6 Dec 1767, Rossington, Yorkshire. Dau of William Merryweather and Female Kitching. Melissa Marr George FRANCE, 28 May 1797, Manchester Cathedral.
Sp. George FRANCE (-) [37].

3. **Edward MERRYWEATHER (1774-) [31].** Born 1774, Red House, Doncaster, Baptised 5 Jul 1774, St. Lawrence, Adwick le Street, Doncaster, Yorkshire. Son of William Merryweather and Female Kitching. Edward married firstly Lucy KAY, 1 Jan 1801, Manchester Cathedral.
Sp. Lucy KAY (-1806) [221]. Died 9 Sept 1806, Walmersley, Bury, Lancashire, in child birth.

4. **Lucy MERRYWEATHER (1806-1806) [222].** Died 9 Sept 1806, Walmersley, Bury, Lancashire.

Edward secondly Marr Catherine MILES, 26 May 1811, Conisbrough, Yorkshire. Edward noted as an Artist. Surname spelt as Merriwether. Edward Merryweather of 57 Merchant's Square, Cheetham Hill, Lancashire, Dealer in Oil Paints – Banes Director of 1824

1841 English Census, Cheetwood, Cheetham, Manchester
Edward MERRYWEATHER, age 60, born 1781, Picture Merchant, Catherine MERRYWEATHER, age 50, born 1791, Julia MERRYWEATHER, age 15, born 1826, Lancashire

1851 English Census, Cleveland Street, Doncaster, Yorkshire, West Riding
Edward MERRYWEATHER, head, married, age 76, born 1775, Red House, Yorkshire, Artist, Catherine MERRYWEATHER, wife, age 59, born 1792, Essex, Julia MERRYWEATHER, dau, unmarr, age 25, born 1826, Cheatham Hill, Lancashire, Milliner and Dress Maker
      Sp. Catherine MILES (1792-1867) [27]. Born 1792, Essex. Catherine died Dec 1867, Manchester, age 75. Name spelt as Merreweather.

1861 English Census, 11 Harris Street, Hulme, Manchester
Catherine MERRYWEATHER, Widow, age 68, born 1793, London, Assists in the house, Julia MERRYWEATHER, dau, unmarr, age 30, born 1832, Manchester, Florence MERRYWEATHER, dau, age 4, born 1857, Manchester, Henry MERRYWEATHER, son, age 7 months, born 1861, Manchester.

    4. **Emma MERRYWEATHER (1814-) [29].** Baptised 5 Jan 1814, Doncaster, Yorkshire. Dau of Edward Merryweather and Catherine Miles.
    4. **George Edward MERRYWEATHER (1817-) [30].** Baptised 22 Jun 1817, Doncaster, Yorkshire. Son of Edward Merryweather and Catherine Miles. George Marr Hannah.
  Sp. Hannah (1823-) [34]. Born 1823.

      5. **John MERRYWEATHER (1848-) [35].** Born 1848, East Cowton, Yorkshire.

    4. **Julia MERRYWEATHER (1826-) [28].** Born Chetham Hill, Lancashire, baptised 10 Sep 1826, Wesleyan Methodist, Crumpsall, Manchester. Dau of Edward Merryweather and Catherine Miles. In the 1841 English Census, Cheetwood, Cheetham, Manchester and the 1851 English Census, Cleveland Street, Doncaster, Yorkshire, West Riding, living with parents. However, Julia is also noted in 1851 English Census, 3 Paradise Hill, Manchester, living with her cousin Horatio Merryweather.

Julia had two children by 1861 and was living with her mother
1861 English Census, 11 Harris Street, Hulme, Manchester
Catherine MERRYWEATHER, Widow, age 68, born 1793, London, Assists in the house, Julia MERRYWEATHER, dau, unmarr, age 30, born 1832, Manchester, Florence MERRYWEATHER, dau, age 4, born 1857, Manchester, Henry MERRYWEATHER, son, age 7 months, born 1861, Manchester

      5. **Eleanor Florence MERRYWEATHER (1856-) [32].** Baptised 19 Sep 1856, Holy Trinity, Hulme, Manchester. Dau of Julia Merryweather, Spinster of 11 Harris Street, Hulme, Lancashire
      5. **Henry MERRYWEATHER (1860-) [33].** Baptised 19 Feb 1860, Holy Trinity, Hulme, Manchester. Son of Julia Merryweather.

  3. **Mary MANEYWETHERS (1759-) [183].** Born 17 Jan 1759, baptised 18 Jan 1759, Cantley Parish, Yorkshire, daughter of William and Mary Manywethers of Gate, Farmer. There was another reference which stated a Mary born in 1761.

Mary Marr Joseph PEACE, 9 Nov 1782, Doncaster, Yorkshire. Surname also recorded as Pease.
Sp. Joseph PEACE (1761-) [184]. Born 1761.

    4. **Mary PEACE (1789-) [185].** Born 1789, Doncaster, Yorkshire.
    4. **Hannah PEACE (1791-) [186].** Born 1791, Doncaster, Yorkshire.
    4. **George PEACE (1793-) [187].** Born 1793, Doncaster, Yorkshire.
    4. **Henry PEACE (1795-) [188].** Born 1795, Doncaster, Yorkshire.
    4. **Melissa PEACE (1796-) [189].** Born 1796, Doncaster, Yorkshire.
    4. **Joseph PEACE (1800-) [190].** Born 1800, Doncaster, Yorkshire.

  3. **George MANEYWEATHER (1770-) [220].** Baptised 8 Jul 1770, Rossington, Yorkshire. Son of William Maneyweather.
  3. **Elizabeth MANEYWETHERS (1755-) [191].** Baptised 29 Nov 1755, Cantley, Yorishire. Dau of William and Mary Maneyweather, of Gate, Farmer. Elizabeth Marr George HANLEY, 1 Nov 1774, St. Lawrence, Adwick-le-Street, Doncaster.
Sp. George HANLEY (-) [192].

2. John MERRYWEATHER (1742-) [193]. Born 1742, Throapham, Yorkshire.
Sp. (unknown).

> **3. Charlotte MERRYWEATHER (1763-) [194].** Baptised 30 May 1763, Throapham,
> Yorkshire. Dau of John Merryweather.
> **3. John MERRYWEATHER (1776-) [195].** Born 1776, Doncaster, Yorkshire. Likely to be the
> son of this John Merryweather. John Marr Martha SAVILLE, 11 Jan 1814, Rotherham.
> Yorkshire. Although not confirmed it is likely this is the son of John and it was this John
> who married Martha.
> **Sp. Martha SAVILLE (-) [196].**

> > **4. Alfred John MERRYWEATHER (1815-) [197].** Born 1 Aug 1815, Doncaster, baptised
> > 15 Aug 1815, Ebenezer Chapel, Aldgate, Doncaster, Yorkshire. Son of John
> > Merryweather and Martha Saville.

PHOTOGRAPHS

- Family of Five Generations
- James (Toffee) Dean. A Founder Member of the Guild and its President 1894 – 95 - 99
- Betsy Dean
- William Dean and Ethel Warner
- William Dean
- Ethel Dean
- Harold Dean
- Amy Dean
- Estella Dean
- Nora Fitzsimmons nee Cooper and family
- Gilbert Fearns Set of Chair Planes
- Mitchell's Ark
- Wombwell's Bostock Menagerie, Hull Fair 1919
- Robert Dixon
- Robert Dixon's Pan am
- Swing Boats
- Gilbert Dixon
- Betsy Dixon 1908 -1983
- Gilbert Dixon and Gilbert Verdin Dixon
- Daisy Manders
- Daisy Manders and friends
- Daisy and Nancy Manders
- Edward (Teddy) Dixon
- Betsy Price nee Manders, Margaret Dixon nee Clough, Edward (Teddy) Dixon
- James Fearns
- Gilbert Fearns and the Silcock Brothers
- Margaret Ellen Dixon nee Clough
- Betsy Dixon, Nelly Manders, Sammy Clough, Daisy Clouch, Willie Clough
- John Cordwell
- John Cordwell and family
- Sarah Ellen Cordwell 1866-1933
- Robert Hines, Betsy Dixon, at Nelly Manders Wedding
- James Griffiths born 1886
- Joseph Merryweather 1928-2006
- Joseph Merryweather and the banjo quintet

INDEX OF SURNAMES included in the book

SEE DETAILS OF ALL PUBLICATIONS BY IRISH ANCESTORS 4U Ltd

www.irishancestors4u.com